CONCISE DICTIONARY OF RELIGIOUS QUOTATIONS

Concise Dictionary of
RELIGIOUS
QUOTATIONS

COMPILED BY

William Neil PhD, DD

Reader in Biblical Studies, Nottingham University

William B. Eerdmans Publishing Company
Grand Rapids, Michigan

Printed in the United States of America
This edition is published by special arrangement with
A. R. Mowbray & Co Ltd, The Alden Press, Osney Mead, Oxford,
England.

Library of Congress Cataloging in Publication Data

Neil, William, 1909-   *comp.*
Concise dictionary of religious quotations.

Bibliography: p. 213
1. Religion — Quotations, maxims, etc.
I. Title.
PN6084.R3N4   *808.88'2*   *74-17470*
ISBN 0-8028-3451-1

Contents

v

Preface

THERE are already well-known dictionaries of quotations which include among other things some items of a religious character. All quotations in this book are, however, specifically religious, though not exclusively Christian and not all necessarily sympathetic to religion. It is hoped that the book will be found useful for those who have to write or speak, teach or preach, and wish to check on the authorship or source of a well-remembered quotation or the exact words of a half-remembered quotation. In the process they may find under the subject headings unfamiliar quotations from a variety of sources which they would wish to employ. Perhaps not the least valuable use of this book may be to stimulate further thought and reflection along devotional lines.

The primary source of religious quotations in a Christian context is of course the Bible itself, and in this connection the New English Bible has been used throughout. Christian verse, ancient and modern, must also be included and the Book of Common Prayer has many eminently quotable lines. Christian theologians, from St Augustine to the present day, have said or written things that are illuminating and memorable and many of these have been included, as well as significant thoughts from religious thinkers of other faiths. The overriding consideration has been that every contribution should be short enough to be quotable.

Indexes

Other users will be looking for quotable phrases or, perhaps, just wondering what great men have said on a particular subject. As well as looking under subject headings, the searcher will be able to use an extensive *subject index* which gives cross-references to quotations which might well have been listed in several places. There is also a *source index*: here the searcher will find the subjects on which authors have been quoted as well as the pages on which their contributions may be found.

Alphabetical Arrangement

Within the subject headings, entries have been arranged in alphabetical order of author or source: extracts from the Bible and the Book of Common Prayer appear at the beginning of each theme and they follow the order in which they fall within these books. The index follows the same plan.

A Personal Note

This is a concise dictionary, which therefore makes no claim to be exhaustive; it is also one man's selection and must inevitably draw on his tastes, experience and interests. I hope that not too many readers and users of the book will be aggrieved because their favourite passages have not been included.

Acknowledgements

I owe a deep debt of gratitude to Canon William Purcell, Literary Adviser to Mowbrays, for his invaluable help throughout the compilation of this book. I am also indebted to Miss Kathleen Downham who compiled the indexes.

WILLIAM NEIL

ADAM: SECOND ADAM

1 The man said, 'The woman you gave me for a companion, she gave me the fruit from the tree and I ate it.'
Gen. 3.12

2 As through the disobedience of the one man the many were made sinners, so through the obedience of the one man the many will be made righteous.
Rom. 5.19

3 For since it was a man who brought death into the world, a man also brought resurrection of the dead.
1 Cor. 15.21

4 As in Adam all men die, so in Christ all will be brought to life.
1 Cor. 15.22

5 As we have worn the likeness of the man made of dust, so we shall wear the likeness of the heavenly man.
1 Cor. 15.49

6 We thinke that Paradise and Calvarie,/ Christ's Crosse, and Adam's tree, stood in one place;/ Looke Lord, and finde both Adams met in me;/As the first Adam's sweat surrounds my face,/May the last Adam's blood my soule embrace.
JOHN DONNE *Hymne to God, my God, in my sicknesse*

7 Adam ambitious desires to be wise,/ Casts out obedience, then lusts with his eyes;/Grasps his sweet fruit, 'As God I shall be'./Lord, forgive Adam, For Adam is me.
RICHARD G. JONES *100 Hymns for Today*

8 The greatness of God is infinite; for while with one die man impresses many coins and all are exactly alike, the King of Kings, The Holy One (blessed be He) with one die impresses the same image of Adam on all men, and yet not one of them is like his neighbour.
The Talmud

ADULTERY

9 You shall not commit adultery.
Ex. 20.14

10 Drink water from your own cistern and running water from your own spring.
Prov. 5.15

11 Can a man kindle fire in his bosom without burning his clothes?
Prov. 6.27

12 One who commits adultery is a senseless fool: he dishonours the woman and ruins himself.
Prov. 6.32

13 You have learned that they were told, 'Do not commit adultery.' But what I tell you is this: If a man looks on a woman with a lustful eye, he has already committed adultery with her in his heart.
Matt. 5.27–28

14 Whoever divorces his wife and marries another commits adultery against her: so too, if she divorces her husband and marries another, she commits adultery.
Mark 10.11–12

ADVERSITY

15 The Lord may give you bread of adversity and water of affliction.
Isa. 30.20

16 Take your share of hardship, like a good soldier of Christ Jesus.
2 Tim. 2.3

1

1 Almighty God, who seest that we have no power of ourselves to help ourselves; Keep us both outwardly in our bodies, and inwardly in our souls; that we may be defended from all adversities which may happen to the body, and from all evil thoughts which may assault and hurt the soul; through Jesus Christ our Lord.
BOOK OF COMMON PRAYER *Collect for the Second Sunday in Lent*

2 Comfort and succour all them, who in this transitory life are in trouble, sorrow, need, sickness, or any other adversity.
BOOK OF COMMON PRAYER From the *Order for Holy Communion*

3 Then welcome each rebuff/That turns earth's smoothness rough,/Each sting that bids not sit nor stand, but go!/
ROBERT BROWNING *Rabbi ben Ezra*

4 He knows not his own strength that hath not met adversity. Heaven prepares good men with crosses.
BEN JONSON *Discoveries*

5 Turn cynic if you will. Curse God and die./You've ample reason for it. There's enough/Of bitterness, God knows, to answer why./The road of life is rough,/But then there is the glory of the sky./
G. A. STUDDERT KENNEDY *The Unutterable Beauty*

6 Adversity reminds men of religion.
LIVY *Annals*

7 Sweet are the uses of adversity/Which, like the toad ugly and venomous,/Wears yet a precious jewel in his head.
WILLIAM SHAKESPEARE *As You Like It*

8 That common chances common men could bear;/That when the sea was calm all boats alike/Show'd mastership in floating.
WILLIAM SHAKESPEARE *Coriolanus*

ADVICE

9 Accept a greeting from everyone,/but advice from only one in a thousand.
Ecclus 6.6

10 We may give advice, but we can never prompt behaviour.
DUC DE LA ROCHEFOUCAULD *Les Maximes*

11 If one's words have been ever a help and never a hindrance, that surely is a useful life and no other justification needed for it, even if it has accomplished nothing more tangible.
FREYA STARK *Beyond Euphrates*

ANGELS

12 He (Jacob) dreamt that he saw a ladder, which rested on the ground with its top reaching to heaven, and angels of God were going up and down upon it.
Gen. 28.12

13 When the sun rises, do you not see a round disk of fire something like a gold piece? O no, no, I see an innumerable company of the Heavenly host crying 'Holy, Holy, Holy, is the Lord God Almighty.'
WILLIAM BLAKE *The Vision of Judgment*

14 Do not talk what thou wouldst do if thou wast an angel, but consider what thou canst do as thou art a man.
WILLIAM LAW *A Practical Treatise upon Christian Perfection*

15 Fools rush in where angels fear to tread.
ALEXANDER POPE *Essay on Criticism*

ANGER

16 The fool is destroyed by his own angry passions.
Job 5.2

17 A soft answer turns away anger.
Prov. 15.1

18 If you are angry, do not let anger lead you into sin; do not let sunset find you still nursing it.
Eph. 4.26

1 The sun must not set upon anger; much less will I let the sun set upon the anger of God towards me.
JOHN DONNE *Sermons*

ANGUISH

2 The Lord is close to those whose courage is broken and he saves those whose spirit is crushed.
Ps. 34.18

3 Out of the depths have I called to thee, O Lord; Lord, hear my cry.
Ps. 130.1–2

4 Is it of no concern to you who pass by?/ If only you would look and see:/is there any agony like mine,/like these my torments/with which the Lord has cruelly punished me/in the day of his anger?
Lam. 1.12

ANIMALS

5 The dove came back to him towards evening with a newly plucked olive leaf in her beak.
Gen. 8.11

6 Countless are the things thou hast made, O Lord./Thou hast made all by thy wisdom;/and the earth is full of thy creatures,/beasts great and small.
Ps. 104.24–25

7 A righteous man cares for his beast.
Prov. 12.10

8 The boy and the angel left the house together, and the dog came out with him and accompanied them.
Tob. 6.1

9 I listen with reverence to the birdsong cascading/At dawn from the oasis, for it seems to me/There is no better evidence for the existence of God/Than in the bird that sings, though it knows not why./

From a spring of untrammelled joy that wells up in its heart.
AN ARAB CHIEFTAIN

10 Hear our humble prayer, O God, for our friends the animals, Thy creatures. We pray especially for all that are suffering in any way; for the overworked and underfed, the hunted, lost or hungry; for all in captivity or ill-treated, and for those that must be put to death.

We entreat for them Thy mercy and pity; and for those who deal with them we ask a heart of compassion, gentle hands and kindly words.

Make us all to be true friends to animals and so more worthy followers of our merciful Saviour, Jesus Christ.
Authorship doubtful

11 For not one sparrow can suffer and the whole Universe not suffer also/In all its Regions, and its Father and Saviour not pity and weep.
WILLIAM BLAKE

12 He prayeth best, who loveth best/ All things both great and small;/ For the dear God who loveth us,/ He made and loveth all.
S. T. COLERIDGE *The Ancient Mariner*

13 O Thou who lovest Thy whole creation, give us strength, we beseech Thee, to put an end to the pain and fear of Thy hunted beasts, the same which they suffer for the careless pleasure of men.
Contemporary British

14 For those, O Lord, the humble beasts, that bear with us the burden and heat of the day, and offer their guileless lives for the well-being of their countries: we supplicate Thy tenderness of heart, for Thou hast promised to save both man and beast, and great is Thy loving kindness, O Master, Saviour of the world.
Eastern Church

15 When I travel in my coach to teach thy Law, give me thought for the mare that carries me, and guard her from my impatience: when I walk through thy woods, may my right foot and my left

foot be harmless to the little creatures that move in its grasses: as it is said by the mouth of thy prophet, They shall not hurt nor destroy in all my holy mountain.
RABBI MOSHE HAKOTUN

1 So I laugh when I hear them make it plain/That dogs and men never meet again./For all their talk who'd listen to them,/With the soul in the shining eyes of him?/Would God be wasting a dog like Tim?
w. M. LETTS *Songs of Leinster*

2 O heavenly Father, protect and bless all things that have breath: guard them from all evil and let them sleep in peace.
ALBERT SCHWEITZER

ANXIETY

3 The mother of Sisera peered through the lattice,/through the window she peered and shrilly cried,/'Why are his chariots so long coming?/Why is the clatter of his chariots so long delayed?'
Judg. 5.28

4 Do not be anxious about tomorrow; tomorrow will look after itself.
Matt. 6.34

5 Martha, Martha, you are fretting and fussing about so many things, but one thing is necessary. The part that Mary has chosen is best.
Luke 10.42

6 The next day is the first link of the chain which fetters a man in a gang with thousands to that superfluous anxiety which is the evil one . . . This anxiety the bird has not.
SÖREN KIERKEGAARD *Christian Discourses*

ARGUMENT

7 Argument, generally speaking in religion, can do no more than clear the track; it cannot make the engine move.
EDWYN BEVAN *Hellenism and Christianity*

8 Whoso seeks God, and takes the intellect for guide,/God drives him forth, in vain distraction to abide/With wild confusion He confounds his inmost heart,/So that, distraught, he cries: 'I know not if Thou art.'
HALLAJ (Sufi)

9 Myself when young did eagerly frequent/ Doctor and Saint and heard great Argument/About it and about, but evermore/ Came out by the same door as in I went.
OMAR KHAYYAM *Rubaiyat*

10 The starting point for natural theology is not argument but sharpened awareness. For the moment it is better for us that the arguments have fallen to pieces.
A. R. VIDLER *Soundings*

ARIDITY

11 O Soul, canst thou not understand/Thou art not left alone,/As a dog to howl and moan/ His master's absence? Thou art as a book/Left in a room that He forsook,/ But returns to by and by,/A book of His dear choice,—/That quiet waiteth for His Hand,/That quiet waiteth for His Eye,/ That quiet waiteth for His Voice.
'MICHAEL FIELD'

12 The Blessed Angela de Foligno says that the prayer which is most acceptable to God is that which we make by force and constraint, the prayer to which we apply ourselves not for any relish we find in it, not by inclination, but purely to please God.
ST FRANCIS DE SALES *Introduction to the Devout Life*

13 There are great drynesses even in the way of meditation; the bread of prayer is often without taste.
FRANÇOIS MALAVAL *A Simple Method of Raising the Soul to Contemplation*

14 Let him who is in consolation think how it will be with him in the desolation that will follow, laying up fresh strength for that time.
ST IGNATIUS OF LOYOLA *The Spiritual Exercises*

1 When it is dull and cold and weary weather with us, when the light is hidden, and the mists are thick, and the sleet begins to fall, still we may get on with the work which can be done as well in the dark days as in the bright.
FRANCIS PAGET *The Spirit of Discipline*

THE ASCENSION

2 Therefore God raised him to the heights and bestowed on him the name above all names, that at the name of Jesus every knee should bow—in heaven, on earth, and in the depths—and every tongue confess, 'Jesus Christ is Lord', to the glory of God the Father.
Phil. 2.9–11

3 As sign and wonder this exaltation is a *pointer* to the revelation that occurred in His resurrection, of Jesus Christ as the heart of all powers in heaven and earth.
KARL BARTH *Credo*

4 Look, ye saints! the sight is glorious;/ See the Man of Sorrows now;/From the fight returned victorious,/Every knee to Him shall bow:/Crown Him! crown Him!/Crowns become the Victor's brow.
THOMAS KELLY *Hymn*

5 The Head that once was crowned with thorns/Is crowned with glory now;/A royal diadem adorns/The mighty Victor's brow.
THOMAS KELLY *Hymn*

6 The Ascension is a festival of the future of the world. The flesh is redeemed and glorified, for the Lord has risen for ever. We Christians are, therefore, the most sublime of materialists.
KARL RAHNER

7 In the days of His earthly ministry, only those could speak to Him who came where He was. If He was in Galilee, men could not find Him in Jerusalem; if He was in Jerusalem, men could not find Him in Galilee. But His Ascension means that He is perfectly united with God; we are with Him wherever we are present to God; and this is everywhere and always.
WILLIAM TEMPLE

8 Jesus, the Saviour, reigns,/The God of truth and love;/When He had purged our stains,/He took His seat above:/Lift up your heart, lift up your voice;/Rejoice; again I say, 'Rejoice.'
CHARLES WESLEY *Hymn*

ASPIRATION

9 O Lord, I, a beggar, ask of Thee more than a thousand kings may ask of Thee. Each one has something he needs to ask of Thee; I have come to ask Thee to give me Thyself.
AL-ANSARI (Sufi)

10 O Lord our God, grant us grace to desire thee with our whole heart; that, so desiring, we may seek, and, seeking, find thee; and so finding thee, may love thee; and loving thee, may hate those sins from which thou hast redeemed us.
ST ANSELM

11 O for a closer walk with God,/A calm and heavenly frame,/A light to shine upon the road/That leads me to the Lamb!
WILLIAM COWPER *Hymn*

12 I asked for Peace—/My sins arose,/And bound me close,/I could not find release.
I asked for Truth—/My doubts came in,/And with their din/They wearied all my youth.
I asked for Love—/My lovers failed,/And griefs assailed/Around, beneath, above.
I asked for Thee—/And Thou didst come/To take me home/Within Thy heart to be.
D. M. DOLBEN

13 O God! if I worship Thee in fear of Hell, burn me in Hell; and if I worship Thee in hope of Paradise, exclude me from Paradise; but if I worship Thee for Thine own sake, withhold not Thine Everlasting Beauty!
RABI 'A (Sufi)

1 God be in my head/And in my understanding;/God be in myne eyes,/And in
my looking;/God be in my mouth,/And
in my speaking;/God be in my heart,/
And in my thynking;/God be at my end,/
And at my departing.
SARUM MISSAL

2 I have immortal longings in me.
WILLIAM SHAKESPEARE *Antony and Cleo-
patra*

3 Thou hidden Love of God, whose height,/
Whose depth unfathomed, no man
knows,/ I see from far Thy beauteous
light,/ Inly I sigh for Thy repose;/My
heart is pained, nor can it be/At rest till
it finds rest in Tfiee.
GERHARD TERSTEEGEN *Hymn*

ATHEISM

4 The impious fool says in his heart,/
'There is no God.'
Ps. 14.1

5 The hope of a godless man is like down
flying on the wind.
Wisd. 5.14

6 Atheism is rather in the lip than in the
heart of man.
FRANCIS BACON *Of Atheism*

7 It is true, that a little philosophy inclines
man's mind to atheism; but depth in
philosophy bringeth men's minds about
to religion.
FRANCIS BACON *Of Atheism*

8 God knows, I'm not the thing I should
be,/ Nor am I even the thing I could be./
But twenty times I rather would be/An
Atheist clean,/Than under gospel colours
hid be/ Just for a screen.
ROBERT BURNS *Epistle to the Reverend
John McMath*

9 The atheist who is moved by love is moved
by the spirit of God; an atheist who lives
by love is saved by his faith in the God
whose existence (under that name) he
denies.
WILLIAM TEMPLE

THE ATONEMENT

10 Among you, whoever wants to be great
must be your servant, and whoever wants
to be first must be the willing slave of all
—like the Son of Man; he did not come
to be served, but to serve, and to give up
his life as a ransom for many.
Matt. 20.26–28

11 I am the good shepherd; the good shepherd lays down his life for the sheep.
John 10.11

12 It is more to your interest that one man
should die for the people, than that the
whole nation should be destroyed.
John 11.50

13 Christ died for us while we were yet
sinners.
Rom. 5.8

14 If, when we were God's enemies, we were
reconciled to him through the death of
his Son, how much more, now that we are
reconciled, shall we be saved by his life!
Rom. 5.10

15 He has reconciled us men to himself
through Christ, and he has enlisted us in
this service of reconciliation.
2 Cor. 5.18

16 God was in Christ reconciling the world
to himself.
2 Cor. 5.19

17 In Jesus, however, we do see one who for
a short while was made lower than the
angels, crowned now with glory and
honour because he suffered death, so
that, by God's gracious will, in tasting
death he should stand for us all.
Heb. 2.9

18 Should anyone commit a sin, we have
one to plead our cause with the Father,
Jesus Christ, and he is just. He is himself
the remedy for the defilement of our sins,
not our sins only but the sins of all the
world.
1 John 2.1

1 Why should his unstain'd breast make good/My blushes with his own heart-blood?
O my Saviour, make me see/How dearly thou hast paid for me
That lost again my life may prove/As then in death, so now in love.
RICHARD CRASHAW *The Dear Bargain*

2 He was a gambler too, my Christ,/He took His life and threw/ It for a world redeemed./And ere His agony was done,/ Before the westering sun went down,/ Crowning that day with its crimson crown,/ He knew that He had won.
G. A. STUDDERT KENNEDY *The Unutterable Beauty*

AUTHORITY

3 Where there is no one in authority, the people break loose.
Prov. 29.18

4 Every person must submit to the supreme authorities. There is no authority but by act of God, and the existing authorities are instituted by him.
Rom. 13.1

5 No morality can be founded on authority, even if the authority were divine.
A. J. AYER *Essay on Humanism*

6 The peril of the hour is a religious subjectivism which is gliding down into religious decadence for want of an objective authority.
P. T. FORSYTH

BAPTISM

1 I baptize you with water, for repentance;
but the one who comes after me is
mightier than I. I am not fit to take off
his shoes. He will baptize you with the
Holy Spirit and with fire.
Matt. 3.11

2 By baptism we were buried with him, and
lay dead, in order that, as Christ was
raised from the dead in the splendour of
the Father, so also we might set our feet
upon the new path of life.
Rom. 6.4

3 We receive this Child into the congregation of Christ's flock, and do sign him
with the sign of the Cross, in token that
hereafter he shall not be ashamed to
confess the faith of Christ crucified, and
manfully to fight under his banner,
against sin, the world, and the devil;
and to continue Christ's faithful soldier
and servant unto his life's end.
BOOK OF COMMON PRAYER From the
Baptismal Service

BELIEF, BELIEVING

4 A simple man believes every word he
hears; a clever man understands the need
for proof.
Prov. 14.15

5 I believe in order that I may understand.
ST ANSELM *Proslogion*

6 In one God I believe/Sole and eternal,
moving all the heaven,/Himself unmoved, with love and with desire./For
such belief not only have I proofs/From
physics and from metaphysics, but/'Tis
also given me by the truth which flows/
Through Moses and the Prophets and
the Psalms,/Through the Evangel, and
through you who wrote/As God's
inspired guardians of the truth.
DANTE ALIGHIERI *Paradiso*

7 O my soul, meditate on God and believe
in Him,/Thy inner fire will be quenched
and thou shalt be wise in His wisdom./

Know thyself, and meet thy Lord, to cast
thy doubts away.
The Granth (Sikh)

8 Belief is a moral act for which the believer
is to be held responsible.
H. A. HODGES *Languages, Standpoints and
Attitudes*—Riddell Lectures

9 It is so hard to believe because it is so
hard to obey.
SÖREN KIERKEGAARD

10 A well-bred man keeps his beliefs out of
his conversation.
ANDRÉ MAUROIS

11 We assent, but we do not *believe*. When
men really believe that the Son of God
died for the sins of men and that through
Him we are brought into that kind of
family relation to the Creator of all the
worlds which is typified in Christ's use
of the word 'Abba', they do not keep
the news to themselves.
WILLIAM PATON *The Church and the New
Order*

12 I think when we are alone we sometimes
see things a little bit more simply, more as
they are. Sometimes when we are with
others, especially when we are talking to
others on religious subjects, we persuade
ourselves that we believe more than we do.
FORBES ROBINSON *Letters to his Friends*

13 I believe that the universe is in evolution.
I believe that evolution proceeds towards
the spirit. I believe that in man spirit is
fully realised in persons. I believe that the
supremely personal is the universal
Christ.
P. TEILHARD DE CHARDIN

14 I believe because it is impossible.
TERTULLIAN *De Carne Christi*

BIBLE

15 Every inspired scripture has its use for
teaching the truth and refuting error, or
for reformation of manners and discipline in right living.
2 Tim. 3.16

1 Blessed Lord, who hast caused all holy Scriptures to be written for our learning; Grant that we may . . . hear them, read, mark, learn and inwardly digest them.
BOOK OF COMMON PRAYER From the *Collect for the Second Sunday in Advent*

2 Lord, Thy word abideth,/And our footsteps guideth;/Who its truth believeth/ Light and joy receiveth.
HENRY WILLIAMS BAKER *Hymn*

3 The New Testament is certainly not a blue-print for twentieth-century Christian behaviour.
F. R. BARRY *Christian Ethics and Secular Society*

4 Thanks to God whose Word is published/ in the tongues of every race./See its glory undiminished/by the change of time or place./ God has spoken:/Praise him for his open Word.
R. T. BROOKS *100 Hymns for Today*

5 I have sometimes seen more in a line of the Bible than I could well tell how to stand under; and yet at another time the whole Bible hath been to me as dry as a stick.
JOHN BUNYAN *Grace Abounding*

6 The Bible is none other than the voice of Him that sitteth upon the throne. Every book of it, every chapter of it, every verse of it, every word of it, every syllable of it, (where are we to stop?) every letter of it, is the direct utterance of the Most High. The Bible is none other than the Word of God, not some part of it more, some part of it less, but all alike the utterance of Him who sitteth upon the Throne, faultless, unerring, supreme.
DR BURGON

7 The Bible, I say, the Bible only is the religion of Protestants.
WILLIAM CHILLINGWORTH *The Religion of Protestants: a Safe Way to Salvation*

8 The Spirit breathes upon the word,/ And brings the truth to sight;/Precepts and promises afford/A sanctifying light.
WILLIAM COWPER *Hymn*

9 We present you with this book, the most valuable thing that this world affords. Here is wisdom, this is the Royal Law: these are the lively oracles of God.
From the *Coronation Service*

10 (In the Bible), the Church is the 'true' Israel, Jesus is the 'true' Anointed King, his death is the 'true' sacrifice. The opposite of 'true' in this way of speaking is not (as we might expect) 'false' but 'literal and prefigurative'.
AUSTIN FARRER *A Short Bible-Introduction*

11 The Word of God is in the Bible as the soul is in the body.
P. T. FORSYTH

12 England has two books, the Bible and Shakespeare. England made Shakespeare, but the Bible made England.
VICTOR HUGO

13 When you read God's word, you must constantly be saying to yourself, 'It is talking to me, and about me.'
SÖREN KIERKEGAARD *For Self-Examination*

14 The Bible was written for men with a head upon their shoulders.
MARTIN LUTHER

15 Why are not folk reading the Bible? Because of science? No. Because they cannot find comfort in it for individualist salvation; for the Bible is about salvation for persons in community.
GEORGE F. MACLEOD *Only One Way Left*

16 The Bible is all about community: from the Garden of Eden to the City at the end.
GEORGE F. MACLEOD *Only One Way Left*

17 What we must do for modern man is not to demythologise the Bible but to rehumanise the area and content of our salvation.
GEORGE F. MACLEOD *Only One Way Left*

18 The authority of the Bible reposes in the fact that, in statements some right and some wrong, and in practical application

some of which is disputable and some even more dubious, a unified witness is borne to Him who is at the centre of the Gospel.

J. K. S. REID *The Authority of Scripture*

1 When in 1796 Bishop Richard Watson published "*An Apology for the Bible*", George III commented: "Apology for the Bible! Apology for the Bible! I did not know that the Bible required an apology."

ALAN RICHARDSON *Christian Apologetics*

2 Scripture is full of Christ. From Genesis to Revelation everything breathes of Him, not every letter of every sentence, but the spirit of every chapter.

F. W. ROBERTSON *Sermons*

3 The devil can cite Scripture for his purpose.

WILLIAM SHAKESPEARE *The Merchant of Venice*

4 It is just because the prophets and apostles are so in-dwelt by the Spirit of God that they are so robustly, freely, independently and concretely human. The incoming of God's Spirit does not eliminate their human qualities so that they become mere puppets of God, but in the fullest sense it makes them men of God.

J. D. SMART *The Interpretation of Scripture*

5 We need never tremble *for* the Word of God, though we may tremble *at* it and the demands which it makes upon our faith and courage.

WILLIAM ROBERTSON SMITH

BIBLE CRITICISM

6 It is in keeping with God's choice of a small insignificant and uncouth people, and with His revelation of His profoundest mystery on the Cross at Golgotha, that He gave us His word in a literary document which will give the critics, in the exercise of their task, enough to do for generations to come.

EMIL BRUNNER *Philosophy of Religion*

7 By identifying the new learning with heresy we make orthodoxy synonymous with ignorance.

ERASMUS

8 Draw deep from the well of Biblical criticism, but do not give your congregation too much of the rope to chew.

W. R. MALTBY

BIBLE: OLD TESTAMENT

9 I find it most interesting and not a little odd that, although the Old Testament on occasions offends our Christian feelings, it did not apparently offend Christ's 'Christian feelings'.

JOHN BRIGHT *The Authority of the Old Testament*

10 Reading the Old Testament is like eating a large crab; it turns out to be mostly shell with very little meat in it.

Chinese Pastor

11 The Old Testament challenges us to see this drama (of history) as God's drama and to play our role in the light of the continuing pressure of the purposes of God in all events, the God who has made himself known in that part of the drama which is the history of the Hebrews.

ROBERT DAVIDSON *The Old Testament*

12 If we Christians wish to understand the psalms, we must bear in mind that the roots of their thought lie in the past, in the Old Testament, while their blossoming reaches out into the far future, to the end of the world, to heaven itself.

P. DRIJVERS *The Psalms: their Structure and Meaning*

13 Here you will find the cradle and swaddling clothes in which Christ lies, to which the angel directs the shepherds. They are poor and mean swaddling clothes, but precious is the treasure, Christ, who lies in them.

MARTIN LUTHER

BLESSING

1 The Lord bless thee, and keep thee: the Lord make his face to shine upon thee, and be gracious unto thee: the Lord lift up his countenance upon thee, and give thee peace.
Num. 6.24–26 (Aaronic blessing)

2 God bless me and my son Jim—/Me and my wife, Jim and his wife,/Us four, and no more.
ANON

3 Blessed is he who does good to others and desires not that others should do good to him.
BROTHER GILES From *The Little Flowers of St. Francis*

BOASTING

4 My little finger is thicker than my father's loins. My father laid a heavy yoke on you; I will make it heavier. My father used the whip on you; but I will use the lash.
1 Kings 12.10–11

5 Some boast of chariots and some of horses, but our boast is the name of the Lord our God.
Ps. 20.7

6 Let not the wise man boast of his wisdom/ nor the valiant of his valour;/ let not the rich man boast of his riches;/but if any man would boast, let him boast of this,/ that he understands and knows me.
Jer. 9.23–24

7 They boast of their wisdom, but they have made fools of themselves.
Rom. 1.22

8 God forbid that I should boast of anything but the cross of our Lord Jesus Christ.
Gal. 6.14

BREAD

9 If only we had died at the Lord's hand in Egypt, where we sat round the fleshpots and had plenty of bread to eat!
Ex. 16.3

10 The Lord said to Moses, 'I will rain down bread from heaven for you.'
Ex. 16.4

11 Israel called the food manna; it was white, like coriander seed, and it tasted like a wafer made with honey.
Ex. 16.31

12 The Israelites themselves wept once again and cried, 'Will no one give us meat? Think of it! In Egypt we had fish for the asking, cucumbers and water-melons, leeks and onions and garlic. Now our throats are parched; there is nothing wherever we look except this manna.'
Num. 11.4–6

13 Man cannot live on bread alone.
Deut. 8.3

14 You shall eat . . . the bread of affliction.
Deut. 16.3

15 The tempter approached him and said, 'If you are the Son of God, tell these stones to become bread.' Jesus answered, 'Scripture says, "Man cannot live on bread alone".'
Matt. 4.3–4

16 Give us today our daily bread.
Matt. 6.11

17 I am the bread of life. Whoever comes to me shall never be hungry.
John 6.35

BROTHERHOOD

18 Am I my brother's keeper?
Gen. 4.9

19 How good it is and how pleasant/for brothers to live together!
Ps. 133.1

1 Rich and poor have this in common: the Lord made them both.
Prov. 22.2

2 Let love for our brotherhood breed warmth of mutual affection.
Rom. 12.10

3 In a word, accept one another as Christ accepted us, to the glory of God.
Rom. 15.7

4 Give due honour to everyone: love to the brotherhood, reverence to God, honour to the sovereign.
1 Pet. 2.17

5 A man may say, 'I am in the light'; but if he hates his brother, he is still in the dark.
1 John 2.9

6 We for our part have crossed over from death to life; this we know, because we love our brothers.
1 John 3.14

7 It is by this that we know what love is: that Christ laid down his life for us. And we in our turn are bound to lay down our lives for our brothers.
1 John 3.16

8 But if a man has enough to live on, and yet when he sees his brother in need shuts up his heart against him, how can it be said that the divine love dwells in him?
1 John 3.17

9 If a man says, 'I love God', while hating his brother, he is a liar.
1 John 4.20

10 My bread may be a material matter. My brother's bread is a spiritual matter.
NICHOLAS BERDYAEV

11 Beloved, let us love: love is of God;/ In God alone hath love its true abode . . . Beloved, let us love: for only thus/ Shall we behold that God who loveth us.
HORATIUS BONAR *Hymn*

12 For a' that, and a' that,/It's coming yet for a' that,/That Man to Man the world o'er,/Shall brothers be for a' that.
ROBERT BURNS

13 Standing as I do in view of God and eternity, I realise that patriotism is not enough. I must have no hatred or bitterness towards anyone.
EDITH CAVELL

14 Jesus Christ has gone to heaven;/One day he'll be coming back, sir./ In this house he will be welcome,/ But we hope he won't be black, sir.
SYDNEY CARTER *100 Hymns for Today*

15 Jesus Christ, the Man for Others,/we, your people, make our prayer:/Give us grace to love as brothers/all whose burdens we can share.
STEWART CROSS *100 Hymns for Today*

16 How shall we love Thee, holy, hidden Being,/ If we love not the world which Thou hast made?/ O, give us brother-love, for better seeing/Thy Word made flesh and in a manger laid./Thy Kingdom come, O Lord, Thy will be done.
LAURENCE HOUSMAN *Hymn*

17 Write me as one that loves his fellow-men.
LEIGHT HUNT *Abou Ben Adhem*

18 I met a hundred men going to Delhi and every one of them was my brother.
Indian saying

19 The God who rules this earth/gave life to every race;/He chose its day of birth,/ the colour of its face;/So none may claim superior grade/Within the family he's made.
RICHARD G. JONES *100 Hymns for Today*

20 For the healing of the nations,/Lord, we pray with one accord;/For a just and equal sharing/of the things that earth affords./To a life of love in action/help us rise and pledge our word.
FRED KAAN *100 Hymns for Today*

1 We shall have to repent in this generation, not so much for the evil deeds of the wicked people, but for the appalling silence of the good people.
MARTIN LUTHER KING

2 Teach us delight in simple things,/And mirth that has no bitter springs;/ Forgiveness free of evil done,/And love to all men 'neath the sun!
RUDYARD KIPLING *Hymn*

3 In Germany, the Nazis came for the Communists and I didn't speak up because I was not a Communist. Then they came for the Jews and I didn't speak up because I was not a Jew.
Then they came for the Trade Unionists and I didn't speak up because I was not a Trade Unionist. Then they came for the Catholics and I was a Protestant so I didn't speak up. Then they came for me
. . . .
By that time there was no one to speak up for anyone.
MARTIN NIEMÖLLER

4 We cannot possibly let ourselves get frozen into regarding everyone we do not know as an absolute stranger.
ALBERT SCHWEITZER *Memories of Childhood and Youth*

5 O brother man, fold to thy heart thy brother!/Where pity dwells, the peace of God is there;/To worship rightly is to love each other,/Each smile a hymn, each kindly deed a prayer.
JOHN GREENLEAF WHITTIER *Hymn*

BURDENS

6 Come to me, all whose work is hard, whose load is heavy; and I will give you relief.
Matt. 11.28

7 My yoke is good to bear, my load is light.
Matt. 11.30

8 Help one another to carry these heavy loads, and in this way you will fulfil the law of Christ.
Gal. 6.2

9 For everyone has his own proper burden to bear.
Gal. 6.5

10 I have read in Plato and Cicero sayings that are very wise and very beautiful; but I never read in either of them: 'Come unto me all ye that labour and are heavy laden.'
ST AUGUSTINE

11 I do not pray for a lighter load, but for a stronger back.
PHILLIPS BROOKS

CHANCE

1 Speed does not win the race nor strength the battle. Bread does not belong to the wise, nor wealth to the intelligent, nor success to the skilful; time and chance govern all.
Eccl. 9.11

2 The man who digs a pit may fall into it.
Eccl. 10.8

3 That Power Which erring men call Chance.
JOHN MILTON *Comus*

CHANGES

4 All the changes and chances of this mortal life.
BOOK OF COMMON PRAYER From the *Order for Holy Communion*

5 Change and decay in all around I see:/ O Thou Who changest not, abide with me.
HENRY FRANCIS LYTE *Hymn*

6 Here below to live is to change, and to be perfect is to have changed often.
CARDINAL NEWMAN *Essay on the Development of Christian Doctrine*

CHARITY

7 Be patient with the penniless,/and do not keep him waiting for your charity.
Ecclus 29.8

8 When you do some act of charity, do not let your left hand know what your right is doing.
Matt. 6.3

9 O Lord, who hast taught us that all our doings without charity are nothing worth; send thy Holy Ghost, and pour into our hearts that most excellent gift of charity, the very bond of peace and of all virtues, without which whosoever liveth is counted dead before thee: Grant this for thine only Son Jesus Christ's sake.
BOOK OF COMMON PRAYER *Collect for Quinquagesima*

10 The trouble is that too often charity not only begins but ends at home.
ANON

11 Charity is not any kind of love of God, but that love of God by which He is loved as the object of bliss, to which we are directed by faith and hope.
ST THOMAS AQUINAS *Summa Theologica*

12 Bestow on me, O Lord, a genial spirit and unwearied forbearance; a mild, loving, patient heart, kindly looks, pleasant, cordial speech and manners in the intercourse of daily life; that I may give offence to none, but as much as in me lies live in charity with all men.
JOHANN ARNDT

13 In necessary things, unity; in doubtful things, liberty; in all things, charity.
Motto of RICHARD BAXTER

14 Alas! for the rarity, of Christian charity/ Under the sun!
THOMAS HOOD *The Bridge of Sighs*

15 To do him any wrong was to beget/A kindness to him, for his heart was rich,/ Of such fine mould, that if you sowed therein/The seed of hate, it blossom'd Charity.
LORD TENNYSON *Queen Mary*

CHILDREN

16 Train your children to do what is right and give alms, to keep God in mind at all times and praise his name in sincerity with all their strength.
Tob. 14.9

17 Let the children come to me; do not try to stop them; for the kingdom of Heaven belongs to such as these.
Matt. 19.14

18 'Whoever receives one of these children in my name', he said 'receives me; and whoever receives me, receives not me but the One who sent me.'
Mark 9.37

1 As for the man who is a cause of stumbling to one of these little ones who have faith, it would be better for him to be thrown into the sea with a millstone round his neck.
Mark 9.42

2 'I tell you, whoever does not accept the kingdom of God like a child will never enter it.' And he put his arms round them, laid his hands upon them, and blessed them.
Mark 10.15–16

3 Let every Christian father and mother understand, when their child is three years old, that they have done more than half of all they will ever do for his character.
HORACE BUSHNELL *Christian Nurture*

4 So long as one does not become simple like a child, one does not get divine illumination. Forget all the worldly knowledge that thou hast acquired and become as a child, and then wilt thou get the divine wisdom.
RAMAKRISHNA (Hindu)

5 We are poor children crying for the light; but it is because we are children and we are alive that we long to ask the questions. Dead men never ask questions.
FATHER ARTHUR STANTON *Faithful Stewardship*

6 A parent should never make distinctions between his children.
The Talmud

7 It needs courage to let our children go, but we are trustees and stewards and have to hand them back to life—to God. As the old saying puts it: 'What I gave I have.' We have to love them and lose them.
ALFRED TORRIE

8 Hush! my dear, lie still and slumber,/ Holy Angels guard thy bed!/Heavenly blessings without number/Gently falling on thy head.
ISAAC WATTS *A Cradle Song*

CHRIST

9 'Behold the Man!' said Pilate.
John 19.5

10 King of kings and Lord of lords.
Rev. 19.16

11 Thou art the King of Glory O Christ./ Thou art the everlasting Son of the Father.
BOOK OF COMMON PRAYER From the *Te Deum*

12 Christ, if we call him a philosopher... was the poor man's philosopher, the first and only one that has appeared.
HORACE BUSHNELL *Nature and the Supernatural*

13 Hold to Christ, and for the rest be totally uncommitted.
HERBERT BUTTERFIELD *Christianity and History*

14 Thou art the Way; to Thee alone/ From sin and death we flee;/And he who would the Father seek/Must seek Him, Lord, by Thee.
GEORGE WASHINGTON DOANE *Hymn*

15 O Lord Jesus Christ, Who art the Way, the Truth, and the Life, we pray Thee suffer us not to stray from Thee, who art the Way, nor to distrust Thee, who art the Truth, nor to rest in any other thing than Thee, who art the Life.
Teach us by Thy Holy Spirit what to believe, what to do, and wherein to take our rest.
ERASMUS

16 An undogmatic Christ is the advertisement of a dying faith.
P. T. FORSYTH

17 If Shakespeare should come into this room, we would all rise; but if Jesus Christ should come in, we would all kneel.
CHARLES LAMB

1 The Divine Man is the great attractive centre, the sole gravitating point of a system which owes to Him all its coherency, and which would be but a chaos were He away.
HUGH MILLER *My Schools and Schoolmasters*

2 Alexander, Caesar, Charlemagne, and I have founded empires. But on what did we rest the creations of our genius? Upon force. Jesus Christ founded his empire upon love; and at this hour millions of men would die for him.
NAPOLEON BONAPARTE

3 The heart of a believer affected with the glory of Christ is like the needle touched with the lodestone. It can no longer be quiet, no longer be satisfied in a distance from Him.
JOHN OWEN *On the Glory of Christ*

4 Apart from Christ we know neither what our life nor our death is; we do not know what God is nor what we ourselves are.
BLAISE PASCAL *Pensées*

6 The knowledge of God without that of our wretchedness creates pride. The knowledge of our wretchedness without that of God creates despair. The knowledge of Jesus Christ is the middle way, because in Him we find both God and our wretchedness.
BLAISE PASCAL *Pensées*

7 Christ be with me, Christ within me,/ Christ behind me, Christ before me,/ Christ beside me, Christ to win me,/ Christ to comfort and restore me,/ Christ beneath me, Christ above me,/ Christ in quiet, Christ in danger,/ Christ in hearts of all that love me,/ Christ in mouth of friend and stranger.
ST PATRICK *Breastplate*

8 What does the Church think of Christ? The Church's answer is categorical and uncompromising, and it is this: That Jesus Bar-Joseph, the carpenter of Nazareth, was in fact and in truth, and in the most exact and literal sense of the words, the God 'by whom all things were made.' His body and brain were those of a common man; His personality was the personality of God, so far as that personality could be expressed in human terms. He was in every respect a genuine living man. He was not merely a man so good as to be 'like God'—He was God.
DOROTHY L. SAYERS

9 Thou hast conquered, O pale Galilean!/ The world has grown grey from Thy breath.
A. C. SWINBURNE *Hymn to Proserpine*

10 Jesus shall reign where'er the sun/Does his successive journeys run;/His Kingdom stretch from shore to shore,/Till moons shall wax and wane no more.
ISAAC WATTS *Hymn*

11 Ye servants of God, your Master proclaim,/And publish abroad His wonderful Name;/The Name all-victorious of Jesus extol;/His Kingdom is glorious, and rules over all.
CHARLES WESLEY *Hymn*

CHRIST, DISCIPLESHIP

12 Jesus said to them, 'Come with me, and I will make you fishers of men.' And at once they left their nets and followed him.
Matt. 4.19–20

13 Follow me, and leave the dead to bury their dead.
Matt. 8.22

14 Look, I send you out like sheep among wolves; be wary as serpents, innocent as doves.
Matt. 10.16

15 No man is worthy of me who does not take up his cross and walk in my footsteps.
Matt. 10.38

16 If anyone wishes to be a follower of mine, he must leave self behind; he must take up his cross and come with me.
Matt. 16.24

1 Full authority in heaven and on earth has been committed to me. Go forth therefore and make all nations my disciples.
Matt. 28. 18–19

2 And looking round at those who were sitting in the circle about him he said, 'Here are my mother and my brothers. Whoever does the will of God is my brother, my sister, my mother.'
Mark 3. 34–35

3 I tell you, if my disciples keep silence the stones will shout aloud.
Luke 19.40

4 Peace is my parting gift to you, my own peace, such as the world cannot give. Set your troubled hearts at rest, and banish your fears.
John 14.27

5 It is not ourselves that we proclaim; we proclaim Christ Jesus as Lord, and ourselves as your servants, for Jesus' sake.
2 Cor. 4.5

6 Here is the test by which we can make sure that we know him: do we keep his commands?
1 John 2.3

7 I have this against you: you have lost your early love.
Rev. 2.4

8 Jesus our Lord, and Shepherd of men,/ caring for human needs;/Feeding the hungry, healing the sick,/showing your love in deeds;/Help us in your great work to share;/People in want still need your care./ Lord, we are called to follow you;/ This we ask strength to do.
PATRICK APPLEFORD *100 Hymns for Today*

9 Lord, it is my chief complaint/That my love is weak and faint;/Yet I love Thee, and adore;/O for grace to love Thee more!
WILLIAM COWPER *Hymn*

10 O Son of Man, our Hero strong and tender,/Whose servants are the brave in all the earth,/Our living sacrifice to Thee we render,/ Who sharest all our sorrows, all our mirth.
FRANK FLETCHER *Hymn*

11 God Almighty, Eternal, Righteous, and Merciful, give to us poor sinners to do for thy sake all that we know of thy will, and to will always what pleases thee, so that inwardly purified, enlightened, and kindled by the fire of the Holy Spirit, we may follow in the footprints of thy well-beloved Son, our Lord Jesus Christ.
ST FRANCIS OF ASSISI

12 They may have had their trials too— failing health, declining years, the ingratitude of men—but they have endured as seeing Him who is invisible.
BENJAMIN JOWETT *College Sermons*

13 Whosoever would fully and feelingly understand the words of Christ, must endeavour to conform his life wholly to the life of Christ. . . .

If thou seekest Jesus in all things, thou shalt surely find Jesus. . . .

Set thyself therefore, like a good and faithful servant of Christ, to bear manfully the Cross of thy Lord Who out of love was crucified for thee.
THOMAS À KEMPIS *The Imitation of Christ*

14 O Thou who camest from above,/The pure celestial fire to impart,/Kindle a flame of sacred love/On the mean altar of my heart.
CHARLES WESLEY *Hymn*

CHRIST, THE ETERNAL

15 Be assured, I am with you always, to the end of time.
Matt. 28.20

16 I am the light of the world.
John 8.12

17 Before Abraham was born, I am.
John 8.58

1 I am the way; I am the truth and I am life.
John. 14.6

2 I have conquered the world.
John 16.33

3 He has made known to us his hidden purpose . . .that the universe, all in heaven and on earth, might be brought into a unity in Christ.
Eph. 1.9–10

4 He is the image of the invisible God; his is the primacy over all created things.
Col. 1.15

5 The whole universe has been created through him and for him.
Col. 1.16

6 In him the complete being of God, by God's own choice, came to dwell.
Col. 1.19

7 Christ is all, and is in all.
Col. 3.11

8 He has broken the power of death and brought life and immortality to light through the Gospel.
2 Tim. 1.10

9 Jesus Christ is the same yesterday, today, and for ever.
Heb. 13.8

10 I am the Alpha and the Omega, the first and the last, the beginning and the end.
Rev. 22.13

11 The one thing that makes me even the kind of Christian that I am is that I dare not turn my back on Christ and put Him out of my life.
JAMES DENNEY

12 If Christ has grappled our hearts to Himself at all, then it were surely wise to trust His certainties and not our own doubts, however persistent.
H. H. FARMER *The Healing Cross*

13 He said not: 'Thou shalt not be tempested, thou shalt not be travailed, thou shalt not be afflicted': but He said: 'Thou shalt not be overcome.'
MOTHER JULIAN OF NORWICH *Revelations of Divine Love*

14 Give me the greedy heart and the little creeping treasons,/Give me the proud heart and the blind, obstinate eyes;/ Give me the shallow heart, and the vain lust, and the folly;/Give me the coward heart and the spiritless refusals;/ Give me the confused self that you can do nothing with;/I can do something.
DOROTHY L. SAYERS *The Just Vengeance*

CHRIST, THE HEALER

15 He went round the whole of Galilee, teaching in the synagogues, preaching the gospel of the Kingdom, and curing whatever illness or infirmity there was among the people.
Matt. 4.23

16 If I can only touch his cloak, I shall be cured.
Matt. 9.21

17 The sight of the people moved him to pity: they were like sheep without a shepherd, harassed and helpless.
Matt. 9.36

18 They came to Jesus and saw the madman who had been possessed by the legion of devils, sitting there clothed and in his right mind; and they were afraid.
Mark 5.15

19 Go home to your own folk and tell them what the Lord in his mercy has done for you.
Mark 5.19

20 No one could perform these signs of yours unless God were with him.
John 3.2

21 'It is not that this man or his parents sinned,' Jesus answered; 'he was born blind so that God's power might be displayed in curing him.'
John 9.3

1 All I know is this: once I was blind,
now I can see.
John 9.25

2
Jesus wept.
John 11.35

3 All the world has gone after him!
John 12.19

4 He who has faith in me will do what I am
doing; and he will do greater things still
because I am going to the Father.
John 14.12

5 O Christ, whose touch unveiled the blind,/
Whose presence warmed the lonely soul;/
Your love made broken sinners whole,/
Your faith cast devils from the mind./
Grant us your faith, your love, your care/
To bring to sufferers everywhere.
H. C. A. GAUNT *100 Hymns for Today*

6 O Saviour Christ, Thou too art Man;/
Thou hast been troubled, tempted, tried;/
Thy kind but searching glance can scan/
The very wounds that shame would
hide;
Thy touch has still its ancient power;/
No word from Thee can fruitless fall:/
Hear in this solemn evening hour,/ And
in Thy mercy heal us all.
HENRY TWELLS *Hymn*

7 The healing of His seamless dress/Is by
our beds of pain;/We touch Him in
life's throng and press,/And we are whole
again.
JOHN GREENLEAF WHITTIER *Hymn*

CHRIST, HIS LIFE ON EARTH

8 What sort of man is this? Even the wind
and the sea obey him.
Matt. 8.27

9 The Son of Man came eating and drinking, and they say, 'Look at him! a glutton
and a drinker, a friend of tax-gatherers
and sinners!'
Matt. 11.19

10 Then Jesus turned and said to Peter,
'Away with you, Satan; you are a
stumbling block to me. You think as
men think, not as God thinks.'
Matt. 16.23

11 From time to time he would withdraw to
lonely places for prayer.
Luke 5.16

12 Can anything good come from Nazareth?
John 1.46

13 Jesus made a whip of cords and drove
them out of the temple, sheep, cattle,
and all.
John. 2.15

14 He needed no evidence from others about
a man, for he himself could tell what was
in a man.
John 2.25

15 There is much else that Jesus did. If it
were all to be recorded in detail, I
suppose the whole world could not hold
the books that would be written.
John 21.25

16 Ours is not a high priest unable to sympathize with our weaknesses, but one
who, because of his likeness to us, has
been tested every way, only without sin.
Heb. 4.15

17 The supreme miracle of Christ's character lies in this: that He combines within
Himself, as no other figure in human
history has ever done, the qualities of
every race.
C. F. ANDREWS *What I Owe to Christ*

18 If revelation is by the Word alone, then
Christ *lived* for nothing, and the Word was
made flesh in vain.
D. M. BAILLIE *God was in Christ*

19 If we cannot validly find any revelation of
God in the portrait of Jesus as an historical person, how are we ever to reach
and accept the dogmas about Him?
D. M. BAILLIE *God was in Christ*

20 Jesus Christ, in fact, is also the Rabbi of
Nazareth, historically so difficult to get

information about, and when it is obtained, one who is so apt to impress us as a little commonplace alongside more than one other founder of a religion and even alongside many later representatives of His own religion.

KARL BARTH *The Doctrine of the Word of God*

1 I do indeed think that we can now know almost nothing concerning the life and personality of Jesus, since early Christian sources show no interest in either, are moreover fragmentary and often legendary, and other sources about Jesus do not exist.

RUDOLF BULTMANN *Jesus and the Word*

2 We are all alike wrapped up in the great earth-dream, and He alone was fully awake of all the sons of men; or we men and women of the twentieth century are broad awake to the reality, and He was dreaming His solitary dream.

D. S. CAIRNS *The Faith that Rebels*

3 Christ's life outwardly was one of the most troubled lives that was ever lived: tempest and tumult, tumult and tempest, the waves breaking over it all the time. But the inner life was a sea of glass. The great calm was always there.

HENRY DRUMMOND *The Ideal Life*

4 It seems, then, that the form of the earthly, no less than the heavenly Christ is for the most part hidden from us. For all the inestimable value of the Gospels, they yield us little more than a whisper of his voice; we trace in them but the outskirts of his ways.

R. H. LIGHTFOOT *History and Interpretation in the Gospels*

5 But, in the eternities,/Doubtless we shall compare together, hear/a million alien Gospels, in what guise/He trod the Pleiades, the Lyre, the Bear.
O be prepared, my soul!/To read the inconceivable, to scan/The million forms of God those stars unroll/When, in our turn, we show to them a Man.

ALICE MEYNELL *Poems*

6 It is a delusion to suppose that we can cut out twenty centuries of lived experience and establish a direct relation between ourselves and the historic Jesus.

J. H. OLDHAM *Life is Commitment*

7 Jesus never claims to be God, personally; yet he always claims to bring God, completely.

J. A. T. ROBINSON *Honest to God*

8 Jesus is 'the man for others'.

J. A. T. ROBINSON *Honest to God*

9 The Jesus of Nazareth who came forward publicly as the Messiah, who preached the ethic of the Kingdom of God, who founded the Kingdom of Heaven upon earth, and died to give His work its final consecration never had any existence. . . . He comes to us as one unknown; without a name, as of old by the lakeside He came to those men who knew him not.

ALBERT SCHWEITZER *The Quest of the Historical Jesus*

10 The Son of God came into the world not only by his doctrine to instruct us in the way to happiness, and by his death to make expiation of sin, but by his life to be an example to us of holiness and virtue.

ARCHBISHOP TILLOTSON *Works*

11 The Christ that Harnack sees, looking back through nineteen centuries of Catholic darkness, is only the reflection of a Liberal Protestant face, seen at the bottom of a deep well.

GEORGE TYRRELL *Christianity at the Crossroads*

CHRIST, LAMB OF GOD

12 There is the Lamb of God; it is he who takes away the sin of the world.
John 1.29

13 Worthy is the Lamb, the Lamb that was slain, to receive all power and wealth, wisdom and might, honour and glory and praise!
Rev. 5.12

1 Praise and honour, glory and might, to him who sits on the throne and to the Lamb for ever and ever!
Rev. 5.13

2 O Lord God, Lamb of God, Son of the Father, that takest away the sins of the world, have mercy upon us.
BOOK OF COMMON PRAYER From the *Order for Holy Communion*

3 And did those feet in ancient time
Walk upon England's mountains green?
And was the Holy Lamb of God
On England's pleasant pastures seen?
And did the countenance divine
Shine forth upon our clouded hills?
And was Jerusalem builded here
Among these dark satanic mills?
WILLIAM BLAKE *Hymn*

4 The cross for the first time revealed God in terms of weakness and lowliness and suffering; even, humanly speaking, of absurdity. He was seen thenceforth in the image of the most timid, most gentle and most vulnerable of all living creatures —a lamb. Agnus Dei!
MALCOLM MUGGERIDGE *Jesus Rediscovered*

5 To Him who sits upon the throne,/The God whom we adore,/And to the Lamb that once was slain,/Be glory evermore.
ISAAC WATTS *Doxology*

CHRIST, HIS LOVE

6 I give you a new commandment: love one another; as I have loved you, so you are to love one another.
John 13.34

7 As the Father has loved me, so I have loved you. Dwell in my love. If you heed my commands, you will dwell in my love as I have heeded my Father's commands and dwell in his love.
John 15. 9–10

8 What can separate us from the love of Christ?
Rom. 8.35

9 May you be strong to grasp, with all God's people, what is the breadth and length and height and depth of the love of Christ, and to know it, though it is beyond knowledge.
Eph. 3. 18–19

10 The King of Love my Shepherd is,/Whose goodness faileth never;/I nothing lack if I am His/And He is mine for ever.
HENRY WILLIAMS BAKER *Hymn*

11 Jesus, the very thought of Thee/With sweetness fills my breast;/But sweeter far Thy face to see,/And in Thy presence rest.
Hymn attributed to ST BERNARD OF CLAIRVAUX

12 Jesus, Thou Joy of loving hearts,/Thou Fount of life, Thou Light of men,/From the best bliss that earth imparts/We turn unfilled to Thee again.
Hymn attributed to ST BERNARD OF CLAIRVAUX

13 My song is love unknown;/My Saviour's love to me;/Love to the loveless shown,/That they might lovely be./O, who am I,/That for my sake/My Lord should take/Frail flesh and die?
SAMUEL CROSSMAN *Love Unknown*

14 Is it not a shame that we are always afraid of Christ, whereas there was never in heaven or earth a more loving, familiar, or milder man, in words, works and demeanour, especially towards poor, sorrowful and tormented consciences?
MARTIN LUTHER *Table-Talk*

15 O Love that wilt not let me go,/I rest my weary soul in Thee:/I give Thee back the life I owe,/That in Thine ocean depths its flow/May richer, fuller be.
GEORGE MATHESON *Hymn*

16 Nobody knows the trouble I've seen,/Nobody knows but Jesus.
Negro spiritual

1 One there is, above all others,/Well deserves the name of Friend;/His is love beyond a brother's,/Costly, free, and knows no end:/They who once His kindness prove/Find it everlasting love.
JOHN NEWTON *Hymn*

2 O Lord, Jesus Christ, Who art as the Shadow of a Great Rock in a weary land, Who beholdest Thy weak creatures weary of labour, weary of pleasure, weary of hope deferred, weary of self; in Thine abundant compassion, and fellow feeling with us, and unutterable tenderness, bring us, we pray Thee, unto Thy rest.
CHRISTINA G. ROSSETTI

3 I know Thee, Saviour, who Thou art,/ Jesus, the feeble sinner's Friend;/Nor wilt Thou with the night depart,/But stay and love me to the end:/Thy mercies never shall remove;/Thy nature and Thy Name is Love.
CHARLES WESLEY *Hymn*

CHRIST, HIS PRESENCE

4 Take heart! It is I; do not be afraid.
Matt. 14.27

5 For where two or three have met together in my name, I am there among them.
Matt. 18.20

6 Here I stand knocking at the door; if anyone hears my voice and opens the door, I will come in and sit down to supper with him and he with me.
Rev. 3.20

7 Wherever there are two, they are not without God, and wherever there is one alone, I say, I am with him. Raise the stone, and there shalt thou find me; cleave the wood, and I am there.
Attributed to Jesus (3rd century)

8 Be Thou my Vision,/O Lord of my heart;/Naught be all else to me,/Save that Thou art,—/Thou my best thought,/

By day or by night,/Waking or sleeping,/ Thy presence my light.
Ancient Irish hymn

9 On Thee we fling our burdening woe,/ O Love Divine, for ever dear;/Content to suffer, while we know,/Living and dying, Thou art near!
OLIVER WENDELL HOLMES *Hymn*

10 Dear Master, in whose life I see/All that I would but fail to be,/Let Thy clear light for ever shine/, To shame and guide this life of mine.
Though what I dream and what I do/ In my weak days are always two,/Help me, oppressed by things undone,/O Thou, whose deeds and dreams were one!
JOHN HUNTER *Hymn*

11 Sun of my soul, Thou Saviour dear,/ It is not night if Thou be near;/O may no earth-born cloud arise/To hide Thee from Thy servant's eyes.
JOHN KEBLE *Hymn*

12 The knowledge of the ever-present Christ can reach down into the hidden depths and assure lonely modern man that he is not alone. More than that; it can draw him out of his loneliness to the rediscovery of the human race.
STEPHEN NEILL *The Church and Christian Union*

13 The day is past and over:/All thanks, O Lord, to Thee;/I pray Thee now that sinless/The hours of dark may be./O Jesus, keep me in Thy sight,/And guard me through the coming night.
Sixth-century hymn

14 Lord Jesus, think on me,/ Nor let me go astray;/Through darkness and perplexity/ Point Thou the heavenly way.
SYNESIUS OF CYRENE *Hymn*

15 There is a common belief among devout people that if we are personally devoted to Christ, His Presence will entirely purify us and put us right in every relation of life. Experience shows that this is simply not true.
WILLIAM TEMPLE *Personal Religion and the Life of Fellowship*

1 Christ, whose glory fills the skies,/
Christ, the true, the only Light,/Sun of
Righteousness, arise,/Triumph o'er the
shades of night./Dayspring from on high,
be near;/Daystar, in my heart appear.
CHARLES WESLEY *Hymn*

CHRIST, HIS REJECTION

2 The stone which the builders rejected/
has become the chief corner-stone./This
is the Lord's doing;/it is marvellous in
our eyes.
Ps. 118. 22–23

3 A prophet will always be held in honour,
except in his home town, and in his own
family.
Matt. 13.57

4 The Son of Man is going the way appointed for him in the scriptures; but alas for
that man by whom the Son of Man is
betrayed! It would be better for that man
if he had never been born.
Matt. 26.24

5 At this be broke into curses and declared
with an oath: 'I do not know the man.'
At that moment a cock crew; and Peter
remembered how Jesus had said, 'Before
the cock crows you will disown me three
times.' He went outside, and wept
bitterly.
Matt. 26. 74–75

6 'Is not this the carpenter, the son of
Mary, the brother of James and Joseph
and Judas and Simon? And are not his
sisters here with us?' So they fell foul of
him.
Mark 6.3

7 Whoever listens to you listens to me;
whoever rejects you rejects me. And
whoever rejects me rejects the One who
sent me.
Luke 10.16

8 Even his brothers had no faith in him.
John 7.5

9 We have no king but Caesar.
John 19.15

CHRIST, THE SAVIOUR

10 It was not to judge the world that God
sent his Son into the world, but that
through him the world might be saved.
John 3.17

11 I am the door; anyone who comes into
the fold through me shall be safe.
John 10.9

12 O Saviour of the world, who by thy Cross
and precious Blood hast redeemed us,
Save us, and help us, we humbly beseech
thee, O Lord.
BOOK OF COMMON PRAYER From the *Order
for the Visitation of the Sick*

13 Jesus, Deliverer,/Come Thou to me;/
Soothe Thou my voyaging/Over life's
sea:/Thou, when the storm of death/
Roars, sweeping by,/Whisper, O Truth of
Truth,/'Peace! It is I.'
Eighth-century hymn

14 Lord, save thy world; we strive in vain/
to save ourselves without thine aid;/
What skill and science slowly gain,/is
soon to evil ends betrayed.
ALBERT F. BAYLY *100 Hymns for Today*

15 By His first work He gave me to myself;
and by the next He gave Himself to me.
And when He gave Himself, He gave me
back myself that I had lost.
ST BERNARD OF CLAIRVAUX *De Diligendo
Deo*

16 Light of the world, undimming and
unsetting!/O shine each mist away;/
Banish the fear, the falsehood, and the
fretting;/Be our unchanging Day.
HORATIUS BONAR *Hymn*

17 'For our God hath blessed creation,/
Calling it good. I know/What spirit with
whom you blindly band/Hath blessed
destruction with his hand;/Yet by God's
death the stars shall stand/And the small
apples grow.'
G. K. CHESTERTON *Ballad of the White
Horse*

1 Christ is the world's Redeemer,/The lover of the pure,/The fount of heavenly wisdom,/Our trust and hope secure;/The armour of His soldiers,/The Lord of earth and sky;/Our health while we are living,/Our life when we shall die.
ST COLUMBA *Hymn*

2 Lord, we are blind; the world around/confuses us, although we see./In Christ the pattern is refound;/he sets us free.
DAVID EDGE *100 Hymns for Today*

3 O wet red swathe of earth laid bare,/O truth, O strength, O gleaming share,/O patient eyes that watch the goal,/O ploughman of the sinner's soul./O Jesus, drive the coulter deep/To plough my living man from sleep.
JOHN MASEFIELD *The Everlasting Mercy*

4 Rest of the weary,/Joy of the sad,/Hope of the dreary,/Light of the glad,/Home of the stranger,/Strength to the end,/Refuge from danger,/Saviour and Friend!
JOHN SAMUEL BEWLEY MONSELL *Hymn*

5 Be Thou our great Deliverer still,/Thou Lord of life and death;/Restore and quicken, soothe and bless,/With Thine almighty breath;/To hands that work and eyes that see/Give wisdom's heavenly lore,/ That whole and sick, and weak and strong,/May praise Thee evermore.
EDWARD HAYES PLUMPTRE *Hymn*

6 I have no wit, no words, no tears;/My heart within me like a stone/Is numbed too much for hopes or fears;/Look right, look left, I dwell alone;/I lift mine eyes, but dimmed with grief/No everlasting hills I see;/My life is in the falling leaf:/O Jesus, quicken me.
CHRISTINA G. ROSSETTI *A Better Resurrection*

7 God harden me against myself,/This coward with pathetic voice/Who craves for ease, and rest, and joys:
Myself, arch-traitor to myself;/My hollowest friend, my deadliest foe,/My clog whatever road I go.
Yet One there is can curb myself,/Can roll the strangling load from me,/Break off the yoke and set me free.
CHRISTINA G. ROSSETTI *Who shall deliver me?*

8 Jesu, Lover of my soul,/Let me to Thy bosom fly,/While the nearer waters roll,/While the tempest still is high;/Hide me, O my Saviour, hide,/Till the storm of life is past;/Safe into the haven guide;/O receive my soul at last!
CHARLES WESLEY *Hymn*

9 O for a thousand tongues, to sing/My great Redeemer's praise,/The glories of my God and King,/The triumphs of His grace!
CHARLES WESLEY *Hymn*

10 No condemnation now I dread;/Jesus, and all in Him, is mine!/Alive in Him, my living Head,/And clothed in righteousness divine,/Bold I approach the eternal throne,/And claim the crown, through Christ my own.
CHARLES WESLEY *Hymn*

11 Come, Thou long-expected Jesus,/Born to set Thy people free;/From our fears and sins release us;/Let us find our rest in Thee.
CHARLES WESLEY *Hymn*

CHRIST, HIS SERVICE

12 For the man who has will be given more, till he has enough and to spare; and the man who has not will forfeit even what he has.
Matt. 13.12

13 'Lord, when was it that we saw you hungry and fed you, or thirsty and gave you a drink, a stranger and took you home, or naked and clothed you? When did we see you ill or in prison, and come to visit you?' And the king will answer, 'I tell you this: anything you did for one of my brothers here, however humble, you did for me.'
Matt. 25. 37–40

1 While daylight lasts we must carry on the work of him who sent me; night comes, when no one can work.
John 9.4

2 If I, your Lord and Master, have washed your feet, you also ought to wash one another's feet.
John 13.14

3 We come therefore as Christ's ambassadors.
2 Cor. 5.20

4 We offer in simplicity/our loving gift and labour;/And what we do, we do to thee,/incarnate in our neighbour.
GILES AMBROSE *100 Hymns for Today*

5 Jesus, risen from the dead,/with us always, as you said;/every day in all we do,/help us live and love like you.
PATRICK APPLEFORD *100 Hymns for Today*

6 O Jesus, I have promised/To serve Thee to the end;/Be Thou for ever near me,/My Master and my Friend:/I shall not fear the battle/If Thou art by my side,/Nor wander from the pathway/If Thou wilt be my Guide.
JOHN ERNEST BODE *Hymn*

7 Lord, in the fulness of my might,/I would for Thee be strong:/While runneth o'er each dear delight,/To Thee should soar my song.
O choose me in my golden time;/In my dear joys have part!/For Thee the glory of my prime,/The fulness of my heart!
THOMAS HORNBLOWER GILL *Hymn*

8 The Son of God goes forth to war,/A kingly crown to gain;/His blood-red banner streams afar:/Who follows in His train?/Who best can drink his cup of woe,/Triumphant over pain,/Who patient bears his cross below,/He follows in His train.
REGINALD HEBER *Hymn*

9 The social gospel needs a theology to make it effective; but theology needs the social gospel to vitalize it.
W. RAUSCHENBUSCH *A Theology for the Social Gospel*

10 O most merciful Redeemer, Friend, and Brother,/May we know Thee more clearly,/Love Thee more dearly,/Follow Thee more nearly:/For ever and ever.
ST RICHARD OF CHICHESTER

11 What can I give Him,/Poor as I am?/If I were a shepherd,/I would bring a lamb;/If I were a wise man,/I would do my part;/Yet what I can I give Him—/Give my heart.
CHRISTINA G. ROSSETTI *Hymn*

12 Of myself I can only say that I am an unprofitable servant; but I serve a good Master.
RICHARD ROTHE *Still Hours*

13 Christ believed it possible to bind men to their kind, but on one condition—that they were first bound fast to Himself.
SIR JOHN SEELEY *Ecce Homo*

14 Govern all by Thy wisdom, O Lord, so that my soul may always be serving Thee as Thou dost will, and not as I may choose. Do not punish me, I beseech Thee, by granting that which I wish or ask, if it offend Thy love, which would always live in me. Let me die to myself, that I may serve Thee: let me live to Thee, who in Thyself art the true Life.
ST TERESA OF AVILA

15 Soldiers of Christ! arise,/And put your armour on,/Strong in the strength which God supplies/Through His eternal Son;/Strong in the Lord of hosts,/And in His mighty power;/Who in the strength of Jesus trusts/Is more than conqueror.
CHARLES WESLEY *Hymn*

16 I'm not ashamed to own my Lord,/Or to defend His cause,/Maintain the glory of His Cross,/And honour all His laws.
ISAAC WATTS *Hymn*

CHRIST, SON OF GOD

17 Everything is entrusted to me by my Father; and no one knows the Son but

the Father, and no one knows the Father but the Son and those to whom the Son may choose to reveal him.
Matt. 11.27

1 At the moment when he came up out of the water, he saw the heavens torn open and the Spirit, like a dove, descending upon him. And a voice spoke from heaven: 'Thou art my Son, my Beloved; on thee my favour rests.'
Mark 1. 10–11

2 All that came to be was alive with his life, and that life was the light of men.
John 1.4

3 The word became flesh; he came to dwell among us, and we saw his glory, such glory as befits the Father's only Son, full of grace and truth.
John 1.14

4 No one has ever seen God; but God's only Son, he who is nearest to the Father's heart, he has made him known.
John 1.18

5 The light has come into the world, but men preferred darkness to light because their deeds were evil.
John 3.19

6 Whoever drinks the water that I shall give him will never suffer thirst any more.
John 4.14

7 If anyone is thirsty let him come to me; whoever believes in me, let him drink.
John 7.38

8 My Father and I are one.
John 10.30

9 Accept the evidence of my deeds, even if you do not believe me, so that you may recognize and know that the Father is in me, and I in the Father.
John 10.38

10 Anyone who has seen me has seen the Father.
John 14.9

11 Christ stimulates us, as other great men stimulate us, but we find a power coming from Him into our lives that enables us to respond. That is the experience that proves Him to be the universal Spirit. It does not happen with others.
WILLIAM TEMPLE

CHRIST, HIS SUFFERING

12 My Father, if it is possible, let this cup pass me by. Yet not as I will, but as thou wilt.
Matt. 26.39

13 The spirit is willing, but the flesh is weak.
Matt. 26.41

14 His sweat was like clots of blood falling to the ground.
Luke 22.44

15 Now my soul is in turmoil, and what am I to say? Father, save me from this hour. No, it was for this that I came to this hour. Father, glorify thy name.
John 12.27–28

16 For since he himself has passed through the test of suffering, he is able to help those who are meeting their test now.
Heb. 2.18

17 Son though he was, he learned obedience in the school of suffering, and once perfected, became the source of eternal salvation for all who obey him.
Heb. 5. 8–9

18 Melt, O my soul, with the fire of compassion at the sufferings of that Man of love, whom in the midst of such gentleness thou seest afflicted with so bitter griefs.
ST ANSELM *Meditations*

19 The groaning of creation,/wrung out by pain and care,/The anguish of a million hearts/that break in dumb despair;/O crucified Redeemer,/these are thy cries of pain;/O may they break our selfish hearts,/and love come in to reign.
TIMOTHY REES *100 Hymns for Today*

1 He has entered little into the depths of our Master's character who does not know that the settled tone of his disposition was a peculiar and subdued sadness.
F. W. ROBERTSON *Sermons*

2 O Christ, I see thy crown of thorns in every eye, thy bleeding, naked, wounded body in every soul; thy death liveth in every memory; thy crucified Person is embalmed in every affection; thy pierced feet are bathed in everyone's tears; and it is my privilege to enter with thee into every soul.
THOMAS TRAHERNE

CHRIST, HIS TEACHING

3 How blest are those who know their need of God; the kingdom of Heaven is theirs.
Matt. 5.3

4 How blest are the sorrowful; they shall find consolation.
Matt. 5.4

5 How blest are those of a gentle spirit; they shall have the earth for their possession.
Matt. 5.5

6 How blest are those who hunger and thirst to see right prevail; they shall be satisfied.
Matt. 5.6

7 How blest are those who show mercy; mercy shall be shown to them.
Matt. 5.7

8 How blest are those whose hearts are pure; they shall see God.
Matt. 5.8

9 How blest are the peacemakers; God shall call them his sons.
Matt. 5.9

10 How blest are those who have suffered persecution for the cause of right; the kingdom of Heaven is theirs.
Matt. 5.10

11 Love your enemies and pray for your persecutors; only so can you be children of your heavenly Father, who makes his sun rise on good and bad alike, and sends the rain on the honest and the dishonest.
Matt. 5. 44–45

12 What then of the man who hears these words of mine and acts upon them? He is like a man who had the sense to build his house on rock.
Matt. 7.24

13 But what of the man who hears these words of mine and does not act upon them? He is like a man who was foolish enough to build his house on sand.
Matt. 7.26

14 Heaven and earth will pass away; my words will never pass away.
Matt. 24.35

15 The time has come; the kingdom of God is upon you; repent, and believe the Gospel.
Mark 1.15

16 What is this? A new kind of teaching! He speaks with authority.
Mark 1.27

17 'Which commandment is first of all?' Jesus answered, 'The first is, "Hear, O Israel: the Lord our God is the only Lord; love the Lord your God with all your heart, with all your soul, with all your mind, and with all your strength." The second is this: "Love your neighbour as yourself." There is no other commandment greater than these.'
Mark 12. 28–31

18 Lord, to whom shall we go? Your words are words of eternal life.
John 6.68

19 How is it that this untrained man has such learning?
John 7.15

20 No man ever spoke as this man speaks.
John 7.46

1 If anyone obeys my teaching he shall never know what it is to die.
John 8.51

2 The man who has received my commands and obeys them—he it is who loves me.
John 14.21

3 What God's Son has told me, take for true I do; Truth himself speaks truly or there's nothing true.
ST THOMAS AQUINAS

4 The Humanist suggestion that Jesus was 'morally right but religiously mistaken' defies all psychological probabilities.
F. R. BARRY *Christian Ethics and Secular Society*

5 No teacher ever showed more belief than our Lord in the capacity of the ordinary man to think rightly, if he be only sincere and open-minded. He did not, except rarely, use the dogmatic method. It would seem as if He feared to stunt men's growth from within thereby.
CHARLES GORE *A New Commentary on Holy Scripture*

6 Most people really believe that the Christian commandments (e.g., to love one's neighbour as onself) are intentionally a little too severe, like putting the clock half an hour ahead to make sure of not being late in the morning.
SÖREN KIERKEGAARD *Journals*

7 I am trying here to prevent anyone saying the really foolish thing that people often say about Him: 'I'm ready to accept Jesus as a great moral teacher, but I don't accept His claim to be God.' That is the one thing we must not say. A man who was merely a man and said the sort of things Jesus said would not be a great moral teacher. He would either be a lunatic—or else he would be the Devil of Hell. You must make your choice.
C. S. LEWIS

8 I am pretty sure that we err in treating these sayings as paradoxes. It would be nearer the truth to say that it is life itself which is paradoxical and that the sayings of Jesus are simply a recognition of that fact.
SIR THOMAS TAYLOR

CHRIST, UNION WITH

9 I will not leave you bereft; I am coming back to you. In a little while the world will see me no longer, but you will see me; because I live, you too will live; then you will know that I am in my Father, and you in me and I in you.
John 14. 18–20

10 I am the vine, and you the branches. He who dwells in me, as I dwell in him, bears much fruit; for apart from me you can do nothing.
John 15.5

11 If you dwell in me, and my words dwell in you, ask what you will, and you shall have it.
John 15.7

12 You must regard yourselves as dead to sin and alive to God, in union with Christ Jesus.
Rom. 6.11

13 There is no condemnation for those who are united with Christ Jesus.
Rom. 8.1

14 We, however, possess the mind of Christ.
1 Cor. 2.16

15 When anyone is united to Christ, there is a new world; the old order has gone, and a new order has already begun.
2 Cor. 5.17

16 The life I now live is not my life, but the life which Christ lives in me.
Gal. 2.20

17 For to me life is Christ, and death gain.
Phil. 1.21

1 I count everything sheer loss, because all is far outweighed by the gain of knowing Christ Jesus my Lord, for whose sake I did in fact lose everything.
Phil. 3.8

2 Christ in you, the hope of a glory to come.
Col. 1.27

3 He died for us so that we, awake or asleep, might live in company with him.
1 Thess. 5.10

4 Here are words you may trust:/'If we died with him, we shall live with him;/ if we endure, we shall reign with him./ If we deny him, he will deny us./ If we are faithless, he keeps faith,/for he cannot deny himself.'
2 Tim. 2. 11–13

5 I have a room./'Tis poor, but 'tis my best, if Thou wilt come/Within so small a cell, where I would fain/Mine and the world's Redeemer entertain./I mean my heart.
SIR MATTHEW HALE

6 Make me a captive, Lord,/And then I shall be free;/Force me to render up my sword,/And I shall conqueror be./I sink in life's alarms/When by myself I stand;/ Imprison me within Thine arms,/And strong shall be my Hand.
GEORGE MATHESON *Hymn*

7 Love divine, all loves excelling,/Joy of heaven, to earth come down,/Fix in us Thy humble dwelling,/All Thy faithful mercies crown.
CHARLES WESLEY *Hymn*

CHRISTIANITY

8 The faith which God entrusted to his people once and for all.
Jude 3

9 What is now called the Christian religion existed among the ancients and has never failed from the beginning of the human race, until Christ came in the flesh; since when true religion, which was already in existence, began to be called Christianity.
ST AUGUSTINE *Retractations*

10 If Christianity were ethics, then Socrates was the Saviour.
WILLIAM BLAKE

11 It is come, I know not how, to be taken for granted, by many persons, that Christianity is not so much as a subject of enquiry; but that it is now at length discovered to be fictitious.
JOSEPH BUTLER *The Analogy of Religion*

12 No great religion was ever a wholly new religion. Christianity could hardly have made its universal appeal if it had not taken up into itself so much of the deepest religious experience of past generations.
C. H. DODD *The Authority of the Bible*

13 The belief in that truth which was revealed through Christ—whether man is passionately opposed to it, or whether he makes every effort to realize it as his own destiny—has been *the* driving force of history ever since.
ERICH FRANK *Philosophical Understanding and Religious Truth*

14 Christianity is Asceticism without Rigorism and Love without Sentimentality.
BARON F. VON HÜGEL

15 This system of beliefs is quite unacceptable in the world of to-day. It is contradicted, as a whole and in detail, by our extended knowledge of the cosmos, of the solar system, of our own planet, of our own species and of our individual selves.
SIR JULIAN HUXLEY

16 As to the Christian religion, Sir, besides the strong evidence which we have for it, there is a balance in its favour from the number of great men who have been convinced of its truth.
SAMUEL JOHNSON Boswell's *Life of Johnson*

17 I have never really doubted the fundamental truth of the Christian faith—though I have constantly found myself questioning its expression.
J. A. T. ROBINSON *Honest to God*

1 Why not give Christianity a trial? The question seems a hopeless one after 2000 years of resolute adherence to the old cry of 'Not this man, but Barabbas.' . . . . 'This man' has not been a failure yet, for nobody has ever been sane enough to try his way.
G. B. SHAW Preface to *Androcles and the Lion*

2 Christianity is the most avowedly materialist of all the great religions.
WILLIAM TEMPLE *Nature, Man and God*

CHRISTIANS

3 You are salt to the world.
Matt. 5.13

4 You are light for all the world.
Matt. 5.14

5 You, like the lamp, must shed light among your fellows, so that, when they see the good you do, they may give praise to your Father in heaven.
Matt. 5.16

6 For he who is not against us is on our side.
Mark 9.40

7 It was in Antioch that the disciples first got the name of Christians.
Acts 11.26

8 We are fools for Christ's sake.
1 Cor. 4.10

9 Be one in thought and feeling, all of you; be full of brotherly affection, kindly and humble-minded.
1 Pet. 3.8

10 The man who is not an artist is not a Christian.
WILLIAM BLAKE

11 To be a Christian does not mean to be religious in a particular way, to cultivate some particular form of asceticism (as a sinner, a penitent, or a saint), but to be a man. It is not some religious act that makes a Christian what he is, but participation in the suffering of God in the life of the world. It is only by living completely in this world that one learns to believe. One must abandon every attempt to make something of oneself, whether it be a saint, a converted sinner, a churchman, a righteous man or an unrighteous one, a sick man or a healthy one. This is what I mean by worldliness—taking life in one's stride, with all its duties and problems, its successes and failures, its experiences and helplessness.
DIETRICH BONHOEFFER *Letters and Papers from Prison*

12 What the world expects of Christians is that they should speak out, loud and clear, and that they should voice their condemnation in such a way that never a doubt, never the slightest doubt, could arise in the heart of the simplest man. They must get away from abstractions and confront the blood-stained face that history has taken on today.
ALBERT CAMUS

13 What the world requires of the Christians is that they should continue to be Christians.
ALBERT CAMUS

14 The greatest of all blessings, as it is the most ennobling of all privileges, is to be indeed a Christian.
S. T. COLERIDGE *Letters*

15 The distinction between Christians and other men, is neither in country nor language nor customs. For they do not dwell in cities in some place of their own, nor do they use any strange variety of dialect, nor practise any extraordinary kind of life. This teaching of theirs has not been discovered by the intellect or thought of busy men, nor are they the advocates of any human doctrine as some men are. Yet while living in Greek and barbarian cities, according as each obtained his lot, and following the local customs, both in clothing and food and in the rest of life, they show forth the wonderful and confessedly strange character of the constitution of their own citizenship. They dwell in their own

fatherlands, but as if sojourners in them: they share all things as citizens, and suffer all things as strangers.

The Epistle to Diognetus

1 I take it for granted that every Christian that is in health is up early in the morning.

WILLIAM LAW *A Serious Call to a Devout and Holy Life*

2 There is a sense in which no man is a Christian—the paradoxical sense that a man is a Christian only when he acknowledges that he is not completely one.

A. D. LINDSAY *The Two Moralities*

3 Just as our neighbour is in need and lacks that in which we abound, so we also have been in need before God and have lacked his mercy. Hence, as our heavenly Father has in Christ freely come to our help, we also ought freely to help our neighbour through our body and its works, and each should become as it were a Christ to the other, that we may be Christs to one another and Christ may be the same in all; that is, that we may be truly Christians.

MARTIN LUTHER *On the Liberty of the Christian Man*

4 The Christian is one who has forever given up the hope of being able to think of himself as a good man.

LESSLIE NEWBIGIN *Christian Freedom in the Modern World*

5 Knowing that Christ has come, we see that because of him there have been many Christs in the world who, like him, have 'loved righteousness and hated iniquity'.

ORIGEN *Contra Celsum*

6 The first (mark of a Christian) is a deep reverence for persons as destined for eternity with God. The second is a kind of heavenly serenity which is able to draw the sting of suffering. And the third is the humility of a man or woman who has known authentically the presence of God.

ARCHBISHOP A. M. RAMSEY

7 You are the light of the world/You are the light of the world/But the tallest candlestick/Ain't much good without a wick/You gotta live right to be the light of the world.

STEPHEN SCHWARTZ *Godspell*

CHRISTMAS

8 Then they opened their treasures and offered him gifts: gold, frankincense, and myrrh.

Matt. 2.11

9 Tonight for the first time the prison gates/ Have opened. Music and sudden light/ Have interrupted our routine to-night,/ And swept the filth of habit from our hearts.

W. H. AUDEN *A Christmas Oratorio*

10 Now blessed be the tow'rs/that crown England so fair/That stand up strong in prayer/unto God for our souls:/Blessed be their founders/(said I) an' our country folk/Who are ringing for Christ/in the belfries to-night/With arms lifted to clutch/the rattling ropes that race/Into the dark above/and the mad romping din.

ROBERT BRIDGES *Noel: Christmas Eve 1913*

11 O Holy Child of Bethlehem,/Descend to us, we pray;/Cast out our sin, and enter in;/Be born in us today./ We hear the Christmas angels/The great glad tidings tell;/O come to us, abide with us,/ Our Lord Immanuel!

PHILLIPS BROOKS *Hymn*

12 To Thee, meek Majesty, soft King/Of simple graces and sweet loves!/Each of us his lamb will bring,/Each his pair of silver doves!/At last, in fire of Thy fair eyes,/Ourselves become our own best sacrifice!

RICHARD CRASHAW *The Shepherd's Hymn*

13 As with gladness men of old/Did the guiding star behold,/As with joy they hailed its light,/Leading onward,beaming bright,—/So, most gracious Lord, may we/Evermore be led to Thee.

WILLIAM CHATTERTON DIX *Hymn*

1 O come all ye faithful,/Joyful and triumphant,/O come ye, O come ye to Bethlehem;/Come and behold Him/Born the King of angels;/ O come let us adore Him, Christ the Lord.
Eighteenth-century hymn

2 All my heart this night rejoices,/As I hear, far and near,/Sweetest angel voices;/ 'Christ is born!' their choirs are singing,/Till the air, everywhere,/Now with joy is ringing.
PAUL GERHARDT *Hymn*

3 Who is He, in yonder stall,/At whose feet the shepherds fall?/'Tis the Lord! O wondrous story!/'Tis the Lord, the King of Glory!/At His feet we humbly fall;/Crown Him, crown Him Lord of all.
BENJAMIN RUSSELL HANBY *Hymn*

4 Ah! dearest Jesus, Holy Child,/Make Thee a bed, soft, undefiled,/Within my heart, that it may be/A quiet chamber kept for Thee.
MARTIN LUTHER *Hymn*

5 Child in the manger,/Infant of Mary;/Outcast and stranger,/Lord of all!/Child who inherits/All our transgressions/All our demerits/On Him fall.
MARY MACDONALD *Hymn*

6 This is the month, and this the happy morn,/Wherein the Son of Heav'n's eternal King,/Of wedded maid and virgin mother born,/Our great redemption from above did bring;/For so the holy sages once did sing,/That he our deadly forfeit should release,/And with his Father work us a perpetual peace.
JOHN MILTON *On the Morning of Christ's Nativity*

7 Still the night, holy the night!/Shepherds first saw the light,/Heard resounding clear and long,/Far and near, the angel-song,/'Christ the Redeemer is here!'
JOSEPH MOHR *Hymn*

8 Outlanders, whence come ye last?/The snow in the street and the wind on the door./Through what green sea and great have ye passed?/Minstrels and maids, stand forth on the floor.

From far away we come to you,/The snow in the street and the wind on the door./ To tell of great tidings strange and true:/Minstrels and maids, stand forth on the floor.
News, news of the Trinity,/The snow in the street and the wind on the door./To Mary and Joseph from over the sea:/Minstrels and maids, stand forth on the floor.
News of a fair and a marvellous thing,/The snow in the street and the wind on the door./Nowell, nowell, nowell, we sing!/Minstrels and maids, stand forth on the floor.
WILLIAM MORRIS

9 Good Christian men, rejoice/With heart and soul and voice!/Give ye heed to what we say:/News! News!/Jesus Christ is born to-day./Ox and ass before Him bow,/And He is in the manger now:/Christ is born to-day.
JOHN MASON NEALE *Hymn*

10 Love came down at Christmas,/Love all lovely, Love Divine;/Love was born at Christmas,/Star and angels gave the sign.
CHRISTINA G. ROSSETTI *Hymn*

11 The first Nowell the angel did say/Was to certain poor shepherds in fields as they lay:/In fields where they lay a-keeping their sheep/On a cold winter's night that was so deep./Nowell, Nowell, Nowell, Nowell,/Born is the King of Israel.
Traditional Carol

CHURCH, ON EARTH

12 You are Peter, the Rock; and on this rock I will build my church, and the powers of death shall never conquer it.
Matt. 16.18

13 There will then be one flock, one shepherd.
John 10.16

14 Holy Father, protect by the power of thy name those whom thou hast given me, that they may be one, as we are one.
John 17.11

1 They met constantly to hear the apostles teach, and to share the common life, to break bread, and to pray.
Acts 2.42

2 The whole body of believers was united in heart and soul. Not a man of them claimed any of his possessions as his own, but everything was held in common.
Acts 4.32

3 There can be no other foundation beyond that which is already laid; I mean Jesus Christ himself.
1 Cor. 3.11

4 You are Christ's body, and each of you a limb or organ of it.
1 Cor. 12.27

5 There is the responsibility that weighs on me every day, my anxious concern for all our congregations.
2 Cor. 11.28

6 There is no such thing as Jew and Greek, slave and freeman, male and female; for you are all one person in Christ Jesus.
Gal. 3.28

7 (God) appointed him as supreme head to the church, which is his body.
Eph. 1. 22–23

8 You are built upon the foundation laid by the apostles and prophets, and Christ Jesus himself is the foundation-stone.
Eph. 2.20

9 One Lord, one faith, one baptism.
Eph. 4.5

10 Inspire continually the universal Church with the spirit of truth, unity and concord.
BOOK OF COMMON PRAYER From the *Order for Holy Communion*

11 The Church, as it now stands, no human power can save.
DR THOMAS ARNOLD

12 He cannot have God for his Father who refuses to have the Church for his mother.
ST AUGUSTINE

13 To walk together to the kirk/And all together pray,/While each to his great Father bends,/Old men, and babes, and loving friends,/And youths and maidens gay.
S. T. COLERIDGE *The Ancient Mariner*

14 Every private Christian is the better for it; he does his service with real cheerfulness when he has all his companions and fellow servants to join with him in it; the worse a great deal if he wants them.
JOHN COSIN *Sermons*

15 There shall always be the Church and the World/And the Heart of Man/Shivering and fluttering between them, choosing and chosen,/Valiant, ignoble, dark and full of light/Swinging between Hell Gate and Heaven Gate./And the Gates of Hell shall not prevail./Darkness now, then/light.
T. S. ELIOT *The Rock*

16 A Church of sanctified egoisms would be no Church.
P. T. FORSYTH

17 We need to think of the Church as the body through which our risen and ascended Lord is seeking to redeem the world from all the evil with which it is infected.
LEONARD HODGSON *The Doctrine of Atonement*

18 For the might of Thine arm we bless Thee, our God, our fathers' God;/Thou hast kept Thy pilgrim people by the strength of Thy staff and rod;/Thou hast called us to the journey which faithless feet ne'er trod;/For the might of Thine arm we bless Thee, our God, our fathers' God.
CHARLES SILVESTER HORNE *Hymn*

19 To be of no Church is dangerous. Religion, of which the rewards are distant, and which is animated only by Faith and Hope, will glide by degrees out of the mind, unless it be invigorated and reimpressed by external ordinances, by stated calls to worship, and the salutary influence of example.
SAMUEL JOHNSON

1 City of God, how broad and far/Outspread thy walls sublime!/The true thy chartered freemen are,/Of every age and clime.
DR SAMUEL JOHNSON *Hymn*

2 Christ is made the sure foundation,/ Christ the head and corner-stone,/ Chosen of the Lord, and precious,/ Binding all the Church in one,/Holy Zion's help for ever,/And her confidence alone.
Latin hymn

3 He wanted life in men, energy, impulse; and in His Church He has often found nothing but a certain tame decorum, of which even He can make little.
W. M. MACGREGOR *Jesus Christ the Son of God*

4 The living Church, though never neat, keeps God's world from complete disaster.
GEORGE F. MACLEOD *Only One Way Left*

5 The great criticism of the Church today is that no one wants to persecute it: because there is nothing very much to persecute it about.
GEORGE F. MACLEOD *Only One Way Left*

6 We need a symbol of the sacred in the midst of the secular to remind us that all is sacred and that we all have souls. The Church is a symbol of celebration and joy and leisure and privacy, a sign of transcendence, a pointer of silence and tranquillity; a church is sacred space, symbolizing to us the sacredness of all space.
HUGH MONTEFIORE

7 Glorious things of thee are spoken,/ Zion, city of our God;/He whose word cannot be broken/Formed thee for His own abode./On the Rock of Ages founded,/What can shake thy sure repose?/With salvation's walls surrounded,/Thou mayest smile at all thy foes.
JOHN NEWTON *Hymn*

8 I ask of Thee neither health nor sickness, neither life nor death, but only that Thou disposest of my health and of my sickness, of my life and of my death, for Thy glory, for my salvation, and for the service of the Church and Thy saints.
BLAISE PASCAL

9 Thy hand, O God, has guided/Thy flock, from age to age;/The wondrous tale is written,/Full clear, on every page;/Our fathers owned Thy goodness,/And we their deeds record;/And both of this bear witness,/One Church, one Faith, one Lord.
EDWARD HAYES PLUMPTRE *Hymn*

10 The Church's one foundation/Is Jesus Christ her Lord:/She is His new creation/By water and the word;/From heaven He came and sought her/To be His holy bride:/With His own blood He bought her,/And for her life He died.
SAMUEL JOHN STONE *Hymn*

11 The Church on earth is a sacrament, an outward and visible sign of the Church Universal, and criticism of its outward form no more exhausts its spiritual significance than the geometrical treatment of curves exhausts the significance of their beauty.
WILLIAM TEMPLE

12 I believe in the Church. One Holy, Catholic and Apostolic, and I regret that it nowhere exists.
WILLIAM TEMPLE (attributed)

13 It is the Church of the saints and martyrs and prophets, who have been the light of the world in their several generations, that has the demand upon your allegiance —not the Church which has been corrupted by wealth and worldly power. But the true Church is embedded in the existing Churches—you will not find it elsewhere.
A. R. VIDLER *God's Demand and Man's Response*

CHURCH, TRIUMPHANT

14 These are the men who have passed through the great ordeal; they have washed their robes and made them white in the blood of the Lamb.
Rev. 7.14

1 They shall never again feel hunger or thirst, the sun shall not beat on them nor any scorching heat, because the Lamb who is at the heart of the throne will be their shepherd and will guide them to the springs of the water of life; and God will wipe all tears from their eyes.
Rev. 7. 16–17

2 Moreover, I heard a voice from heaven, saying, 'Write this: "Happy are the dead who die in the faith of Christ! Henceforth", says the Spirit, "they may rest from their labours; for they take with them the record of their deeds". '
Rev. 14.13

3 O what their joy and their glory must be,/Those endless Sabbaths the blessed ones see!/Crown for the valiant; to weary ones rest;/God shall be all, and in all ever blest.
PIERRE ABELARD *Hymn*

4 He wants not friends that hath Thy love,/And may converse and walk with Thee,/And with Thy saints here and above,/With whom for ever I must be.
RICHARD BAXTER *Hymn*

5 From the high eminencies of heaven a great cloud of witnesses are looking down upon earth, not as a scene for the petty anxieties of time, but as a splendid theatre for the ambition of immortal spirits.
THOMAS CHALMERS *Commercial Discourses*

6 For all the saints who from their labours rest,/Who Thee by faith before the world confessed,/Thy Name, O Jesu, be for ever blest./Hallelujah!
WILLIAM WALSHAM HOW *Hymn*

7 For those we love within the veil,/Who once were comrades of our way,/We thank Thee, Lord; for they have won/To cloudless day;
And life for them is life indeed,/The splendid goal of earth's strait race;/And where no shadows intervene/They see Thy face.
WILLIAM CHARTER PIGGOTT *Hymn*

8 How bright these glorious spirits shine!/Whence all their white array?/How came they to the blissful seats/Of everlasting day?
Lo! these are they, from sufferings great/Who came to realms of light,/And in the blood of Christ have washed/Those robes which shine so bright.
ISAAC WATTS *Hymn*

9 Let saints on earth in concert sing/With those whose work is done;/For all the servants of our King/In earth and heaven are one.
CHARLES WESLEY *Hymn*

COMMITMENT

10 Commit your life to the Lord;/trust in him and he will act.
Ps. 37.5

11 Commit your fortunes to the Lord,/and he will sustain you;/he will never let the righteous be shaken.
Ps. 55.22

12 Commit to the Lord all that you do, and your plans will be fulfilled.
Prov. 16.3

13 Then I heard the Lord saying, Whom shall I send? Who will go for me? And I answered, Here am I; send me.
Isa. 6.8

14 O Lord our God,/other lords than thou have been our masters,/but thee alone do we invoke by name.
Isa. 26.13

15 Therefore, my brothers, I implore you by God's mercy to offer your very selves to him: a living sacrifice, dedicated and fit for his acceptance, the worship offered by mind and heart.
Rom. 12.1

16 Whether therefore we live or die, we belong to the Lord.
Rom. 14.8

1 Take my life, and let it be/Consecrated, Lord, to Thee.
FRANCES RIDLEY HAVERGAL *Hymn*

2 Thou rulest heaven and earth and all between,/Lord of the sun and moon and all that starry sheen/The night discloses, when no clouds are seen,/Lord of all life and rocks and stones,/Lord of our hearts, our minds, our blood, our bones,/Lord of all times, Lord of eternity, Who owns/The small things and the great,/Here and Hereafter; and the Gate/Of Paradise is Thine,/O Lord Divine,/To Thee we do submit: we hear Thy Voice: 'Be Mine!'
WILLIAM BASHYR PICKARD *The Divine Divan* (Muslim)

3 I am afraid of saying 'yes', Lord. Where will you take me?
MICHEL QUOIST *Prayers of Life*

COMMUNITY

4 For no one of us lives, and equally no one of us dies, for himself alone.
Rom. 14.7

5 Any man's death diminishes me, because I am involved in mankind; and therefore never send to know for whom the bell tolls; it tolls for thee.
JOHN DONNE *Devotions upon Emergent Occasions*

6 No man is an island.
JOHN DONNE *Devotions upon Emergent Occasions*

7 We need society, and we need solitude also, as we need summer and winter, day and night, exercise and rest.
PHILIP GILBERT HAMERTON *The Intellectual Life*

8 Not that I admire the reserved; for they are next to unnatural that are not communicable. But if reservedness be at any time a virtue, 'tis in throngs or ill company.
WILLIAM PENN *Some Fruits of Solitude*

9 We don't live alone. We are members of one body. We are responsible for each other. And I tell you that the time will soon come when, if men will not learn that lesson, then they will be taught it in fire and blood and anguish.
J. B. PRIESTLEY *An Inspector Calls*

COMPASSION

10 When you reap the harvest in your field and forget a swathe, do not go back to pick it up; it shall be left for the alien, the orphan, and the widow.
Deut. 24.19

11 Happy the man who has a concern for the helpless! The Lord will save him in time of trouble.
Ps. 41.1

12 Man's compassion is only for his neighbour, but the Lord's compassion is for every living thing.
Ecclus. 18.13

13 Go now and wander for the welfare and happiness of many, out of compassion for the world. Let not two of you proceed in the same direction. Proclaim the Dhamma. (Truth).
Buddha's last command to his disciples

14 Perchance that I might learn what pity is,/that I might laugh at erring men no more.
MICHELANGELO BUONARROTI

15 The root of the matter is a very simple and old-fashioned thing, a thing so simple that I am almost ashamed to mention it for fear of the derisive smile with which wise cynics will greet my words. The thing I mean—please forgive me for mentioning it—is love, Christian love, or compassion.
BERTRAND RUSSELL *Impact of Science on Society*

16 The quality of mercy is not strain'd,/It droppeth as the gentle rain from heaven
WILLIAM SHAKESPEARE *The Merchant of Venice*

COMPROMISE

1 When my master goes to the temple of Rimmon to worship, leaning on my arm, and I worship in the temple of Rimmon when he worships there, for this let the Lord pardon me.
2 Kings 5.18

2 For my part I always try to meet everyone half-way.
1 Cor. 10.33

3 The greatness of Christianity did not arise from attempts to make compromises with those philosophical opinions of the ancient world which had some resemblance to its own doctrine, but from the unrelenting and fanatical proclamation and defence of its own teaching.
ADOLF HITLER *Mein Kampf*

CONFESSION

4 If we confess our sins, he is just, and may be trusted to forgive our sins and cleanse us from every kind of wrong.
1 John 1.9

5 We have left undone those things which we ought to have done; And we have done those things which we ought not to have done.
BOOK OF COMMON PRAYER From the *General Confession*

6 We acknowledge and bewail our manifold sins and wickedness, which we, from time to time, most grievously have committed, by thought, word, and deed, against thy Divine Majesty.
BOOK OF COMMON PRAYER From the *Order for Holy Communion*

7 I must humble myself before God for the fault; but then it is very pride and a still worse fault to go on fidgeting about the forgiven fault, calling myself all the bad names in the dictionary.
FATHER CONGREVE *Spiritual Letters*

8 A man who makes it his business not to confess his sin, but to understand it and explain it, no matter how philosophical he may seem, is walking in darkness, and the truth is not in him.
JAMES DENNEY *The Way Everlasting*

9 The General Confession, with its repeated and elaborate protestations of guilt, looks like a desperate attempt to persuade God to accept us on the score of our eating the maximum dust possible.
H. A. WILLIAMS *Soundings*

CONTEMPLATION

10 Contemplation is not in itself 'more spiritual' than recording a vote or managing a business.
F. R. BARRY *Christian Ethics and Secular Society*

11 No person in this life may reach the point at which he can be excused from outward service. Even if he is given to a life of contemplation, still he cannot refrain from going out and taking an active part in life.
MEISTER ECKHART

12 The longest journey is the journey inward. . . .The road to holiness necessarily passes through the world of action.
DAG HAMMERSKJÖLD *Markings*

13 Dispose our soul for tranquillity, O God, that the loving knowledge of contemplation may the more grow and the soul will feel it and relish it more than all other things whatever; because it brings with it peace and rest, sweetness and delight, without trouble.
ST JOHN OF THE CROSS

14 I think there is a place both inside and outside religion for a sort of contemplation of the Good, not just by dedicated experts but by ordinary people; an attention which is not just the planning of particular good actions but an attempt to look right away from self towards a distant transcendent perfection, a source of uncontaminated energy, a source of *new* and quite undreamt of virtue.
IRIS MURDOCH *The Sovereignty of Good*

CONTENTMENT

1 The lines fall for me in pleasant places, indeed I am well content with my inheritance.
Ps. 16.6

2 I know that there is nothing good for man except to be happy and live the best life he can while he is alive.
Eccl. 3.12

3 Better one hand full and peace of mind, than both fists full and toil that is chasing the wind.
Eccl. 4.6

4 Be content with whatever you have,/ and do not get a name for living on hospitality.
Ecclus. 29.23

5 I have learned to find resources in myself whatever my circumstances.
Phil. 4.11

6 Be content with what you have.
Heb. 13.5

7 Pale care, avant,/I'll learn to be content/ With that small stock, Thy bounty gave or lent./What may conduce/To my most healthful use,/Almighty God, me grant;/ But that, or this,/That hurtful is/Deny Thy suppliant.
ROBERT HERRICK

8 O Lord, endue me with more contentedness in what is present, and less solicitude about what is future; with a patient mind to submit to any loss of what I have, or to any disappointment of what I expect.
BISHOP SIMON PATRICK

9 Contentment is a sleepy thing!/If it in death alone must die;/A quiet mind is worse than poverty;/Unless it from enjoyment spring!
THOMAS TRAHERNE *Of Contentment*

CONTRITION

10 Saul answered, 'I have done wrong; come back, David my son. You have held my life precious this day, and I will never harm you again. I have been a fool, I have been sadly in the wrong.'
1 Sam. 26.21

11 My sacrifice, O God, is a broken spirit; a wounded heart, O God, thou wilt not despise.
Ps. 51.17

12 The Lord will happiness divine/On contrite hearts bestow;/Then tell me, gracious God, is mine/A contrite heart, or no?
WILLIAM COWPER *A Contrite Heart*

CONVERSION

13 Saul, Saul, why do you persecute me?
Acts 9.4

14 O Lord, convert the world—and begin with me.
A Chinese student's prayer

15 Suddenly I heard the words of Christ and understood them, and life and death ceased to seem to me evil, and instead of despair I experienced happiness and the joy of life undisturbed by death.
LEO TOLSTOY *What I Believe*

16 Five years ago I came to believe in Christ's teaching and my life suddenly changed; I ceased to desire what I had previously desired, and began to desire what I formerly did not want. What had previously seemed to me good seemed evil, and what had seemed evil seemed good. It happened to me as it happens to a man who goes out on some business and on the way suddenly decides that the business is unnecessary and returns home. All that was on his right hand is now on his left, and all that was on his left hand is now on his right.
LEO TOLSTOY *What I Believe*

1 There may have been a neurotic element in the make-up of Saul of Tarsus, John Bunyan and George Fox, and this may account for some features in the story of the conversion of each. But in all three examples, the man is re-made psychologically, morally and intellectually by his vision. This does not happen to the drug addict.
H. G. WOOD *Belief and Unbelief since 1850*

COURAGE

2 Yes, as my swift days near their goal,/ 'Tis all that I implore:/In life and death, a chainless soul,/With courage to endure.
EMILY BRONTË

3 I am not speaking chiefly of the courage that flows from faith. I am thinking of open-eyed faith itself as an act of supreme courage.
P. T. FORSYTH *The Justification of God*

4 Lord, as we rise to leave the shell of worship,/called to the risk of unprotected living,/willing to be at one with all your people,/we ask for courage.
FRED KAAN *100 Hymns for Today*

5 I argue not/Against Heaven's hand or will, not bate a jot/Of heart or hope, but still bear up/And steer right onward.
JOHN MILTON

COVETOUSNESS

6 You shall not covet.
Ex. 20.17

7 I should never have known what it was to covet, if the law had not said, 'Thou shalt not covet.'
Rom. 7.7

8 My duty towards my neighbour is. . . not to covet nor desire other men's goods; but to learn and labour truly to get mine own living, and to do my duty in that state of life, unto which it shall please God to call me.
BOOK OF COMMON PRAYER *The Catechism*

9 The man who covets is always poor.
CLAUDIAN

CREATED WORLD

10 While the earth lasts/seedtime and harvest, cold and heat,/summer and winter, day and night,/shall never cease.
Gen. 8.22

11 A land flowing with milk and honey.
Ex. 3.8

12 Can you bind the cluster of the Pleiades or loose Orion's belt?
Job 38.31

13 When I look up at thy heavens, the work of thy fingers,/the moon and the stars set in their place by thee,/what is man that thou shouldst remember him,/ mortal man that thou shouldst care for him?
Ps. 8.3

14 The heavens tell out the glory of God, the vault of heaven reveals his handiwork.
Ps. 19.1

15 The earth is the Lord's and all that is in it,/the world and those who dwell therein.
Ps. 24.1

16 Thou dost crown the year with thy good gifts.
Ps. 65.11

17 Others there are who go to sea in ships/ and make their living on the wide waters./ These men have seen the acts of the Lord/ and his marvellous doings in the deep.
Ps. 107. 23–24

18 Three things there are which are too wonderful for me,/four which I do not understand:/the way of a vulture in the sky,/the way of a serpent on the rock,/ the way of a ship out at sea,/and the way of a man with a girl.
Prov. 30. 18–19

1 Who can count the sand of the sea,/the drops of rain, or the days of unending time?
Ecclus 1.2

2 What a masterpiece is the clear vault of the sky!/How glorious is the spectacle of the heavens!
Ecclus 43.1

3 Consider how the lilies grow in the fields; they do not work, they do not spin; and yet, I tell you, even Solomon in all his splendour was not attired like one of these.
Matt. 6. 28–29

4 His everlasting power and deity, have been visible, ever since the world began, to the eye of reason, in the things he has made.
Rom. 1.20

5 The created universe waits with eager expectation for God's sons to be revealed.
Rom. 8.19

6 Up to the present, we know, the whole created universe groans in all its parts as if in the pangs of childbirth.
Rom. 8.22

7 That it may please thee to give and preserve to our use the kindly fruits of the earth, so as in due time we may enjoy them; We beseech thee to hear us, good Lord.
BOOK OF COMMON PRAYER From *The Litany*

8 What though in solemn silence all/Move round the dark terrestrial ball?/What though no real voice nor sound/Amidst their radiant orbs be found?/In reason's ear they all rejoice,/And utter forth a glorious voice,/Forever singing, as they shine,/'The hand that made us is divine.'
JOSEPH ADDISON *The Spectator*

9 Grant that, this day and every day, we may keep our shock of wonder at each new beauty that comes upon us as we walk down the paths of life.
ANON Contemporary

10 When I can go just where I want to go,/There is a copse of birch-trees that I know;/And, as in Eden Adam walked with God,/When in that quiet aisle my feet have trod/I have found peace among the silver trees,/Known comfort in the cool kiss of the breeze/Heard music in its whisper, and have known/Most certainly that I was not alone!
FATHER ANDREW *The Birch Copse*

11 I asked the whole frame of the world about my God; and it answered me, 'I am not He, but He made me.'
ST AUGUSTINE *Confessions*

12 God Almighty first planted a garden.
FRANCIS BACON *Of Gardens*

13 Almighty One, in the woods I am blessed. Happy is everyone in the woods. Every tree speaks through thee. O God! What glory in the woodland! On the heights is peace—peace to serve Him.
LUDWIG VAN BEETHOVEN

14 The tree which moves some to tears of joy is in the eyes of others only a green thing which stands in the way.
WILLIAM BLAKE

15 Nature hath made one World, and Art another. In brief, all things are artificial; for Nature is the Art of God.
SIR THOMAS BROWNE *Religio Medici*

16 The year's at the spring,/And day's at the morn;/Morning's at seven;/The hillside's dew-pearled;/The lark's on the wing;/The snail's on the thorn;/God's in His heaven—/All's right with the world!
ROBERT BROWNING *Pippa Passes*

17 All created things are living in the Hand of God. The senses see only the action of the creatures; but faith sees in everything the action of God.
J. P. DE CAUSSADE *Abandonments to Divine Providence*

18 We plough the fields, and scatter/The good seed on the land,/But it is fed and watered/By God's almighty hand;/He

sends the snow in winter,/The warmth to swell the grain,/The breezes and the sunshine/And soft refreshing rain./All good gifts around us/Are sent from heaven above;/Then thank the Lord, O thank the Lord,/For all His love.
MATTHIAS CLAUDIUS *Hymn*

1 Either God is in the whole of Nature, with no gaps, or He's not there at all.
C. A. COULSON *Science and Christian Belief*

2 The world is one, and the knowledge that is in it is one—because God made it so, and for no other reason; it is his hallmark that is stamped upon it.
C. A. COULSON

3 God made the country, and man made the town.
WILLIAM COWPER *The Task*

4 Lord, how rich the times are now!/A rainbow and a cuckoo's song/May never come together again.
W. H. DAVIES *A Great Time*

5 Praised be my Lord for our mother the earth, the which doth sustain and keep us, and bringeth forth divers fruits, and flowers of many colours, and grass.
ST FRANCIS OF ASSISI *The Canticle of the Creatures*

6 There is a sufficiency in the world for man's need but not for man's greed.
MAHATMA GANDHI

7 The glory of the spring how sweet!/The new-born life how glad!/What joy the happy earth to greet,/In new, bright raiment clad!
Divine Renewer, Thee I bless;/I greet Thy going forth;/I love Thee in the loveliness/Of Thy renewed earth.
THOMAS HORNBLOWER GILL *Hymn*

8 One is nearer God's heart in a garden/Than anywhere else on earth.
DOROTHY FRANCES GURNEY *God's Garden*

9 Blessed art thou, O Lord our God, King of the universe, who hast given of the

wisdom of thy hands to flesh and blood, that beautiful cities might rise for thy glory.
RABBI MOSHE HAKOTUN

10 Blessed art thou, O Lord our God, King of the universe, who createst thy world every morning afresh.
Hebrew, contemporary

11 The failure of Rationalism is that it tries to find a place for God in its picture of the world. But God, whose centre is everywhere and His circumference nowhere, cannot be fitted into a diagram. He is rather the canvas on which the picture is painted, or the frame in which it is set.
W. R. INGE *Faith and its Psychology*

12 The universe begins to look more like a great thought than like a great machine.
SIR JAMES JEANS *The Mysterious Universe*

13 This is the great delight of this awakening: to know the creatures through God and not God through the creatures.
ST JOHN OF THE CROSS *The Living Flame*

14 There is a book, who runs may read,/Which heavenly truth imparts,/And all the lore its scholars need,/Pure eyes and Christian hearts.
JOHN KEBLE *Hymn*

15 As far as meaning is from speech, as beauty from a rose,/As far as music is from sound, as poetry from prose,/As far as love from friendship is, as reason is from Truth,/As far as laughter is from joy, and early years from youth,/As far as love from shining eyes, as passion from a kiss,/So far is God from God's green earth, so far that world from this.
G. A. STUDDERT KENNEDY *The Unutterable Beauty*

16 Wherever, in anything that God has made, in the glory of it, be it sky or flower or human face, we see the glory of God, there a true imagination is beholding a truth of God.
GEORGE MACDONALD *Unspoken Sermons*

1 The saint sees practically that creatures are nothing in comparison with the God whom he loves. But the more he despises creatures as God's rivals, the more he cherishes them in as much as they are loved by God.
JACQUES MARITAIN *True Humanism*

2 What does it take to make a rose,/Mother mine?/It takes the world's eternal wars,/It takes the moon and all the stars,/It takes the might of heaven and hell,/And the everlasting love as well,/Little child.
ALFRED NOYES *The Forest of Wild Thyme*

3 O never harm the dreaming world,/the world of green, the world of leaves,/but let its million palms unfold/the adoration of the trees. . . .
KATHLEEN RAINE *Collected Poems*

4 What is Paradise? All things that are; for all are goodly and pleasant, and therefore may fitly be called a Paradise. It is said also that Paradise is an outer court of Heaven. Even so this world is verily an outer court of the Eternal, or of Eternity.
Theologia Germanica

5 St Francis ordered a plot to be set aside for the cultivation of flowers when the convent garden was made, in order that all who saw them might remember the Eternal Sweetness.
THOMAS OF CELANO

6 Not Shelley, not Wordsworth himself, ever drew so close to the heart of Nature as did the Seraph of Assisi, who was close to the Heart of God.
FRANCIS THOMPSON *Works*

CREEDS

7 The articles and dogmas of a religion are man-made things, and if you cling to them and shut yourself up in a code of life made out for you, you would not know and cannot know the Truth of the Spirit that lies beyond all codes and dogmas, wide and large and free. When you stop at a religious creed and tie yourself up in it, taking it for the only truth in the world, you stop the advance and widening of your inner soul.
AUROBINDO (Hindu)

8 The change in our conception of God necessitates the stressing of religious experience as such, as against belief in particular dogma, or in the efficacy of special ritual.
JULIAN HUXLEY *Essays of a Biologist*

9 There lives more faith in honest doubt,/Believe me, than in half the creeds.
LORD TENNYSON *In Memoriam*

10 Great God! I'd rather be/A Pagan suckled in a creed outworn;/So might I, standing on this pleasant lea,/Have glimpses that would make me less forlorn;/Have sight of Proteus rising from the sea;/Or hear old Triton blow his wreathed horn.
WILLIAM WORDSWORTH *The World is Too Much with Us*

THE CROSS

11 This doctrine of the cross is sheer folly to those on their way to ruin, but to us who are on the way to salvation it is the power of God.
1 Cor. 1.18

12 Jews call for miracles, Greeks look for wisdom; but we proclaim Christ—yes, Christ nailed to the cross; and though this is a stumbling-block to Jews and folly to Greeks, yet to those who have heard his call, Jews and Greeks alike, he is the power of God and the wisdom of God.
1 Cor. 1. 22–24

13 He died on the cross in weakness, but he lives by the power of God.
2 Cor. 13.4

14 We can write over the manger, 'So God loved the world, that He gave His only begotten Son, that whosoever believeth on Him should not perish, but have

everlasting life,' and that ought to have been sufficient. But since it was not sufficient to write those letters in the whiteness of the innocency of Christ, they had to be written in the redness of the agony of His sacrifice.
FATHER ANDREW

1 The cross is 'I' crossed out.
ANON

2 In the Cross of Christ I glory,/Towering o'er the wrecks of Time;/All the light of sacred story/Gathers round its head sublime.
JOHN BOWRING *Hymn*

3 In this sign thou shalt conquer.
CONSTANTINE THE GREAT

4 O Saviour, as thou hang'st upon the tree;/ I turn my back to thee, but to receive/ Corrections, till thy mercies bid thee leave./O think me worth thine anger, punish me,/Burn off my rusts, and my deformity,/Restore thine image, so much, by thy grace,/That thou may'st know me, and I'll turn my face.
JOHN DONNE *Good Friday, 1613*

5 We need less homilies on 'Fret not' or 'Study to be quiet', and more sermons on 'Through Him, the world is crucified to me, and I to the world.'
P. T. FORSYTH

6 To remember Jesus is to remember first of all his Cross.
JOHN KNOX *The Church and the Reality of Christ*

7 The Cross is where history and life, legend and reality, time and eternity, intersect. There, Jesus is nailed for ever to show us how God could become a man and a man become God.
MALCOLM MUGGERIDGE *Jesus Rediscovered*

8 The Way of the Cross winds through our towns and cities, our hospitals and factories, and through our battlefields; it takes the road of poverty and suffering in every form.
   It is in front of these new Stations of the Cross that we must stop and meditate and pray to the suffering Christ for strength to love him enough to act.
MICHEL QUOIST *Prayers of Life*

9 Jesus hath now many lovers of the heavenly kingdom, but few bearers of His Cross.
THOMAS À KEMPIS *The Imitation of Christ*

10 Nothing in my hand I bring,/Simply to Thy Cross I cling.
AUGUSTUS MONTAGUE TOPLADY *Hymn*

11 When I survey the wondrous Cross/On which the Prince of Glory died,/My richest gain I count but loss,/And pour contempt on all my pride.
ISAAC WATTS *Hymn*

THE CRUCIFIXION

12 'He saved others,' they said, 'but he cannot save himself. King of Israel, indeed! Let him come down now from the cross, and then we will believe him.'
Matt. 27.42

13 My God, my God, why hast thou forsaken me?
Matt. 27.46

14 Father, forgive them; they do not know what they are doing.
Luke 23.34

15 Today you shall be with me in Paradise.
Luke 23.43

16 Father, into thy hands I commit my spirit.
Luke 23.46

17 I shall draw all men to myself, when I am lifted up from the earth.
John 12.32

18 Pilate replied, 'What I have written, I have written.'
John 19.22

19 'It is accomplished!' He bowed his head and gave up his spirit.
John 19.30

1 We know that the man we once were has been crucified with Christ, for the destruction of the sinful self.
Rom. 6.6

2 If we thus died with Christ, we believe that we shall also come to life with him.
Rom. 6.8

3 There is a green hill far away,/Without a city wall,/Where the dear Lord was crucified,/Who died to save us all.
CECIL FRANCES ALEXANDER *Hymn*

4 Our attitude to the Crucifixion must be that of self-identification with the rest of human nature—we must say '*We* did it'; and the inability to adopt something of the same attitude in the case of twentieth-century events has caused our phenomenal failure to deal with the problem of evil in our time.
HERBERT BUTTERFIELD *History and Human Relations*

5 You can blame it on to Adam,/You can blame it on to Eve,/You can blame it on the apple,/But that I can't believe./It was God that made the Devil/And the Woman and the Man,/And there wouldn't be an apple/If it wasn't in the plan./It's God they ought to crucify/Instead of you and me,/I said to the carpenter/A-hanging on the tree.
SYDNEY CARTER *Friday Morning*

6 I simply argue that the Cross be raised again at the centre of the market place as well as on the steeple of the church. I am recovering the claim that Jesus was not crucified in a Cathedral between two candles, but on a Cross between two thieves; on the town garbage heap; at a crossroad so cosmopolitan that they had to write his title in Hebrew and in Latin and in Greek (or shall we say in English, in Bantu and in Afrikaans?); at the kind of place where cynics talk smut, and thieves curse, and soldiers gamble.

Because that is where He died. And that is what He died about. And that is where churchmen should be and what churchmen should be about.
GEORGE F. MACLEOD *Only One Way Left*

7 Were you there when they crucified my Lord?/Were you there when they crucified my Lord?/Oh! Sometimes it causes me to tremble, tremble, tremble./Were you there when they crucified my Lord?
Negro spiritual

CYNICISM

8 Emptiness, emptiness, says the Speaker, emptiness, all is empty. What does man gain from all his labour and his toil here under the sun?
Eccl. 1. 2–3

9 What has happened will happen again, and what has been done will be done again, and there is nothing new under the sun.
Eccl. 1.9

10 The wise man has eyes in his head, but the fool walks in the dark. Yet I saw also that one and the same fate overtakes them both.
Eccl. 2.14

11 I counted the dead happy because they were dead, happier than the living who are still in life. More fortunate than either I reckoned the man yet unborn, who had not witnessed the wicked deeds done here under the sun.
Eccl. 4. 2–3

12 Your laughter has killed more hearts than ever were pierced with swords and more than blood is lost in the weary battle of words.
ALFRED NOYES

DEATH

1 Dust you are, to dust you shall return.
Gen. 3.19

2 But now that he is dead, why should I fast? Can I bring him back again? I shall go to him; he will not come back to me.
2 Sam. 12.23

3 Naked I came from the womb,/naked I shall return whence I came./The Lord gives and the Lord takes away;/blessed be the name of the Lord.
Job 1.21

4 There the wicked man chafes no more,/ there the tired labourer rests.
Job 3.17

5 If a man dies, can he live again?/He shall never be roused from his sleep.
Job 14.12

6 For man is a creature of chance and the beasts are creatures of chance, and one mischance awaits them all: death comes to both alike.
Eccl. 3.19

7 All go to the same place: all came from the dust, and to the dust all return.
Eccl. 3.20

8 It is not in man's power to restrain the wind, and no one has power over the day of death.
Eccl. 8.8

9 For man goes to his everlasting home, and the mourners go about the streets.
Eccl. 12.5

10 Remember him before the silver cord is snapped and the golden bowl is broken, before the pitcher is shattered at the spring and the wheel broken at the well, before the dust returns to the earth as it began and the spirit returns to God who gave it.
Eccl. 12. 6–7

11 Let us eat and drink; for tomorrow we die.
Isa. 22.13

12 We have made a treaty with Death.
Isa. 28.15

13 Death has climbed in through our windows,/it has entered our palaces,/ it sweeps off the children in the open air/ and drives young men from the streets.
Jer. 9.21

14 Call no man happy before he dies,/for not until death is a man known for what he is.
Ecclus 11.28

15 For he is destined to reign until God has put all enemies under his feet; and the last enemy to be abolished is death.
1 Cor. 15.25–26

16 O Death, where is your victory? O Death, where is your sting?
1 Cor. 15.55

17 We brought nothing into the world; for that matter we cannot take anything with us when we leave.
1 Tim. 6.7

18 Earth to earth, ashes to ashes, dust to dust.
BOOK OF COMMON PRAYER From the *Order for the Burial of the Dead*

19 Man that is born of a woman hath but a short time to live, and is full of misery. He cometh up, and is cut down, like a flower; he fleeth as it were a shadow, and never continueth in one stay./In the midst of life we are in death.
BOOK OF COMMON PRAYER From the *Order for the Burial of the Dead*

20 Because my faltering feet may fail to dare/The first descendant of the steps of Hell/Give me the Word in time that triumphs there./I too must pass into the misty hollow/Where all our living laughter stops: and hark!/The tiny stuffless voices of the dark/Have called me, called me, till I needs must follow:/ Give me the Word and I'll attempt it well.
HILAIRE BELLOC

1 In the hour of death, after this life's whim,/When the heart beats low, and the eyes grow dim,/And pain has exhausted every limb – /The lover of the Lord shall trust in Him.
R. D. BLACKMORE

2 They say that the Dead die not, but remain/Near to the rich heirs of their grief and mirth./I think they ride the calm mid-heaven, as these,/In wise majestic melancholy train,/And watch the moon, and the still-raging seas,/And men, coming and going on the earth.
RUPERT BROOKE *Collected Poems*

3 So he passsd over, and all the trumpets sounded for him on the other side.
JOHN BUNYAN *The Pilgrim's Progress*

4 I would be willing to live to be further serviceable to God and his people, but my work is done.
Last words of OLIVER CROMWELL

5 O harmless Death! whom still the valiant brave,/The wise expect, the sorrowful invite,/And all the good embrace, who know the grave/A short dark passage to eternal light.
SIR WILLIAM DAVENANT

6 Since I am coming to that holy room,/Where, with thy choir of saints for evermore,/I shall be made thy music; as I come/I tune the instrument here at the door,/And what I must do then, think here before.
JOHN DONNE *Hymn to God, my God, in my Sickness*

7 And thou, most kind and gentle death,/Waiting to hush our latest breath,/O praise Him, Alleluia!/Thou leadest home the child of God,/And Christ our Lord the way hath trod.
ST FRANCIS OF ASSISI *The Canticle of the Creatures*

8 Be near me, Lord, when dying;/O show Thy Cross to me;/And, for my succour flying,/Come, Lord, to set me free;/These eyes, new faith receiving,/From Thee shall never move;/For he who dies believing/Dies safely through Thy love.
PAUL GERHARDT *Hymn*

9 The paths of glory lead but to the grave.
THOMAS GRAY *Elegy written in a Country Churchyard*

10 Human Nature is so subject to deception that it can frustrate, by some pollution or other, almost every dispensation but death.
SARAH GRUBB *Journal*

11 Turn up the lights; I don't want to go home in the dark.
O. HENRY (Last words)

12 The conquest of death is the final achievement of religion. No religion is worth its name unless it can prove itself more than a match for death.
L. P. JACKS *The Inner Sentinel*

13 'Depend upon it, Sir, when a man knows he is to be hanged in a fortnight, it concentrates his mind wonderfully.'
SAMUEL JOHNSON Boswell's *Life of Johnson*

14 I know well there is no comfort for this pain of parting: the wound always remains, but one learns to bear the pain, and learns to thank God for what He gave, for the beautiful memories of the past, and the yet more beautiful hope for the future.
MAX MÜLLER *Life and Letters*

15 Lord, grant that my last hour my be my best hour.
Old English prayer

16 No man can die cheerfully or comfortably who lives not in a constant resignation of the time and season of his death unto the will of God.
JOHN OWEN *On the Glory of Christ*

17 The Lord shall raise me up, I trust.
SIR WALTER RALEIGH'S epitaph by himself

18 Thou in me and I in thee. Death! what is death? There is no death: in thee it is impossible, absurd.
MARK RUTHERFORD *More Pages from a Journal*

1 Golden lads and girls all must,/As chimney-sweepers, come to dust.
WILLIAM SHAKESPEARE *Cymbeline*

2 The undiscover'd country from whose bourn/No traveller returns.
WILLIAM SHAKESPEARE *Hamlet*

3 Tomorrow, and tomorrow, and to-morrow,/Creeps in this petty pace from day to day/To the last syllable of recorded time,/And all our yesterdays have lighted fools/The way to dusty death.
WILLIAM SHAKESPEARE *Macbeth*

4 Sceptre and crown/Must tumble down/And in the dust be equal made/With the poor crooked scythe and spade.
JAMES SHIRLEY *The Contention of Ajax and Ulysses*

5 Since Nature's works be good, and death doth serve/As Nature's work, why should we fear to die?
SIR PHILIP SIDNEY

6 Home is the sailor,/Home from the sea,/And the hunter home from the hill.
R. L. STEVENSON *Requiem*

7 For tho' from out our bourne of Time and Place/The flood may bear me far,/I hope to see my Pilot face to face/When I have crost the bar.
LORD TENNYSON *Crossing the Bar*

8 O, hear a supliant heart all crush'd/And crumbled into contrite dust!/My hope, my fear—my Judge, my Friend!/Take charge of me, and of my end!
THOMAS OF CELANO (attributed)

9 Death, the only immortal who treats us all alike, whose pity and whose peace and whose refuge are for all—the soiled and the pure, the rich and the poor, the loved and the unloved.
MARK TWAIN, last words of

DECEIT

10 The voice is Jacob's voice, but the hands are the hands of Esau.
Gen. 27.22

11 Their speech is smoother than butter.
Ps. 55.21

12 Keep your mouth from crooked speech/and your lips from deceitful talk.
Prov. 4.24

13 One man pretends to be rich, although he has nothing;/another has great wealth but goes in rags.
Prov. 13.7

DELIVERANCE

14 How lovely on the mountains are the feet of the herald/who comes to proclaim prosperity and bring good news,/the news of deliverance.
Isa. 52.7

15 The hour of favour has now come; now, I say, has the day of deliverance dawned.
2 Cor. 6.2

16 From all the deceits of the world, the flesh, and the devil, Good Lord, deliver us.
BOOK OF COMMON PRAYER From *The Litany*

17 From lightning and tempest; from plague, pestilence, and famine; from battle and murder, and from sudden death, Good Lord, deliver us.
BOOK OF COMMON PRAYER From *The Litany*

18 From all blindness of heart; from pride, vain-glory, and hypocrisy; from envy, hatred, and malice, and all uncharitableness, Good Lord, deliver us.
BOOK OF COMMON PRAYER From *The Litany*

19 From all evil and mischief; from sin, from the crafts and assaults of the devil; from thy wrath, and from everlasting damnation, Good Lord, deliver us.
BOOK OF COMMON PRAYER From *The Litany*

1 In all time of our tribulation; in all time of our wealth; in the hour of death, and in the day of judgement, Good Lord, deliver us.
BOOK OF COMMON PRAYER From *The Litany*

2 From all that terror teaches,/From lies of tongue and pen,/From all the easy speeches/That comfort cruel men,/From sale and profanation/Of honour, and the sword,/From sleep and from damnation,/Deliver us, good Lord!
G. K. CHESTERTON *Hymn*

3 To deliver us from evil is not merely to take us out of hell, it is to take us into heaven.
P. T. FORSYTH *The Work of Christ*

DERELICTION

4 If I go forward, he is not there;/if backward, I cannot find him;/when I turn left, I do not descry him;/I face right but I see him not.
Job 23. 8–9

5 Ah my deare angrie Lord,/Since thou dost iove, yet strike;/Cast down, yet help afford;/Sure I will do the like.
I will complain, yet praise;/I will bewail, approve:/And all my sowre-sweet dayes/I will lament, and love.
GEORGE HERBERT

6 Show Thy mercy to me, O Lord, to glad my heart withal. Lo, here the man that was caught of thieves, wounded, and left for half-dead, as he was going towards Jericho. Thou kind-hearted Samaritan, take me up.
ST JEROME

7 O Lord my God, I have hoped in Thee,/Jesus beloved, now set me free./In harshest chain, in wretched pain,/In weakness and in sorrow sair,/Upon my knees and at my prayer,/I beg Thee that Thou freest me.
MARY, QUEEN OF SCOTS

8 Lord, since Thou hast taken from me all that I had of Thee, yet of Thy grace leave me the gift which every dog has by nature: that of being true to Thee in my distress, when I am deprived of all consolation. This I desire more fervently than Thy heavenly Kingdom!
MECHTHILD OF MAGDEBURG

9 Alas, my God, that we should be/Such strangers to each other!/O that as friends we might agree,/And walk and talk together!
THOMAS SHEPHERD

10 When the heart is hard and parched up, come upon me with a shower of mercy./When grace is lost from life, come with a burst of song./When tumultuous work raises its din on all sides shutting me out from beyond, come to me, my Lord of silence, with thy peace and rest./When my beggarly heart sits crouched, shut up in a corner, break open the door, my king, and come with the ceremony of a king./When desire blinds the mind with delusion and dust, O thou holy One, thou wakeful, come with thy light and thy thunder.
RABINDRANATH TAGORE

11 Come down, O Christ, and help me! reach Thy hand,/For I am drowning in a stormier sea/Than Simon on Thy Lake of Galilee:/The wine of life is spilled upon the sand,/My heart is as some famine-murdered land/Whence all good things have perished utterly,/And well I know my soul in Hell must lie/If I this night before God's throne should stand.
OSCAR WILDE

DESPAIR

12 I am in despair, I would not go on living;/leave me alone, for my life is but a vapour.
Job 7.16

13 Why hast thou made me thy butt,/and why have I become thy target?
Job 7.20

1 I am sickened of life.
Job 10.1

2 God himself has flung me down in the mud,/no better than dust or ashes.
Job 30.19

3 How could we sing the Lord's song/in a foreign land?
Ps. 137.4

4 Alas, alas, my mother, that you ever gave me birth!/a man doomed to strife, with the whole world against me.
Jer. 15.10

5 A curse on the day when I was born!/ Be it for ever unblessed,/the day when my mother bore me!
Jer. 20.14

6 My mind reels confusedly in the darkness. . . . /Desolation envelops my understanding. . . . /Nothing gives peace to my fevered mind.
The Bhagavad Gita (Hindu)

7 This then is the formula which describes the condition of the self when despair is completely eradicated: relating itself to its own self and by willing to be itself the self is grounded transparently in the Power which posited it.
SÖREN KIERKEGAARD *The Sickness unto Death*

8 Lord, it is dark!/Lord, are you there in my darkness?/Where are you, Lord?/ Do you love me still?/I haven't wearied you?/Lord, answer me!/Answer!/It is so dark!
MICHEL QUOIST

THE DEVIL

9 The day came when the members of the court of heaven took their places in the presence of the Lord, and Satan was there among them. The Lord asked him where he had been. 'Ranging over the earth', he said, 'from end to end'.
Job 1. 6–7

10 I watched how Satan fell, like lightning, out of the sky.
Luke 10.18

11 Stand up to the devil and he will turn and run.
Jas. 4.7

12 Awake! be on the alert! Your enemy the devil, like a roaring lion, prowls round looking for someone to devour.
1 Pet. 5.8

13 The Devil's best ruse is to persuade us that he does not exist.
CHARLES BAUDELAIRE *Petits Poèmes*

14 Why should the Devil have all the good tunes?
ROWLAND HILL *Sermons*

15 It is so stupid of modern civilization to have given up believing in the devil when he is the only explanation of it.
RONALD KNOX *Let Dons Delight*

16 Speak the truth and shame the Devil.
FRANÇOIS RABELAIS

17 He must have a long spoon that shall eat with the devil.
WILLIAM SHAKESPEARE *The Comedy of Errors*

DISCRETION

18 When men talk too much, sin is never far away;/common sense holds its tongue.
Prov. 10.19

19 Keep a guard over your lips and tongue/ and keep yourself out of trouble.
Prov. 21.23

20 Argue your own case with your neighbour,/but do not reveal another man's secrets.
Prov. 25.9

21 For lack of fuel a fire dies down/and for want of a tale-bearer a quarrel subsides.
Prov. 26.20

1 Have you heard a rumour? Let it die
with you. Never fear, it will not make you
burst.
Ecclus. 19.10

2 Better a slip on the stone floor than a slip
of the tongue.
Ecclus. 20.18

3 He who knows does not talk; he who
talks does not know.
LAO TZE (Taoist)

4 Speak as little as may be of thy neighbour
or of anything that concerns him,
unless an opportunity offers to say
something good of him.
LORENZO SCUPOLI *The Spiritual Combat*

DOUBT

5 Unless I see the mark of the nails on his
hands, unless I put my finger into the
place where the nails were, and my hand
into his side, I will not believe it.
John 20.25

6 Help us to free ourselves from fearful
doubt,/for when we begin to doubt then
doubt has no end./Thou hast no voice,
O God, thy form is unseen,/yet we can
hear thy words and know Thee near.
BUNJIRO (Shinto)

7 Insecurity welcomes manacles to prevent
its hands shaking.
WALTER LIPPMANN

8 O God, if you are there, save me, if you
can!
R. K. NARAYAN (Hindu)

9 O God, if there be a God, save my soul, if
I have a soul.
UPTON SINCLAIR *O Shepherd Speak*

10 Cleave ever to the sunnier side of doubt,/
And cling to Faith beyond the forms of
Faith.
LORD TENNYSON *The Ancient Sage*

11 Doubt as to the validity of historic evidence is no obstacle to the victory of
faith.
BROOKE FOSS WESTCOTT

All fanaticism is a strategy to prevent
doubt from becoming conscious.
H. A. WILLIAMS *The True Wilderness*

12 God will provide—ah, if only He would!
Yiddish Proverb

DUTY

13 'Do the Duty which lies nearest thee',
which thou knowest to be a Duty! Thy
second Duty will already have become
clearer.
THOMAS CARLYLE *Sartor Resartus*

14 Keep us, Lord, so awake in the duties of
our callings that we may sleep in thy
peace and wake in thy glory.
JOHN DONNE

15 Stern Daughter of the Voice of God.
WILLIAM WORDSWORTH *Ode to Duty*

EVIL

1 The triumph of the wicked is short-lived,/
the glee of the godless lasts but a moment.
Job 20.5

2 Though you offer countless prayers,/I
will not listen./There is blood on your
hands;/wash yourselves and be clean./
Put away the evil of your deeds,/away
out of my sight.
Isa. 1.15–16

3 Our fight is not against human foes, but
against cosmic powers, against the
authorities and potentates of this dark
world, against the superhuman forces of
evil in the heavens.
Eph. 6.12

4 The fact of evil produces the paradox of
an all-powerful and malevolent, or bene-
volent but sterile, God.
ALBERT CAMUS

5 Boredom is the root of all evil—the
despairing refusal to be oneself.
SÖREN KIERKEGAARD

6 It is one of the curious ironies of modern
culture that in the very moment when a
rationalistic type of Christianity tended
to consider the possibilities of human
perfection in terms of its purely conscious activity, a secular science in the
form of psychology on the one hand, and
of social economics on the other,
revealed the labyrinthian depths of the
unconscious and of the endless possibilities of evil which were hidden there.
Both Marx and Freud have, each in his
own way, discovered the unconscious
dishonesties which dog human actions
and corrupt human ideals, even though
the conscious mind is intent upon
virtue.
REINHOLD NIEBUHR *Beyond Tragedy*

7 Men never do evil so completely and
cheerfully as when they do it from
religious conviction.
BLAISE PASCAL *Pensées*

8 The evil in the world is not God's responsibility, either directly or permiss-
ively: it is a brute fact attaching to
creation as such.
NORMAN PITTENGER

9 Of two evils we should always choose the
less.
THOMAS À KEMPIS *The Imitation of Christ*

FAITH

1 Abram put his faith in the Lord, and the Lord counted that faith to him as righteousness.
Gen. 15.6

2 Put no faith in princes.
Ps. 146.3

3 If you have faith no bigger even than a mustard-seed, you will say to this mountain, 'Move from here to there!', and it will move; nothing will prove impossible for you.
Matt. 17.20

4 'I have faith', cried the boy's father; 'help me where faith falls short.'
Mark 9.24

5 Increase our faith.
Luke 17.5

6 Because you have seen me you have found faith. Happy are they who never saw me and yet have found faith.
John 20.29

7 A way that starts from faith and ends in faith.
Rom. 1.17

8 When hope seemed hopeless, his (Abraham's) faith was such that he became 'father of many nations'.
Rom. 4.18

9 Faith gives substance to our hopes, and makes us certain of realities we do not see.
Heb. 11.1

10 By faith Abraham obeyed the call to go out to a land destined for himself and his heirs, and left home without knowing where he was to go.
Heb. 11.8

11 So with faith; if it does not lead to action, it is in itself a lifeless thing.
Jas. 2.17

12 For what is faith unless it is to believe what you do not see?
ST AUGUSTINE

13 O for a faith that will not shrink,/Though pressed by many a foe,/That will not tremble on the brink/Of poverty or woe,/That will not murmur nor complain/Beneath the chastening rod,/But, in the hour of grief or pain,/Can lean upon its God.
WILLIAM HILEY BATHURST *Hymn*

14 Faith without knowledge leads to the conceit of ignorance, and knowledge without faith begets a stony heart. Therefore only as these two are well blended do they become the basis of good deeds.
Buddhist scripture

15 God has no voice, his form is unseen. With Him there is neither night nor day, neither far nor near. Pray to Him simply, with a heart of faith. He is your friend.
BUNJIRO (Shinto)

16 I should count a life well spent, and the world well lost, if, after tasting all its experiences and facing all its problems, I had no more to show at its close, or to carry with me to another life, than the acquisition of a real, sure, humble, and grateful faith in the Eternal and Incarnate Son of God.
P. T. FORSYTH

17 Although faith be an intellectual habit of the mind, and have her seat in the understanding, yet an evil moral disposition wedded to the love of darkness dampeth the very light of heavenly illumination.
RICHARD HOOKER *Ecclesiastical Polity*

18 I want to live, live out, not wobble through/My life somehow, and then into the dark./I must have God. This life's too dull without,/Too dull for aught but suicide.
G. A. STUDDERT KENNEDY *The Unutterable Beauty*

1 Yet have I looked into my mother's eyes,/And seen the light that never was on sea/Or land, the light of Love, pure Love and true,/And on that Love I bet my life.
G. A. STUDDERT KENNEDY *The Unutterable Beauty*

2 I back the scent of life/Against its stink. That's what Faith works out at/Finally.
G. A STUDDERT KENNEDY *The Unutterable Beauty*

3 Faith consists in a man's lying 'constantly out upon the deep and with 70,000 fathoms of water under him'.
SÖREN KIERKEGAARD *Stages on Life's Way*

4 What words can tell the state of those who live in faith and trust,/Who make His Will their own?/The Soul mounts high, Reason and mind grow clear.
GURU NANAK *Japji* (Sikh)

5 Faith is the assertion of a possibility against all probabilities. . . . Such a faith has nothing else than Jesus Christ in the middle of a world which scoffs at all our hopes and fears.
ETHELBERT STAUFFER *New Testament Theology*

6 From the point of view of religion, not only of the Christian religion, faith is something nobler in its own kind than certainty. For us finite beings in this world that which most of all calls forth our noblest capacities into action is always a hazard of some kind, never a certainty. It is when we are ready to stake our lives on something being so, or to make something so that is not so, that nobility begins to appear in human nature.
WILLIAM TEMPLE

7 Strong Son of God, immortal Love,/Whom we, that have not seen thy face,/By faith, and faith alone, embrace,/Believing where we cannot prove.
LORD TENNYSON *In Memoriam*

8 Saints by the power of God are kept,/Till the salvation come:/We walk by faith as strangers here:/But Christ shall call us home.
ISAAC WATTS *Hymn*

FAITHFULNESS

9 Where you go, I will go, and where you stay, I will stay. Your people shall be my people, and your God my God. Where you die, I will die, and there I will be buried.
Ruth 1. 16–17

10 A precious thing in the Lord's sight/is the death of those who die faithful to him.
Ps. 116.15

11 Loyalty brings its own reward.
Prov. 11.17

12 The righteous man will live by being faithful.
Hab. 2.4

13 'Well done, my good and trusty servant!' said the master. 'You have proved trustworthy in a small way; I will now put you in charge of something big. Come and share your master's delight.'
Matt. 25.21

14 Happy the man who remains steadfast under trial, for having passed that test he will receive for his prize the gift of life promised to those who love God.
Jas. 1.12

15 It is, however, only by fidelity in little things that a true and constant love to God can be distinguished from a passing fervour of spirit.
F. DE LA M. FÉNELON *Letters and Reflections*

16 When the Pro-Consul pressed him and said: 'Take the oath and I let you go, revile Christ,' Polycarp said: 'Eighty and six years have I served him, and he hath done me no wrong: how then can I blaspheme my King who saved me?'
POLYCARP (at his martyrdom)

1 Faithfulness is consecration in overalls.
EVELYN UNDERHILL *Fruits of the Spirit*

FAMILY

2 Delightful and dearly loved were Saul and Jonathan; in life, in death, they were not parted.
2 Sam. 1.23

3 Trust no neighbour, put no confidence in your closest friend;/seal your lips even from the wife of your bosom./For son maligns father,/daughter rebels against mother, . . ./and a man's enemies are his own household.
Micah 7. 5–6

4 If a man does not know how to control his own family, how can he look after a congregation of God's people?
1 Tim. 3.5

5 For all the blesssings life has brought,/For all its sorrowing hours have taught,/For all we mourn, for all we keep,/The hands we clasp, the loved that sleep,
We thank Thee, Father: let Thy grace/Our loving circle still embrace,/Thy mercy shed its heavenly store,/Thy peace be with us evermore.
OLIVER WENDELL HOLMES *Hymn*

6 Examine yourselves—ask yourselves, each of you, Have I been a good brother? . . . son? . . . husband? . . . father? . . . servant? If not, all professions of religion will avail me nothing.
CHARLES KINGSLEY *True words for Brave Men*

7 May young and old together find/in Christ the Lord of every day,/That fellowship our homes may bind/ in joy and sorrow, work and play./ Our Father, on the homes we love/Send down thy blessing from above.
HUGH MARTIN *100 Hymns for Today*

FEAR

8 Every morning you will say, 'Would God it were evening!', and every evening, 'Would God it were morning!', for the fear that lives in your heart and the sights that you see.
Deut. 28.67

9 Fear is nothing but an abandonment of the aid that comes from reason.
Wisd. 17.12

10 Do not fear those who kill the body, but cannot kill the soul.
Matt. 10.28

11 Thus conscience does make cowards of us all.
WILLIAM SHAKESPEARE *Hamlet*

FIRE

12 Moses noticed that, although the bush was on fire, it was not being burnt up.
Ex. 3.2

13 And all the time the Lord went before them, by day a pillar of cloud to guide them on their journey, by night a pillar of fire to give them light, so that they could travel night and day.
Ex. 13.21

14 I have come to set fire to the earth, and how I wish it were already kindled!
Luke 12.49

FOLLY: FOOL

15 A clever man conceals his knowledge,/but a stupid man broadcasts his folly.
Prov. 12.23

16 A man's own folly wrecks his life,/and then he bears a grudge against the Lord.
Prov. 19.3

17 Like a dog returning to its vomit/is a stupid man who repeats his folly.
Prov. 26.11

1 The laughter of a fool is like the crackling of thorns under a pot.
Eccl. 7.6

2 To shame the wise, God has chosen what the world counts folly, and to shame what is strong, God has chosen what the world counts weakness.
1 Cor. 1.27

3 Carlyle said that men were mostly fools. Christianity, with a surer and more reverend realism, says that they are all fools.
G. K. CHESTERTON *Heretics*

FORGIVENESS

4 Be gracious to me, O God, in thy true love;/in the fullness of thy mercy blot out my misdeeds.
Ps. 51.1

5 Let the wicked abandon their ways/and evil men their thoughts:/let them return to the Lord, who will have pity on them,/return to our God, for he will freely forgive.
Isa. 55.7

6 So I will make good the years/that the swarm has eaten.
Joel 2.25

7 Forgive us the wrong we have done,/as we have forgiven those who have wronged us.
Matt. 6.12

8 If you do not forgive others, then the wrongs you have done will not be forgiven by your Father.
Matt. 6.15

9 'Lord, how often am I to forgive my brother if he goes on wronging me? As many as seven times?' Jesus replied, 'I do not say seven times; I say seventy times seven.'
Matt. 18.21–22

10 And when you stand praying, if you have a grievance against anyone, forgive him,

so that your Father in heaven may forgive you the wrongs you have done.
Mark 11.25

11 Where little has been forgiven, little love is shown.
Luke 7.47

12 Bring the fatted calf and kill it, and let us have a feast to celebrate the day. For this son of mine was dead and has come back to life; he was lost and is found.
Luke 15.23–24

13 Almighty and everlasting God, who hatest nothing that thou hast made, and dost forgive the sins of all them that are penitent; Create and make in us new and contrite hearts, that we worthily lamenting our sins, and acknowledging our wretchedness, may obtain of thee, the God of all mercy, perfect remission and forgiveness; through Jesus Christ our Lord.
BOOK OF COMMON PRAYER *Collect for Ash Wednesday*

14 Grant, we beseech thee, merciful Lord, to thy faithful people pardon and peace, that they may be cleansed from all their sins, and serve thee with a quiet mind.
BOOK OF COMMON PRAYER *From the Collect for the Twenty-first Sunday after Trinity*

15 Forgive me my sins, O Lord; forgive me the sins of my youth and the sins of mine age, the sins of my soul and the sins of my body, my secret and my whispering sins, the sins I have done to please myself and the sins I have done to please others. Forgive those sins which I know, and the sins which I know not; forgive them, O Lord, forgive them all of Thy great goodness.
ANON

16 If forgiveness meant letting off the criminal it would be a violation of the love-commandment. We have no right to be turning other people's cheeks, leaving other people's children to be raped or lonely old ladies to be beaten up, allowing thieves and murderers to run loose. But in Christian theology, for-

giveness does not mean being let off the consequences. Forgiveness means reconciliation.

F. R. BARRY *Christian Ethics and Secular Society*

1 Though a man be soiled/With the sins of a lifetime,/Let him but love me,/Rightly resolved,/In utter devotion:/I see no sinner,/That man is holy.
The Bhagavad Gita (Hindu)

2 To forgive our enemies, yet hope that God will punish them, is not to forgive enough. To forgive them ourselves, and not to pray God to forgive them, is a partial piece of charity. Forgive thine enemies totally, and without any reserve that however God will revenge thee.
SIR THOMAS BROWNE *Christian Morals*

3 Good to forgive; Best, to forget!
ROBERT BROWNING *La Saisiaz*

4 'Twas the soul of Judas Iscariot,/Strange, and sad, and tall,/Stood all alone at dead of night/Before a lighted hall.
'Twas the Bridegroom stood at the open door,/And beckon'd smiling sweet;/'Twas the soul of Judas Iscariot/Stole in, and fell at his feet.
'The Holy Supper is spread within,/And the many candles shine,/And I have waited long for thee/Before I pour'd the wine!'
The supper wine is pour'd at last,/The lights burn bright and fair,/Iscariot washes the Bridegroom's feet,/And dries them with his hair.
ROBERT WILLIAMS BUCHANAN *Judas Iscariot*

5 If we are sinners forgiven, we ought to behave as forgiven, welcomed home, crowned with wonderful love in Christ, and so cheer and encourage all about us, who often go heavily because we reflect our gloom upon them instead of our grateful love, hope, confidence.
FATHER CONGREVE *Spiritual Letters*

6 Wilt thou forgive that sinne where I begunne,/Which is my sin, though it were done before?/Wilt thou forgive those sinnes, through which I runne,/And

do run still: though still I do deplore?/When thou hast done, thou hast not done,/For, I have more.
Wilt thou forgive that sinne by which I have wonne/Others to sinne? and, made my sinne their doore?/Wilt thou forgive that sinne which I did shunne/A yeare, or two: but wallowed in, a score?/When thou hast done, thou hast not done,/For I have more.
I have a sinne of feare, that when I have spunne/My last thred, I shall perish on the shore;/Sweare by thy selfe, that at my death thy sonne/Shall shine as he shines now, and heretofore;/And having done that, Thou haste done,/I feare no more.
JOHN DONNE *Hymn to God the Father*

7 Forgiveness to the injured doth belong,/But they ne'er pardon who have done the wrong.
JOHN DRYDEN *The Conquest of Granada*

8 God will forgive me: that is His business.
Dying words of HEINRICH HEINE

9 The one final and utter failure of the Church would be its ceasing to be able to bring to sinners the assurance of forgiveness.
LEONARD HODGSON *The Doctrine of Atonement*

10 Here lie I, Martin Elginbrodde;/Ha'e mercy o' my soul, Lord God;/As I wad do, were I Lord God,/And ye were Martin Elginbrodde.
GEORGE MACDONALD *David Elginbrod*

11 To err is human, to forgive divine.
ALEXANDER POPE *An Essay on Criticism*

12 Only one petition in the Lord's prayer has any condition attached to it: it is the petition for forgiveness.
WILLIAM TEMPLE *Personal Religion and the Life of Fellowship*

13 Know all and you will pardon all.
THOMAS À KEMPIS *The Imitation of Christ*

14 I felt my heart strangely warmed. I felt I did trust in Christ, Christ alone, for

salvation; and an assurance was given me that he had taken away my sins, even mine, and saved me from the bore of sin and death.

JOHN WESLEY *Journal*

1 The best of what we do and are,/Just God, forgive!

WILLIAM WORDSWORTH *Thoughts suggested on the Banks of Nith*

FREEDOM

2 Christ set us free, to be free men. Stand firm, then, and refuse to be tied to the yoke of slavery again.

Gal. 5.1

3 Live as free men, not however as though your freedom were there to provide a screen for wrongdoing, but as slaves in God's service.

1 Pet. 2.16

4 A Christian man is the most free lord of all, and subject to none; a Christian man is the most dutiful servant of all, and subject to everyone.

MARTIN LUTHER

FREE WILL

5 When he made man in the beginning,/he left him free to take his own decisions;/if you choose, you can keep the commandments;/whether or not you keep faith is yours to decide.

Ecclus 15.15

6 All theory is against freedom of the will; all experience for it.

SAMUEL JOHNSON

7 Analytic psychology as well as analytic sociology, has shown how destiny and freedom, tragedy and responsibility, are interwoven in every human being from early childhood on, and in all social and political groups in the history of mankind.

PAUL TILLICH *Systematic Theology*

FRIEND, FRIENDSHIP

8 I grieve for you, Jonathan my brother;/dear and delightful you were to me;/your love for me was wonderful,/surpassing the love of women.

2 Sam. 1.26

9 A friend is a loving companion at all times,/and a brother is born to share troubles.

Prov. 17.17

10 A friend may stick closer than a brother.

Prov. 18.24

11 The blows a friend gives are well meant.

Prov. 27.6

12 A faithful friend is beyond price;/his worth is more than money can buy.

Ecclus 6.15

13 The man who fears the Lord keeps his friendships in repair,/for he treats his neighbour as himself.

Ecclus 6.17

14 Do not desert an old friend;/a new one is not worth as much,/A new friend is like new wine;/you do not enjoy drinking it until it has matured.

Ecclus 9.10

15 There is no greater love than this, that a man should lay down his life for his friends.

John 15.13

16 I have called you friends.

John 15.15

17 Friendship is in loving rather than in being lov'd.

ROBERT BRIDGES *The Testament of Beauty*

18 A friend will be sure to act the part of an advocate before he will assume that of a judge.

ROBERT SOUTH *Sermons*

THE FUTURE

1 Let your eyes look straight before you,/
fix your gaze upon what lies ahead.
Prov. 4.25

2 You never know what a day will bring
forth.
Prov. 27.1

3 When things go well, be glad; but when
things go ill, consider this: God has set
the one alongside the other in such a way
that no one can find out what is to happen
next.
Eccl. 7.14

4 I have set before you an open door,
which no one can shut.
Rev. 3.8

5 All that he left when living/was through/
Was a mountain of things he intended/
to do—Tomorrow.
Untraced

GENEROSITY

1 Do not be hard-hearted or close-fisted with your countryman in his need. Be openhanded towards him.
Deut. 15. 7–8

2 The wicked man borrows and does not pay back,/but the righteous is a generous giver.
Ps. 37.21

3 He who despises a hungry man does wrong,/but he who is generous to the poor is happy.
Prov. 14.21

4 He who is generous to the poor lends to the Lord,/he will repay him in full measure.
Prov. 19.17

5 He who gives to the poor will never want.
Prov. 28.27

6 Where a man has been given much, much will be expected of him.
Luke 12.48

7 Be generous to one another, tender-hearted, forgiving one another as God in Christ forgave you.
Eph. 4.32

GIFTS: GIVING

8 A lavish giver has the world for his friend.
Prov. 19.6

9 Let your almsgiving match your means. If you have little, do not be ashamed to give the little you can afford.
Tob. 4.8

10 As water quenches a blazing fire,/so almsgiving atones for sin.
Ecclus 3.30

11 Do not keep your hand open to receive/ and close it when it is your turn to give.
Ecclus 4.31

12 If, when you are bringing your gift to the altar, you suddenly remember that your brother has a grievance against you, leave your gift where it is before the altar. First go and make your peace with your brother, and only then come back and offer your gift.
Matt. 5. 23–24

13 Give when you are asked to give; and do not turn your back on a man who wants to borrow.
Matt. 5.42

14 You received without cost; give without charge.
Matt. 10.8

15 This poor widow has given more than any of the others; for those others who have given had more than enough, but she, with less than enough, has given all that she had to live on.
Mark 12.44

16 Give, and gifts will be given you. Good measure, pressed down, shaken together, and running over, will be poured into your lap; for whatever measure you deal out to others will be dealt to you in return.
Luke 6.38

17 God loves a cheerful giver.
2 Cor. 9.7

18 Each of us has been given his gift, his due portion of Christ's bounty.
Eph. 4.7

19 All good giving, every perfect gift, comes from above, from the Father of the lights of heaven.
Jas. 1.17

20 When people say they have not anything to give for good causes, they are as a rule telling the truth. They have nothing to give because they have already spent everything.
JAMES DENNEY *The Way Everlasting*

21 Alms are but the vehicles of prayer.
JOHN DRYDEN

1 Grant, O Lord, that I may give Thee choice gifts,/three lighted, and dazzling torches:/my spirit, my soul and my body./ My spirit to the Father,/my soul to the Son,/my body to the Holy Ghost./O Father, sanctify my spirit!/O Son, sanctify my soul!/O Holy Ghost, sanctify my sin-soiled body!
Eastern Church

GOD

2 Happy is the nation whose God is the Lord.
Ps. 33.12

3 The works of God should be acknowledged publicly.
Tob. 12.7

4 Pay Caesar what is due to Caesar, and pay God what is due to God.
Matt. 22.21

5 Everything is possible for God.
Mark 10.27

6 God has no favourites.
Rom. 2.11

7 It is a terrible thing to fall into the hands of the living God.
Heb. 10.31

8 The voice of the people is the voice of God.
ALCUIN *Epistolae*

9 God explained, is God explained away.
ANON

10 Man proposes, God disposes.
LUDOVICO ARIOSTO *Orlando Furioso*

12 Thou hast made us for Thyself, and the heart of man is restless until it finds its rest in Thee.
ST AUGUSTINE *Confessions*

13 It were better to have no opinion of God at all, than such an opinion as is unworthy of Him.
FRANCIS BACON *Of Superstition*

14 God said: Know, O Man, by whom this universe is upheld. I am the producer and destroyer of the whole universe. There is nothing else . . . all this is woven upon me like numbers of pearls upon a thread. I am the taste in water; I am the light of the sun and moon; I am the OM, the sound in space and in all scriptures, and the manliness in human beings; I am the fragrant smell of the earth and the brightness of fire; I am life in all beings. Know me to be the eternal seed of all beings. I am the discernment of the discerning and the glory of the glorious. I am the strength of the strong, I am love. All goodness is from me.
The Bhagavad Gita (Hindu)

15 God is the 'beyond' in the midst of our life.
DIETRICH BONHOEFFER *Letters and Papers from Prison*

16 It is so much more comfortable to have a pantheistic philosophy than to believe in a Lord God . . . A God who is neuter makes no claims; He simply allows Himself to be looked at.
EMIL BRUNNER *Man in Revolt*

17 God is the Thou which by its very nature cannot become it.
MARTIN BUBER *I and Thou*

18 Our picture of God must resemble more the violence of a sunset painting by Turner than, as one of my friends once put it, a watery wash by a maiden aunt!
C. A. COULSON *Science and Christian Belief*

19 I have never been able to conceive mankind without Him.
F. DOSTOEVSKY

20 God can no more do without us than we can do without Him.
MEISTER ECKHART

21 The best way to find the heart of God is to trust our own best affections whatever we are looking at.
AUSTIN FARRER

1 Now stands no more between the Truth and me/Or reasoned demonstration,/Or proof, or revelation;/Now, brightly blazing forth, Truth's luminary/Hath driven out of sight/Each flickering, lesser light.
This I have proven, this I now declare,/This is my faith unbending,/And this my joy unending:/There is no god but God! No rivals share/His peerless majesty,/His claimed supremacy.
HALLAJ (Sufi)

2 The language of 'transcendence', the thought of God as a personal being, wholly other to man, dwelling apart in majesty—this talk may well collapse into meaninglessness, in the last analysis. And yet to sacrifice it seems at once to take one quite outside Christianity.
R. W. HEPBURN *Christianity and Paradox*

3 In vain our labours are, whatso'er they be,/Unless God gives the *Benedicite*.
ROBERT HERRICK *Noble Numbers*

4 We cannot make too sure of this: that religion, communion with God, is not luxury, but a necessity for the soul. We must have God.
G. A. STUDDERT KENNEDY *The New Man in Christ*

5 In order to sew we must first have a knot in the thread.
SÖREN KIERKEGAARD

6 Though the mills of God grind slowly/Yet they grind exceeding small;/Though with patience He stands waiting,/With exactness grinds He all.
HENRY WADSWORTH LONGFELLOW *Retribution*

7 God is always on the side of the big battalions.
NAPOLEON BONAPARTE

8 The imagination enlarges little objects so as to fill our soul with its fantastic estimate, and by a rash insolence belittles the great to its own measure, as when it speaks of God.
BLAISE PASCAL

9 To know that there is a beauty greater than any we ourselves have seen or can imagine should not make us discontented with the drabness of our own lives but help us to appreciate more deeply such beauty as may be given to us either now or in the future.
E. ALLISON PEERS *Spirit of Flame*

10 We can be certain about God, but tentative about theology.
IAN RAMSEY

11 Almost the only statement about the Hebrew names of God which would command general acceptance from modern scholars is that their original meaning is unknown.
H. WHEELER ROBINSON

12 Then opened the heavenly door, and Thy face showed!
RICHARD ROLLE

13 He who believes in the good is for this very reason directly under subjection and responsibility to God, even although he himself may be quite unaware of the fact.
RICHARD ROTHE *Still Hours*

14 When God shuts a door, He opens a window.
JOHN RUSKIN

15 O Lord, who art our ultimate hypothesis and our eternal hope.
Scottish minister

16 The old doctrine of transcendence is nothing more than an assertion of an outmoded view of the world.
R. GREGOR SMITH *The New Man*

17 We have been all too ready, especially since the great breakthrough of the Renaissance, to fight a kind of battle against the world on behalf of God.
R. GREGOR SMITH *The New Man*

18 God tempers the wind to the shorn lamb.
LAURENCE STERNE *A Sentimental Journey*

1 To adore . . . that means to lose oneself in the unfathomable, to plunge into the inexhaustible, to find peace in the incorruptible, to be absorbed in defined immensity, to offer oneself to the fire and the transparency, to annihilate oneself as one becomes more deliberately conscious of oneself, and to give of one's deepest to that whose depth has no end.
P. TEILHARD DE CHARDIN *Le Milieu Divin*

2 The old order changeth, yielding place to new,/And God fulfils himself in many ways,/Lest one good custom should corrupt the world.
LORD TENNYSON *The Passing of Arthur*

3 Let nothing disturb thee;/Let nothing dismay thee;/All things pass:/God never changes./Patience attains/All that it strives for./He who has God/Finds he lacks nothing:/God alone suffices.
ST TERESA'S Bookmark

4 The name of this infinite and inexhaustible depth and ground of all being is *God.*
PAUL TILLICH *The Shaking of the Foundations*

5 You must forget everything traditional that you have learned about God, perhaps even that word itself.
PAUL TILLICH *The Shaking of the Foundations*

GOD, ARMOUR OF

6 Put on all the armour which God provides, so that you may be able to stand firm against the devices of the devil.
Eph. 6.11

7 Stand firm, I say. Fasten on the belt of truth; for coat of mail put on integrity; let the shoes on your feet be the gospel of peace, to give you firm footing; and, with all these, take up the great shield of faith, with which you will be able to quench all the flaming arrows of the evil one.
Eph. 6. 14–16

8 Take salvation for helmet; for sword, take that which the Spirit gives you—the words that come from God.
Eph. 6.17

9 We, who belong to daylight, must keep sober, armed with faith and love for coat of mail, and the hope of salvation for helmet.
1 Thess. 5.8

10 Fight gallantly, armed with faith and a good conscience.
1 Tim. 1.19

11 Almighty God, give us grace that we may cast away the works of darkness and put upon us the armour of light.
BOOK OF COMMON PRAYER From the *Collect for the First Sunday in Advent*

12 Bread of Thy Body give me for my fighting,/Give me to drink Thy Sacred Blood for wine,/While there are wrongs that need me for the righting,/While there is warfare splendid and divine.
Give me, for light, the sunshine of Thy sorrow,/Give me, for shelter, shadow of Thy Cross;/Give me to share the glory of Thy morrow,/Gone from my heart the bitterness of Loss.
G. A. STUDDERT KENNEDY *The Unutterable Beauty*

GOD, BELIEF IN

13 Elijah stepped forward and said to the people, 'How long will you sit on the fence? If the Lord is God, follow him; but if Baal, then follow him.'
1 Kings 18.21

14 To believe in God is to know/that all the rules will/be fair and that there will/be wonderful surprises.
UGO BETTI

15 God does not die on the day when we cease to believe in a personal deity; but we die on the day when our lives cease to be illuminated by the steady radiance renewed daily, of a wonder, the source of which is beyond all reason.
DAG HAMMARSKJÖLD

GOD, CARE OF

1 Though my father and my mother forsake me,/the Lord will take me into his care.
Ps. 27.10

2 I know every bird on those hills,/the teeming life of the fields is my care.
Ps. 50.11

3 For the Lord, high as he is, cares for the lowly,/and from afar he humbles the proud.
Ps. 138.6

4 Look at the birds of the air; they do not sow and reap and store in barns, yet your heavenly Father feeds them. You are worth more than the birds!
Matt. 6.26

5 God, who made the earth,/The air, the sky, the sea,/Who gave the light its birth,/Careth for me.
SARAH BETTS RHODES *Hymn*

GOD, COMPASSION OF

6 Then the Lord passed in front of him and called aloud, 'Jehovah, the Lord, a god compassionate and gracious, long-suffering, ever constant and true, maintaining constancy to thousands, forgiving iniquity, rebellion, and sin, and not sweeping the guilty clean away; but one who punishes sons and grandsons to the third and fourth generation for the iniquity of their fathers.'
Ex. 34. 6–7

7 Does not the consolation of God suffice you,/a word whispered quietly in your ear?
Job 15.11

8 Thou, Lord, art God, compassionate and gracious,/forbearing, ever constant and true.
Ps. 86.15

9 As a father has compassion on his children,/so has the Lord compassion on all who fear him,/For he knows how we were made,/he knows full well that we are dust.
Ps. 103. 13–14

10 He will tend his flock like a shepherd/and gather them together with his arm;/he will carry the lambs in his bosom/and lead the ewes to water.
Isa. 40.11

11 I alone, I am He,/who for his own sake wipes out your transgressions,/who will remember your sins no more.
Isa. 43.25

12 As a mother conforts her son,/so will I myself comfort you.
Isa. 66.13

13 How can I give you up, Ephraim,/how surrender you, Israel?. . . .
My heart is changed within me,/my remorse kindles already. . . .
I will not turn round and destroy Ephraim;/for I am God, and not a man.
Hos. 11.8 and 9

14 Those things, which for our unworthiness we dare not, and for our blindness we cannot ask, vouchsafe to give us.
BOOK OF COMMON PRAYER From the *Order for Holy Communion*

GOD, CREATOR

15 In the beginning of creation, when God made heaven and earth, the earth was without form and void, with darkness over the face of the abyss, and a mighty wind that swept over the surface of the waters. God said, 'Let there be light', and there was light.
Gen. 1. 1–3

16 God saw all that he had made, and it was very good.
Gen. 1.31

17 Who is this whose ignorant words/cloud my design in darkness?
Where were you when I laid the earth's foundations?
Job 38.2 and 4

1 When the morning stars sang together/
and all the sons of God shouted aloud.
Job 38.7

2 The day is thine, and the night is thine
also.
Ps. 74.16

3 Do you not know, have you not heard?/
The Lord, the everlasting God, creator of
the wide world,/grows neither weary nor
faint;/no man can fathom his understanding.
Isa. 40.28

4 We are the clay, thou the potter,/and all
of us are thy handiwork.
Isa. 64.8

5 All existing things are dear to thee and
thou hatest nothing that thou hast
created—why else wouldst thou have
made it?
Wisd. 11.24

6 Thou sparest all things because they are
thine, our Lord and master who lovest all
that lives; for thy imperishable breath is
in them all.
Wisd. 12.1

7 The greatness and beauty of created
things give us a corresponding idea of
their Creator.
Wisd. 13.5

8 We have seen but a small part of his
works, and there remain many mysteries
greater still.
Ecclus 43.32

9 The stars shone at their appointed
stations and rejoiced; he called them and
they answered, 'We are here!' Joyfully
they shone for their Maker.
Baruch 3.34

10 Everything that God created is good, and
nothing is to be rejected when it is taken
with thanksgiving.
1 Tim. 4.4

11 O Maker of the material world, thou
Holy One...Who established the sunlit
days and the star glistering sphere and the
Milky Way?... Who apart from Thee!
AVESTA (Zoroastrian)

12 Any child knows that the earth was not
made in six days. But not everyone knows
that God made the world through his
Spirit and man in his own image.
DIETRICH BONHOEFFER *No Rusty Swords*

13 O this beauty of the Universe!/How did
you, my Lord, come to create it?/In what
outburst of ecstasy/Allowed you your
Being to be manifested?/Some say you
took fancy in the play of form,/Giving in
delight your Absolute Being an appearance./Dadu understands you need him/
In thy play of creation.
DADU (Hindu)

14 Himself the Lord, created the creation../
Himself the Lord, He pervadeth all; Him-
self/the Lord, He is above and beyond
all.
The Granth (Sikh)

15 How long wilt thou give the reins into
the hand of Doubt?/For every one there
is a pathway and approach to God;/To
every one is pledged the certainty of His
existence;/On the heart of every thought-
ful man is painted His image,/And for
every painting there must be a painter
.../When thou beholdest before thee the
architecture of the universe/How is it
that thy mind is not busied with the
Architect?/When thou seest the work,
turn thy face towards the Workman.
JAMI (Muslim)

16 'I had no need of that hypothesis.'
LAPLACE to Napoleon

17 Songs of praise the angels sang,/Heaven
with hallelujahs rang,/When creation was
begun,/When God spake, and it was
done.
JAMES MONTGOMERY *Hymn*

18 There are millions and millions of worlds
below and above ours,/Man's mind is
tired of this great search,/It cannot reach
the end of His vastness./How can the
Infinite be reduced to the finite?/All
attempts to describe Him are futile/ ...
He alone knows how great He is .../
None knoweth the Lord's beginning nor
His end ...
GURU NANAK (Sikh)

GOD, DELIVERER

1 When your children ask you, 'What is the meaning of this rite?' you shall say, 'It is the Lord's Passover, for he passed over the houses of the Israelites in Egypt when he struck the Egyptians but spared our houses.'
Ex. 12. 26–27

2 Sing to the Lord, for he has risen up in triumph;/the horse and his rider he has hurled into the sea.
Ex. 15.21

3 I am the Lord your God who brought you out of Egypt, out of the land of slavery./You shall have no other god to set against me.
Ex. 20. 2–3

4 How deep I am sunk in misery,/groaning in my distress:/yet I will wait for God;/I will praise him continually,/my deliverer, my God.
Ps. 42.5

5 Arise and come to our help;/for thy love's sake set us free.
Ps. 44.26

6 In truth he is my rock of deliverance,/my tower of strength, so that I am unshaken.
Ps. 62.6

7 Blessed be the Lord God of Israel: for he hath visited, and redeemed his people.
BOOK OF COMMON PRAYER From the *Benedictus*

8 O Lord, raise up thy power, and come among us, and with great might succour us; that whereas, through our sins and wickedness, we are sore let and hindered in running the race that is set before us, thy bountiful grace and mercy may speedily help and deliver us.
BOOK OF COMMON PRAYER From the *Collect for the Fourth Sunday in Advent*

9 Yet dearly I love you, and would be loved fain,/But am betroth'd unto your enemy:/Divorce me, untie, or break that knot again,/Take me to you, imprison me, for I/Except you enthrall me, never shall be free,/Nor ever chaste, except you ravish me.
JOHN DONNE *Holy Sonnets*

10 A safe stronghold our God is still,/A trusty shield and weapon;/He'll help us clear from all the ill/That hath us now o'ertaken./The ancient prince of hell/Hath risen with purpose fell;/Strong mail of craft and power/He weareth in this hour;/On earth is not his fellow.
MARTIN LUTHER *Hymn*

11 But (when so sad thou canst not sadder)/Cry;—and upon thy so sore loss/Shall shine the traffic of Jacob's ladder/Pitched betwixt Heaven and Charing Cross.
Yea, in the night, my Soul, my daughter,/Cry,—clinging Heaven by the hems;/And lo, Christ walking on the water/Not of Gennesareth, but Thames!
FRANCIS THOMPSON *The Kingdom of God*

GOD, DISCIPLINE OF

12 Happy the man whom God rebukes!/therefore do not reject the discipline of the Almighty.
Job 5.17

13 Those whom he loves the Lord reproves,/and he punishes a favourite son.
Prov. 3.12

14 See how I tested you, not as silver is tested,/but in the furnace of affliction; there I purified you.
Isa. 48.10

15 For you alone have I cared/among all the nations of the world;/therefore will I punish you/for all your iniquities.
Amos 3.2

16 I might for the present avoid man's punishment, but, alive or dead, I shall never escape from the hand of the Almighty.
2 Macc. 6.26

1 Batter my heart, three-person'd God; for, you/As yet but knock, breathe, shine, and seek to mend;/That I may rise, and stand, o'erthrow me, and bend/Your force, to break, blow, burn and make me new.
JOHN DONNE *Holy Sonnets*

2 Throw away Thy rod,/Throw away Thy wrath;/O my God,/Take the gentle path. Throw away Thy rod:/Though man frailties hath,/Thou art God:/Throw away Thy wrath.
GEORGE HERBERT *Discipline*

3 Hear me, O God!/A broken heart/Is my best part:/Use still thy rod,/That I may prove/Therein, thy love.
BEN JONSON *A Hymn to God the Father*

4 Disappointments that come not by our own folly, they are the trials or corrections of heaven: and it is our own fault if they prove not to our advantage.
WILLIAM PENN *Some Fruits of Solitude*

5 Only with God's good hand and strict bridle can the soul be helped to give its best.
NATHAN SÖDERBLOM *Life*

GOD, ETERNAL

6 For in thy sight a thousand years are as yesterday.
Ps. 90.4

7 Long ago thou didst lay the foundations of the earth,/and the heavens were thy handiwork./They shall pass away, but thou endurest;/like clothes they shall all grow old;/thou shalt cast them off like a cloak,/and they shall vanish;/but thou art the same and thy years shall have no end.
Ps. 102.25–27

8 It is I, the Lord, I am the first,/and to the last of them I am He.
Isa. 41.4

9 I am the first and I am the last,/and there is no god but me.
Isa. 44.6

10 In every relationship in which we stand we are regarding the hem of the garment of the eternal Thou; from each there reaches us a waft of His breath; in each Thou we address the eternal Thou.
MARTIN BUBER *I and Thou*

GOD, EXISTENCE OF

11 The only way to be honest is to recognize that we have to live in the world *etsi deus non daretur*—even if God is not 'there'.
DIETRICH BONHOEFFER *Letters and Papers from Prison*

12 What the gods are is a matter of dispute but that they are is denied by nobody.
CICERO *On the Nature of the Gods*

13 In the case of our human friends we take their existence for granted, not caring whether it is proven or not. Our relationship is such that we could read philosophical arguments designed to prove the non-existence of each other, and perhaps even be convinced by them—and then laugh together over so odd a conclusion. I think that it is something of the same kind of security we should seek in our relationship with God.
SIR ARTHUR EDDINGTON *Science and the Unseen World*

14 The most flawless proof of the existence of God is no substitute for it; and if we have that relationship, the most convincing disproof is turned harmlessly aside. If I may say it with reverence, the soul and God laugh together over so odd a conclusion.
SIR ARTHUR EDDINGTON *Science and the Unseen World*

15 If God did not exist we should have to invent him.
VOLTAIRE

GOD, FAITHFULNESS OF

1 Know then that the Lord your God is God, the faithful God; with those who love him and keep his commandments he keeps covenant and faith for a thousand generations.
Deut. 7.9

2 God's every promise has stood the test.
Prov. 30.5

3 God's promises can never fail.
Luke 1.37

GOD, FATHERHOOD OF

4 In thee the fatherless find a father's love.
Hos. 14.3

5 Have we not all one father? Did not one God create us?
Mal. 2.10

6 Are not sparrows two a penny? Yet without your Father's leave not one of them can fall to the ground.
Matt. 10.29

7 Even if I have gone astray, I am thy child, O God; thou art my father and mother.
ARJAN (Sikh)

8 I am the father of the whole universe, the mother, the creator, the Lord, the friend.
The Bhagavad Gita (Hindu)

9 May we not worry but believe in Thee, our Great Parent.
BUNJIRO (Shinto)

10 He does not say, 'No man knoweth God save the Son'. That would be to deny the truth of the Old Testament revelation. What He does say is that He alone has a deeper secret, the essential Fatherhood of the Sovereign Power.
D. S. CAIRNS *The Riddle of the World*

11 If we address Him as children, it is because He tells us He is our Father. If we unbosom ourselves to Him as a Friend, it is because He calls us friends.
WILLIAM COWPER *Letters*

12 The Father is our Fount and Origin, in whom our life and being is begun.
JOHN OF RUYSBROECK *The Spiritual Espousals*

13 If the earth is our mother, God is our Father, and we need faith in God as our Father to save us from a mother-fixation to earth.
H. G. WOOD *Belief and Unbelief since 1850*

GOD, FEAR OF

14 It is God who makes me faint-hearted/ and the Almighty who fills me with fear.
Job 23.16

15 Arise, Lord, give man no chance to boast his strength;/summon the nations before thee for judgement./Strike them with fear, O Lord,/let the nations know that they are but men.
Ps. 9. 19–20

16 If there is any man who fears the Lord,/ he shall be shown the path that he should choose.
Ps. 25.12

17 The fear of the Lord is the beginning of wisdom.
Ps. 111.10

18 The fear of the Lord is the beginning of knowledge.
Prov. 1.7

19 Fear God and obey his commands; there is no more to man than this.
Eccl. 12.13

20 The fear of the Lord gladdens the heart;/ it brings cheerfulness and joy and long life.
Ecclus 1.12

21 The man who fears the Lord will have nothing else to fear.
Ecclus 34.14

GOD, GLORY OF

1 O Lord, I love the beauty of thy house,/
the place where thy glory dwells.
Ps. 26.8

2 Holy, holy, holy is the Lord of Hosts:/
the whole earth is full of his glory.
Isa. 6.3

3 For the earth shall be full of the knowledge of the glory of the Lord as the
waters fill the sea.
Hab. 2.14

4 Let us exult in the hope of the divine
splendour that is to be ours.
Rom. 5.2

GOD, GLORY TO

5 Not to us, O Lord, not to us,/but to thy
name ascribe the glory,/for thy true love
and for thy constancy.
Ps. 115.1

6 Ascribe glory to the Lord your God/
before the darkness falls.
Jer. 13.16

7 Now to him who is able to do immeasurably more than all we can ask or conceive,
by the power which is at work among us,
to him be glory in the church and in
Christ Jesus from generation to generation evermore!
Eph. 3. 20–21

8 Now to the King of all worlds, immortal,
invisible, the only God, be honour and
glory for ever and ever!
1 Tim. 1.17

9 Now to the One who can keep you from
falling and set you in the presence of his
glory, jubilant and above reproach, to
the only God our Saviour, be glory and
majesty, might and authority, through
Jesus Christ our Lord, before all time,
now, and for evermore.
Jude 24–25

10 Glory be to God on high, and in earth
peace, good will towards men.
BOOK OF COMMON PRAYER From the *Order
for Holy Communion*

GOD, GOODNESS OF

11 For everything comes from thee, and it is
only of thy gifts that we give to thee.
1 Chr. 29.14

12 Well I know that I shall see the goodness
of the Lord/in the land of the living.
Ps. 27.13

13 Bless the Lord, my soul,/and forget none
of his benefits./He pardons all my guilt/
and heals all my suffering.
Ps. 103. 2–3

14 He contents me with all good in the prime
of life,/and my youth is ever new like an
eagle's.
Ps. 103.5

15 Jesus said to him, 'Why do you call me
good? No one is good except God alone.'
Mark 10.18

16 Almighty and everlasting God, who art
always more ready to hear than we to
pray, and art wont to give more than
either we desire, or deserve; pour down
upon us the abundance of thy mercy.
BOOK OF COMMON PRAYER From the
*Collect for the Twelfth Sunday after
Trinity*

17 O Lord, in Mercy grant my soul to live/,
And patience grant, that hurt I may not
grieve:/How shall I know what thing is
best to seek?/Thou only knowest: what
Thou knowest, give!
AL-ANSARI (Sufi)

18 What a man has, not from himself but
from God, he ought to regard as not so
much his own as God's. For no one has
from himself the truth which he teaches,
or a righteous will, but from God.
ST ANSELM *Cur Deus Homo*

1 Father, who on man dost shower/Gifts of plenty from Thy dower,/To Thy people give the power/All Thy gifts to use aright.
PERCY DEARMER *Hymn*

2 There's a wideness in God's mercy,/Like the wideness of the sea;/There's a kindness in His justice,/Which is more than liberty.
FREDERICK WILLIAM FABER *Hymn*

3 (It is) much more easy to have faith in the goodness of providence when that goodness seems safe in one's pocket in the form of bank-notes.
CHARLES KINGSLEY *Two Years Ago*

GOD, GUIDANCE OF

4 He renews life within me,/and for his name's sake guides me in the right path.
Ps. 23.3

5 Man plans his journey by his own wit,/but it is the Lord who guides his steps.
Prov. 16.9

6 It is the Lord who directs a man's steps;/how can mortal man understand the road he travels?
Prov. 20.24

7 O Self-existent One/Who art beyond comprehension,/O Thou omnipotent One/Who hast no equal in power and greatness,/Who art without a second:/O Thou merciful One/Who guidest stray souls to the right path,/Thou art truly our God.
AL-ANSARI (Sufi)

8 If He stood by Paul, saying 'Fear not', just as really and maybe as evidently will He stand by you. If He guided him in his work, restraining him from preaching here, and calling him to service there, He will give you also leadings just as certain and maybe as distinct.
J. RENDEL HARRIS *Memoranda Sacra*

9 All my hope on God is founded;/He doth still my trust renew./Me through change and chance He guideth,/Only good and

only true./God unknown,/He alone/Calls my heart to be His own.
Yattendon Hymnal

GOD, HEALER

10 O Lord my God, I cried to thee and thou didst heal me.
Ps. 30.2

11 It is he who heals the broken in spirit/and binds up their wounds.
Ps. 147.3

12 Come, let us return to the Lord;/for he has torn us and will heal us,/he has struck us and he will bind up our wounds.
Hos. 6.1

13 For you who fear my name, the sun of righteousness shall rise with healing in his wings.
Mal. 4.2

GOD, HOUSE OF

14 But can God indeed dwell on earth? Heaven itself, the highest heaven, cannot contain thee; how much less this house that I have built!
1 Kings 8.27

15 How dear is thy dwelling-place,/thou Lord of Hosts!
Ps. 84.1

16 Happy are those who dwell in thy house;/they never cease from praising thee.
Ps. 84.4

17 Better one day in thy courts/than a thousand days at home.
Ps. 84.10

18 I rejoiced when they said to me,/'Let us go to the house of the Lord'.
Ps. 122.1

19 My house shall be called/a house of prayer for all nations.
Isa. 56.7

1 You keep saying, 'This place is the temple of the Lord, the temple of the Lord, the temple of the Lord!' This catchword of yours is a lie; put no trust in it. Mend your ways and your doings, deal fairly with one another, do not oppress the alien, the orphan, and the widow, shed no innocent blood in this place, do not run after other gods to your own ruin.
Jer. 7. 4–6

2 Scripture says, 'My house shall be called a house of prayer'; but you are making it a robbers' cave.
Matt. 21.13

3 Did you not know that I was bound to be in my Father's house?
Luke 2.49

4 Go out on to the highways and along the hedgerows and make them come in; I want my house to be full.
Luke 14.23

5 There are many dwelling-places in my Father's house; if it were not so I should have told you; for I am going there on purpose to prepare a place for you.
John 14.2

GOD, JUSTICE OF

6 Shall not the judge of all the earth do what is just?
Gen. 18.25

7 For the Lord is just and loves just dealing;/his face is turned towards the upright man.
Ps. 11.7

8 And men shall say,/'There is after all a reward for the righteous;/after all, there is a God that judges on earth.'
Ps. 58.11

9 One thing God has spoken,/two things I have learnt:/'Power belongs to God'/ and 'True love, O Lord, is thine';/thou dost requite a man for his deeds.
Ps. 62. 11–12

10 Let us humble ourselves, let us strive to know the Lord,/whose justice dawns like morning light,/and its dawning is as sure as the sunrise.
Hos. 6.3

11 If you say 'our father' to the One who judges every man impartially on the record of his deeds, you must stand in awe of him while you live out your time on earth.
1 Pet. 1.17

GOD, KINGDOM OF

12 Set your mind on God's kingdom and his justice before everything else, and all the rest will come to you as well.
Matt. 6.33

13 Thus will the last be first, and the first last.
Matt. 20.16

14 For though many are invited, few are chosen.
Matt. 22.14

15 No one who sets his hand to the plough and then keeps looking back is fit for the kingdom of God.
Luke 9.62

16 In fact the kingdom of God is among you.
Luke 17.21

17 Unless a man has been born over again he cannot see the kingdom of God.
John 3.3

18 In truth I tell you, no one can enter the kingdom of God without being born from water and spirit.
John 3.5

19 Christ leads me through no darker rooms/ Than He went through before;/He that into God's Kingdom comes/Must enter by this door.
RICHARD BAXTER *Hymn*

1 So be it, Lord! Thy throne shall never,/
Like earth's proud empires, pass away;/
Thy Kingdom stands and grows for ever,/
Till all Thy creatures own Thy sway.
JOHN ELLERTON *Hymn*

2 The core of all that Jesus teaches about
the Kingdom is the immediate apprehension and acceptance of God as King
in his own life.
T. W. MANSON *The Teaching of Jesus*

3 If only we knew how to look at life as God
sees it, we should realize that nothing is
secular in the world, but that everything
contributes to the building of the kingdom of God.
MICHEL QUOIST *Prayers of Life*

GOD, KNOWLEDGE OF

4 No longer need they teach one another
to know the Lord: all of them, high and
low alike, shall know me, says the Lord,
for I will forgive their wrongdoing and
remember their sin no more.
Jer. 31.34

5 As I was going round looking at the
objects of your worship, I noticed among
other things an altar bearing the inscrip-
tion 'To an Unknown God.' What you
worship but do not know—this is what I
now proclaim.
Acts 17.23

6 O depth of wealth, wisdom, and knowledge in God! How unsearchable his
judgements, how untraceable his ways!
Rom. 11.33

7 If by knowledge only, and reason, we
could come to God, then none should
come but they that are learned and have
good wits. . . .But God hath made His
way 'viam regiam'—the King's highway.
LANCELOT ANDREWES

8 Bestow upon me, O Lord my God,
understanding to know Thee, diligence
to seek Thee, wisdom to find Thee, and a
faithfulness that may finally embrace
Thee.
ST THOMAS AQUINAS

9 As people who do not know the country
walk again and again over a gold treasure
that has been hidden somewhere in the
earth and do not discover it, thus do all
those who day after day live in the spirit
world and yet do not discover it; because
they are carried away by untruth, they
do not discover the true Self in Brahman
(God).
Chandogya Upanishad (Hindu)

10 God cannot be known by mere exercise
of intellect. The only way to know God is
to cherish an intense desire to realize His
true nature, and constantly to be mindful
of Him. The most indispensable requisite
is to purify the mind by keeping it fixed on
Him and by doing good to others. So
long as the mirror is unclean the image
cannot be reflected in it.
DADU (Hindu)

11 Within the cave of the mind is an inexhaustible Treasure;/Within it resides the
Unknowable, Infinite, He/Who Himself
is Manifest, Unmanifest,/Yea, through
the Lord's Word, one loseth one's self
and knoweth Him.
The Granth (Sikh)

12 He who knows his own self knows God.
MUHAMMAD *Hadith* (Muslim)

13 He who leaveth home in search of knowledge walketh in the path of God.
MUHAMMAD *Hadith* (Muslim)

14 Do that much of the will of God which
is plain to you, and 'you shall know of
the doctrine, whether it be of God.'
F. W. ROBERTSON *Sermons*

15 Thou askest what God is? I answer
shortly to thee: such a one so great is He
that none other is or ever may be of like
kind . . . . If thou wilt know properly to
speak what God is, I say thou shalt never
find an answer to this question . . . .How
wouldest thou know what is unknown?
. . . If thou knew what God is thou
shouldest be as wise as God . . . If thou
desirest to know what God is, thou
desirest to be God . . . It is enough for
thee to know that God is.
RICHARD ROLLE *The Fire of Love*

1 He truly knows God perfectly that feels Him incomprehensible and unable to be known.
RICHARD ROLLE *The Fire of Love*

2 In all forms of love, we wish to have knowledge of what is loved, not for purposes of power, but for the ecstasy of contemplation. In knowledge of God stands our eternal life, but not because knowledge of God gives us any power over Him.
BERTRAND RUSSELL *The Scientific Outlook*

3 The only really vital thing in religion is to become acquainted with God.
MRS PEARSALL SMITH *The Unselfishness of God*

4 God would not be God if he could be fully known to us, and God would not be God if he could not be known at all.
H. G. WOOD *Belief and Unbelief since 1850*

GOD, HIS KNOWLEDGE OF US

5 Lord, thou hast examined me and knowest me./Thou knowest all, whether I sit down or rise up;/thou hast discerned my thoughts from afar.
Ps. 139. 1–2

6 Thou knowest me through and through.
Ps. 139.14

7 Almighty God, unto whom all hearts be open, all desires known, and from whom no secrets are hid; Cleanse the thoughts of our hearts by the inspiration of thy Holy Spirit, that we may perfectly love thee, and worthily magnify thy holy Name.
BOOK OF COMMON PRAYER From the *Order for Holy Communion*

GOD, LAW OF

8 The law of the Lord is perfect and revives the soul./The Lord's instruction never fails,/and makes the simple wise.
Ps. 19.7

9 Every day I take my life in my hands,/ yet I never forget thy law.
Ps. 119.109

10 Thy law is my continual delight.
Ps. 119.174

GOD, LIFE IN

11 He is not God of the dead but of the living.
Matt. 22.32

12 Now your life lies hidden with Christ in God.
Col. 3.3

13 If we walk in the light as he himself is in the light, then we share together a common life, and we are being cleansed from every sin by the blood of Jesus his Son.
1 John 1.7

14 'No man ever saw God and lived'; and yet I shall not live till I see God; and when I have seen Him I shall never die.
JOHN DONNE *Fifty Sermons*

15 The eye with which I see God is the same with which God sees me.
MEISTER ECKHART

16 Ah now, my inner fire is quenched, my body and mind are cool-comforted . . ./ The Lord hath become manifest . . .He Himself hath united me with Himself . . ./ I am wholly fulfilled.
The Granth (Sikh)

17 I looked at God and He looked at me, and we were one forever.
C. H. SPURGEON

18 There is in God (some say)/A deep, but dazzling darkness; as men here/Say it is late and dusky, because they/See not all clear;/O for that night! where I in him/ Might live invisible and dim.
HENRY VAUGHAN *The Night*

GOD, LIGHT

1 God is light, and in him there is no darkness at all.
1 John 1.5

2 I presumed to fix my look on the eternal light so long that I consumed my sight thereon.
DANTE ALIGHIERI _Paradiso_

3 Therefore we thank Thee for our little light, that is dappled with shadow./ We thank Thee who hast moved us to building, to finding, to forming at the ends of our fingers and beams of our eyes./And when we have built an altar to the Invisible Light, we may set thereon the little lights for which our bodily vision is made./And we thank Thee that darkness reminds us of light./O Light Invisible, we give Thee thanks for Thy great glory!
T. S. ELIOT _The Rock_

4 In Thee, Beloved, is light;/And the light doth shine/In darkness of the world./ And the world knows it not!
MIRA (Hindu)

5 You know how things look when the sun's beams are on them, the very air then appears full of impurities which, before it came out, were not seen. So it is with our souls. We are full of stains and corruptions, we see them not, they are like the air before the sun shines; but though we see them not, God sees them: He pervades us as the sunbeam.
CARDINAL NEWMAN

6 I believe Thee to be the best being of all, the source of light for the whole world. O beneficent spirit, Divine Being. Thou, O Lord, shalt be unto us as the Everlasting Light.
Zoroastrian

GOD, LOVE OF

7 Know that the Lord has shown me his marvellous love;/the Lord hears when I call to him.
_Ps. 4.3_

8 Goodness and love unfailing, these will follow me/all the days of my life,/and I shall dwell in the house of the Lord/my whole life long.
_Ps. 23.6_

9 I will sing the story of thy love, O Lord, for ever;/I will proclaim thy faithfulness to all generations.
_Ps. 89.1_

10 Can a woman forget the infant at her breast,/or a loving mother the child of her womb?/Even these forget, yet I will not forget you.
Isa. 49.15

11 I will betroth you to myself for ever, betroth you in lawful wedlock with unfailing devotion and love; I will betroth you to myself to have and to hold, and you shall know the Lord.
Hos. 2.19–20

12 When Israel was a boy, I loved him;/I called my son out of Egypt;/but the more I called, the further they went from me.
Hos. 11.1–2

13 I am convinced that there is nothing in death or life, in the realm of spirits or superhuman powers, in the world as it is or the world as it shall be, in the forces of the universe, in heights or depths— nothing in all creation that can separate us from the love of God in Christ Jesus our Lord.
Rom. 8.38–39

14 God is love; he who dwells in love is dwelling in God, and God in him.
1 John 4.16

15 The flame of Thy love glows/In the darkness of my night.
AL-ANSARI (Sufi)

16 Even the most elementary and familiar of our spiritual experiences are robbed of their true meaning if they be regarded otherwise than as part of the soul's dealings with One who all our lives through is seeking us out in love.
JOHN BAILLIE _Our Knowledge of God_

1 It is but right that our hearts should be on God, when the heart of God is so much on us.
RICHARD BAXTER *The Saints' Everlasting Rest*

2 Judge not the Lord by feeble sense,/But trust Him for His grace;/Behind a frowning providence/He hides a smiling face.
WILLIAM COWPER *Hymn*

3 Behold my needs which I know not myself; see and do according to Thy tender mercy.
F. DE LA M. FÉNELON

4 Lord of all being, throned afar,/Thy glory flames from sun and star;/Centre and soul of every sphere,/Yet to each loving heart how near!
OLIVER WENDELL HOLMES *Hymn*

5 But all shall be well, and all shall be well, and all manner of thing shall be well.
MOTHER JULIAN OF NORWICH *Revelations of Divine Love*

6 Thou, my God, who art Love, art Love that loveth, and Love that is loveable, and Love that is the bond between these twain.
NICOLAS OF CUSA

7 For, ah, who can express/How full of bonds and simpleness/Is God,/How narrow is He,/And how the wide, waste field of possibility/Is only trod/Straight to His homestead in the human heart,/And all His art/Is as the babe's that wins his Mother to repeat/Her little song so sweet!
COVENTRY PATMORE

8 Come sing about love, that caused us first to be/Come sing about love, that made the stone and tree/Come sing about love, love, love that draws us lovingly/We beseech Thee, hear us.
STEPHEN SCHWARTZ *Godspell*

9 The God of love, if omnipotent and omniscient, must be the god of cancer and epilepsy as well.
G. B. SHAW

10 I fled Him, down the nights and down the days;/I fled Him, down the arches of the years;/I fled Him, down the labyrinthine ways/Of my own mind; and in the mist of tears/I hid from Him, and under running laughter.
FRANCIS THOMPSON *The Hound of Heaven*

11 Here in the maddening maze of things,/When tossed by storm and flood,/To one fixed ground my spirit clings:/I know that God is good.
I know not where His islands lift/Their fronded palms in air;/I only know I cannot drift/Beyond His love and care.
JOHN GREENLEAF WHITTIER *Hymn*

GOD, LOVE TOWARDS

12 Hear, O Israel, the Lord is our God, one Lord, and you must love the Lord your God with all your heart and soul and strength.
Deut. 6.4–5

13 I offer you the choice of life or death, blessing or curse. Choose life and then you and your descendants will live; love the Lord your God, obey him and hold fast to him.
Deut. 30.19–20

14 Pour into our hearts such love toward thee, that we, loving thee above all things, may obtain thy promises, which exceed all that we can desire.
BOOK OF COMMON PRAYER From the *Collect for the Sixth Sunday after Trinity*

GOD, LOYALTY TO

15 I will leave seven thousand in Israel, all who have not bent the knee to Baal, all whose lips have not kissed him.
1 Kings 19.18

16 If there is a god who is able to save us from the blazing furnace, it is our God whom we serve, and he will save us from

your power, O king; but if not, be it
known to your majesty that we will
neither serve your god nor worship the
golden image that you have set up.
Dan. 3.17–18

1 All peoples may walk, each in the name
of his god,/but we will walk in the name
of the Lord our God/for ever and ever.
Micah 4.5

GOD, MAJESTY OF

2 So now you must circumcise the foreskin
of your hearts and not be stubborn any
more, for the Lord your God is God of
gods and Lord of lords, the great,
mighty, and terrible God. He is no
respecter of persons and is not to be
bribed; he secures justice for widows and
orphans, and loves the alien who lives
among you, giving him food and clothing.
Deut. 10.16–18

3 Thine, O Lord, is the greatness, the
power, the glory, the splendour, and the
majesty; for everything in heaven and on
earth is thine.
1 Chr. 29.11

4 O Lord our sovereign,/how glorious is
thy name in all the earth!
Ps. 8.1

5 Lift up your heads, you gates,/Lift them
up, you everlasting doors,/that the king
of glory may come in./Who then is the
king of glory?/The king of glory is the
Lord of Hosts.
Ps. 24.9–10

6 Bow down to the Lord in the splendour
of holiness,/and dance in his honour, all
men on earth.
Ps. 96.9

7 The Lord is king, let the earth be glad.
Ps. 97.1

8 O Lord my God, thou art great indeed,/
clothed in majesty and splendour,/and
wrapped in a robe of light.
Ps. 104.1–2

9 It is not the constant thought of their
sins, but the vision of the holiness of
God that makes the saints aware of
their own sinfulness.
METROPOLITAN ANTHONY (BLOOM)

10 Exalted art thou above my praise and the
praise of anyone beside me, above my
description and the description of all who
are in heaven and all who are on earth.
BAHA'U'UAH (Bahai)

GOD, MYSTERY OF

11 Can you fathom the mystery of God,/can
you fathom the perfection of the Almighty?
Job 11.7

12 For as the heavens are higher than
the earth,/so are my ways higher than
your ways/and my thoughts than your
thoughts.
Isa. 55.9

13 How can any man learn what is God's
plan? How can he apprehend what the
Lord's will is?
Wisd. 9.13

14 The reason why the element of paradox
comes into all religious thought and
statement is because God cannot be
comprehended in any human words or
in any of the categories of our finite
thought.
D. M. BAILLIE *God was in Christ*

15 God is the Being . . . that may properly
only be addressed, not expressed.
MARTIN BUBER *I and Thou*

16 'God is inescapable. He is God only
because he is inescapable. And only that
which *is* inescapable is God . . . it is
safe to say that a man who has never
tried to flee God has never experienced
the God who is really God . . . A god
whom we can easily bear, a god from
whom we do not have to hide, a god
whom we do not hate in moments, a god
whose destruction we never desire, is not
God at all, and has no reality.'
PAUL TILLICH *The Shaking of the Foundations*

1 There is ever a Beyond of mystery; for the more we know, the more we wonder.
GEORGE TYRRELL *Oil and Wine*

2 What none can comprehend with the mind but that by which the mind is comprehended—may we know this alone to be God, and not lesser things that we worship.
Sama Veda (Hindu)

GOD, NAME OF

3 God answered, 'I AM; that is who I am.'
Ex. 3.14

4 Moses prayed, 'Show me thy glory.' The Lord answered, 'I will make all my goodness pass before you, and I will pronounce in your hearing the name Jehovah. I will be gracious to whom I will be gracious, and I will have compassion on whom I will have compassion.' But he added, 'My face you cannot see, for no mortal man may see me and live.'
Ex. 33.18–20

5 To attempt to worship a God without a name, is to attempt the impossible ... Religion is falling in love with God; and it is impossible to fall in love with an abstract God, He must have a name ... The Christian faith says boldly to mankind, 'Come, let us introduce you to God. His name is Jesus, and He was a Carpenter by trade.'
G. A. STUDDERT KENNEDY

GOD, OBEDIENCE TO

6 Obedience is better than sacrifice,/and to listen to him than the fat of rams.
1 Sam. 15.22

7 Teach me thy way, O Lord.
Ps. 27.11

8 We must obey God rather than men.
Acts 5.29

9 Give what Thou commandest, and command what Thou wilt.
ST AUGUSTINE *Confessions*

10 There are three different paths to reach the Highest: the path of I, the path of Thou, and the path of Thou and I.
RAMAKRISHNA (Hindu)

GOD, PEOPLE OF

11 If only you will now listen to me and keep my covenant, then out of all peoples you shall become my special possession; for the whole earth is mine. You shall be my kingdom of priests, my holy nation.
Ex. 19.5–6

12 It was not because you were more numerous than any other nation that the Lord cared for you and chose you, for you were the smallest of all nations; it was because the Lord loved you and stood by his oath to your forefathers.
Deut. 7.7–8

13 You are the sons of the Lord your God.
Deut. 14.1

14 You are a people holy to the Lord your God, and the Lord has chosen you out of all peoples on earth to be his special possession.
Deut. 14.2

15 We will have a king over us; then we shall be like other nations.
1 Sam. 8.20

16 The Lord will seek a man after his own heart.
1 Sam. 13.14

17 I now see how true it is that God has no favourites, but that in every nation the man who is godfearing and does what is right is acceptable to him.
Acts 10.34–35

18 Penniless, we own the world.
2 Cor. 6.10

1 You are a chosen race, a royal priesthood, a dedicated nation, and a people claimed by God for his own.
1 Pet. 2.9

2 Here and now, dear friends, we are God's children; what we shall be has not yet been disclosed, but we know that when it is disclosed we shall be like him, because we shall see him as he is.
1 John 3.2

3 Behold the amazing gift of love/The Father hath bestowed/On us, the sinful sons of men,/To call us sons of God!
Scottish Paraphrases

4 When wilt Thou save the people?/O God of mercy, when?/The people, Lord, the people/Not thrones and crowns, but men!/God save the people, for Thine they are,/Thy children, as Thy angels fair/Save the people from despair/God save the people.
STEPHEN SCHWARTZ *Godspell*

GOD, POWER OF

5 Indeed this I know for the truth,/that no man can win his case against God.
Job 9.2

6 I planted the seed, and Apollos watered it; but God made it grow.
1 Cor. 3.6

7 I know who it is in whom I have trusted, and am confident of his power to keep safe what he has put into my charge.
2 Tim. 1.12

8 God of concrete, God of steel,/God of piston and of wheel,/God of pylon, God of steam,/God of girder and of beam,/God of atom, God of mine,/All the world of power is thine.
RICHARD G. JONES *100 Hymns for Today*

9 No strength of our own or goodness we claim;/Yet, since we have known the Saviour's great Name,/In this our strong tower for safety we hide,—/The Lord is our power, the Lord will provide.
JOHN NEWTON *Hymn*

GOD, PRAISE OF

10 I will praise the Lord for his righteousness,/and sing a psalm to the name of the Lord most High.
Ps. 7.17

11 I will praise thee, O Lord, with all my heart,/I will tell the story of thy marvellous acts.
Ps. 9.1

12 Send forth thy light and thy truth to be my guide/and lead me to thy holy hill, to thy tabernacle,/then shall I come to the altar of God, the God of my joy,/and praise thee on the harp, O God, thou God of my delight.
Ps. 43.3–4

13 Open my lips, O Lord,/that my mouth may proclaim thy praise.
Ps. 51.15

14 But I will wait in continual hope,/I will praise thee again and yet again.
Ps. 71.14

15 O Lord, it is good to give thee thanks,/to sing psalms to thy name, O Most High,/to declare thy love in the morning/and thy constancy every night.
Ps. 92.1–2

16 Come! Let us raise a joyful song to the Lord,/a shout of triumph to the Rock of our salvation./Let us come into his presence with thanksgiving,/and sing him psalms of triumph.
Ps. 95.1–2

17 Sing a new song to the Lord;/sing to the Lord, all men on earth./Sing to the Lord and bless his name,/proclaim his triumph day by day./Declare his glory among the nations,/his marvellous deeds among all peoples.
Ps. 96.1–3

18 Enter his gates with thanksgiving/and his courts with praise./Give thanks to him and bless his name;/for the Lord is good and his love is everlasting,/his constancy endures to all generations.
Ps. 100.4–5

1 It is good to give thanks to the Lord;/
for his love endures for ever.
Ps. 106.1

2 Let everything that has breath praise the
Lord!
Ps. 150.6

3 We praise thee, O God: we acknowledge
thee to be the Lord./All the earth doth
worship thee: the Father everlasting.
BOOK OF COMMON PRAYER From the *Te
Deum*

4 The glorious company of the Apostles
praise thee./The goodly fellowship of the
Prophets praise thee./The noble army
of Martyrs praise thee.
BOOK OF COMMON PRAYER From the *Te
Deum*

5 O all ye Works of the Lord, bless ye
the Lord: praise him, and magnify him
for ever.
BOOK OF COMMON PRAYER From the
Benedicite

6 O ye holy and humble Men of heart,
bless ye the Lord, praise him, and
magnify him for ever.
BOOK OF COMMON PRAYER From the
Benedicite

7 When all Thy mercies, O my God!/My
rising soul surveys,/Transported with the
view, I'm lost/In wonder, love, and
praise.
JOSEPH ADDISON *Hymn*

8 My soul, bear thou thy part,/Triumph in
God above,/And with a well-tuned heart/
Sing thou the songs of love./Let all thy
days/Till life shall end,/Whate'er He
send,/Be filled with praise.
RICHARD BAXTER *Hymn*

9 Every star shall sing a carol;/every
creature, high or low,/Come and praise
the King of Heaven,/by whatever name
you know.
God above, Man below,/Holy is the
name I know.
SYDNEY CARTER *100 Hymns for Today*

10 What else can I do, a lame old man, but
sing hymns to God? If I were a nightingale, I would do the nightingale's part; if
I were a swan, I would do as a swan. But
now I am a rational creature, and I ought
to praise God: this is my work; I do it,
nor will I desert my post, so long as I am
allowed to keep it. And I exhort you to
join me in this same song.
EPICTETUS

11 Dwell on Him alone, O mind, who is
the King of kings./Rest thy hope on Him
alone, who is the Hope of all./Shed all
thy cleverness and come to the feet of
the Lord./Meditate, O my mind, on the
Name, in peace and joy./Day and night
call thou on thy God, and utter His
praises for ever.
The Granth (Sikh)

12 Let all the world in every corner sing,/
'My God and King!'/The heavens are not
too high,/His praise may thither fly;/
The earth is not too low,/His praises
there may grow./Let all the world in
every corner sing,/'My God and King!'
GEORGE HERBERT *Hymn*

13 Of all the creatures both in sea and land/
Onely to Man thou hast made known thy
wayes,/And put the penne alone into his
hand,/And made him Secretarie of thy
praise . . .
GEORGE HERBERT

14 The shepherds sing; and shall I silent be?/
My God, no hymns for Thee?/My soul's
a shepherd too; a flock it feeds/Of
thoughts, and words, and deeds;/The
pasture is thy word; the streams, thy
grace/Enriching all the place./Shepherd
and flock shall sing, and all my powers/
Out-sing the day-light houres.
GEORGE HERBERT

15 Praise God, from whom all blessings
flow;/Praise Him, all creatures here
below;/Praise Him above, ye heavenly
host;/Praise Father, Son, and Holy
Ghost.
THOMAS KEN *Doxology*

1 All praise to Thee, my God, this night,/
For all the blessings of the light!/Keep
me, O keep me, King of kings,/Beneath
Thy own almighty wings.
THOMAS KEN *Hymn*

2 All people that on earth do dwell,/Sing
to the Lord with cheerful voice./Him
serve with mirth, His praise forth tell;/
Come ye before Him and rejoice.
WILLIAM KETHE *Hymn*

3 Hast thou not seen how all in the Heavens
and in the Earth uttereth the praise of
God?—the very birds as they spread
their wings? Every creature knoweth its
prayer and its praise! and God knoweth
what they do.
The Koran (Muslim)

4 Let us with a gladsome mind/Praise the
Lord, for He is kind:/For His mercies aye
endure,/Ever faithful, ever sure.
JOHN MILTON *Hymn*

5 From all that dwell below the skies/Let
the Creator's praise arise: Hallelujah!
Let the Redeemer's Name be sung/
Through every land, in every tongue.
Hallelujah!
ISAAC WATTS *Hymn*

GOD, PRESENCE OF

6 Thou wilt show me the path of life;/
in thy presence is the fullness of joy,/in
thy right hand pleasures for evermore.
Ps. 16.11

7 Even though I walk through a valley
dark as death/I fear no evil, for thou art
with me.
Ps. 23.4

8 But, Lord, do not thou forsake me;/keep
not far from me, my God./Hasten to my
help, O Lord my salvation.
Ps. 38.21

9 Where can I escape from thy spirit?/
Where can I flee from thy presence?/
If I climb up to heaven, thou art there;/

if I make my bed in Sheol, again I find
thee.
Ps. 139.7–8

10 Fear nothing, for I am with you;/be not
afraid, for I am your God.
Isa. 41.10

11 He is not far from each one of us, for in
him we live and move, in him we exist.
Acts 17.27–28

12 Come close to God, and he will come
close to you.
Jas. 4.8

13 Thou wast with me, and I was not with
thee.
ST AUGUSTINE *Confessions*

14 Never forget that you are not alone. The
Divine is with you, helping and guiding.
He is the companion who never fails, the
friend whose love comforts and strengthens. Have faith and He will do everything for you.
AUROBINDO (Hindu)

15 Come near to God. He is your friend.
BUNJIRO (Shinto)

16 Could we pierce the veil, and were we
vigilant and attentive, God would reveal
Himself continuously to us and we
should rejoice in His action in everything that happened to us.
J. P. DE CAUSSADE *Self-abandonment to
Divine Providence*

17 The remarkable thing about the way in
which people talk about God, or about
their relation to God, is that it seems to
escape them completely that God hears
what they are saying.
SÖREN KIERKEGAARD *Journals*

18 There are fixed times for all things, and
it would manifestly be out of order to
do at one moment what we ought to do at
another. But there is no time in which we
ought not to love God and think of
Him.
FRANÇOIS MALAVAL *A Simple Method of
Raising the Soul to Contemplation*

1 Adore God as if you could see Him; for although you cannot see Him, He can see you.
MUHAMMAD *Hadith* (Muslim)

2 Nothing in life need thee dismay,/Is He not by?/Humble thyself and to Him pray./Is He not by?/Cannot He hear thy cry?
W. B. PICKARD *The Divine Divan* (Muslim)

3 God is in the water, God is in the dry land, God is in the heart./God is in the forest, God is in the mountain, God is in the cave./God is in the earth, God is in heaven . . ./Thou art in the tree, thou art in its leaves,/Thou art in the earth, thou art in the firmament.
GOVIND SINGH (Sikh)

4 Lord! it is not life to live,/If Thy presence Thou deny;/Lord! if Thou Thy presence give,/'Tis no longer death—to die.
AUGUSTUS MONTAGUE TOPLADY

GOD, PROTECTOR

5 So the Lord put a mark on Cain, in order that anyone meeting him should not kill him.
Gen. 4.15

6 The Lord himself goes at your head; he will be with you; he will not fail you or forsake you. Do not be discouraged or afraid.
Deut. 31.8

7 I will not fail you or forsake you.
Josh. 1.5

8 Be strong, be resolute; do not be fearful or dismayed, for the Lord your God is with you wherever you go.
Josh. 1.9

9 For look! my witness is in heaven;/there is one on high ready to answer for me.
Job 16.19

10 But in my heart I know that my vindicator lives/and that he will rise last to speak in court;/and I shall discern my witness standing at my side/and see my defending counsel, even God himself,/whom I shall see with my own eyes,/I myself and no other.
Job 19.25–27

11 I lie down and sleep,/and I wake again, for the Lord upholds me.
Ps. 3.5

12 Keep me like the apple of thine eye;/hide me in the shadow of thy wings.
Ps. 17.8

13 The Lord is my stronghold, my fortress and my champion,/my God, my rock where I find safety,/my shield, my mountain refuge, my strong tower.
Ps. 18.2

14 The Lord is my shepherd; I shall want nothing.
Ps. 23.1

15 Blessed is the Lord:/he carries us day by day.
Ps. 68.19

16 The Lord will guard your going and your coming,/now and for evermore.
Ps. 121.8

17 If God is on our side, who is against us?
Rom. 8.31

18 Lighten our darkness, we beseech thee, O Lord; and by thy great mercy defend us from all perils and dangers of this night.
BOOK OF COMMON PRAYER From the *Order for Evening Prayer*

19 In all our dangers and necessities stretch forth thy right hand to help and defend us.
BOOK OF COMMON PRAYER From the *Collect for the Third Sunday after the Epiphany*

20 O God, who knowest us to be set in the midst of so many and great dangers, that by reason of the frailty of our nature we cannot always stand upright; Grant to us such strength and protection, as may support us in all dangers, and carry us through all temptations.
BOOK OF COMMON PRAYER From the *Collect for the Fourth Sunday after the Epiphany*

1 O God, the protector of all that trust in thee, without whom nothing is strong, nothing is holy; Increase and multiply upon us thy mercy; that, thou being our ruler and guide, we may so pass through things temporal, that we finally lose not the things eternal.
BOOK OF COMMON PRAYER From the *Collect for the Fourth Sunday after Trinity*

2 Lead us, heavenly Father, lead us/O'er the world's tempestuous sea;/Guard us, guide us, keep us, feed us,/For we have no help but Thee;/Yet possessing every blessing/If our God our Father be.
JAMES EDMESTON *Hymn*

GOD, PURPOSE OF

3 No one should ask, 'What is this?' or 'Why is that?'/Everything has been created for its own purpose.
Ecclus. 39.21

4 God is working His purpose out, as year succeeds to year:/God is working His purpose out, and the time is drawing near—/Nearer and nearer draws the time—the time that shall surely be,/ When the earth shall be filled with the glory of God, as the waters cover the sea.
ARTHUR CAMPBELL AINGER *Hymn*

5 I can hardly recollect a single plan of mine, of which I have not since seen reason to be satisfied that, had it taken place in season and circumstance just as I proposed, it would, humanly speaking, have proved my ruin; or at least it would have deprived me of the greater good the Lord had designed for me.
JOHN NEWTON *Cardiphonia*

GOD, REFUGE

6 The Lord is my light and my salvation;/ whom should I fear?/The Lord is the refuge of my life;/of whom then should I go in dread?
Ps. 27.1

7 Taste, then, and see that the Lord is good./Happy the man who finds refuge in him!
Ps. 34.8

8 God is our shelter and our refuge,/a timely help in trouble.
Ps. 46.1

9 Lord, thou hast been our refuge/from generation to generation.
Ps. 90.1

10 Thou art my only refuge on the day of disaster.
Jer. 17.17

11 That man is perfect in faith who can come to God in the utter dearth of his feelings and desires, without a glow or an aspiration, with the weight of low thoughts, failures, neglects, and wandering forgetfulness, and say to Him, 'Thou art my refuge.'
GEORGE MACDONALD

GOD, SEEKING AND FINDING

12 For thou, Lord, dost not forsake those who seek thee.
Ps. 9.10

13 Hear, O Lord, when I call aloud;/show me favour and answer me./'Come,'my heart has said,/'seek his face.'/I will seek thy face, O Lord.
Ps. 27.7–8

14 As a hind longs for the running streams,/ so do I long for thee, O God./With my whole being I thirst for God, the living God.
Ps. 42.1–2

15 Let us delight to find Thee by failing to find Thee rather than by finding Thee to fail to find Thee.
ST AUGUSTINE *Confessions*

1 Anything else one may doubt but that he who desires only the Divine shall reach the Divine is a certitude and more certain than two and two make four.
AUROBINDO (Hindu)

2 We should find God in what we do know, not in what we don't; not in problems still outstanding, but in those we have already solved . . . God cannot be used as a stop-gap.
DIETRICH BONHOEFFER *Letters and Papers from Prison*

3 He is to be seen in the light of a cottage window as well as in the sun or the stars.
ARTHUR CLUTTON-BROCK *Studies in Christianity*

4 I said: 'I will find God', and forth I went/To seek Him in the clearness of the sky./But over me stood unendurably/Only a pitiless, sapphire firmament/Ringing the world——blank splendour; yet intent/Still to find God. 'I will go seek', said I,/'His way upon the waters', and drew nigh/An ocean marge weed-strewn, and foam besprent;/And the waves dashed on idle sand and stone,/And very vacant was the long, blue sea;/But in the evening as I sat alone,/My window open to the vanishing day,/Dear God! I could not choose but kneel and pray,/And it sufficed that I was found of Thee.
EDWARD DOWDEN

5 The paths to God are more in number than the breathings of created beings.
Parsee

6 The sun meets not the springing bud that stretches towards him with half that certainty as God, the source of all good, communicates Himself to the soul that longs to partake of Him.
WILLIAM LAW *Spirit of Power*

7 Thou dost guide to Thyself those who turn to Thee.
Muslim

8 Seek His will—that is to live.
GURU NANAK *Japji* (Sikh)

9 Console thyself, thou wouldst not seek Me, if thou hadst not found Me.
BLAISE PASCAL *Pensées*

10 As one can ascend to the top of a house by means of a ladder or a bamboo or a staircase or a rope, so divers are the ways and means to approach God, and every religion in the world shows one of these ways.
RAMAKRISHNA (Hindu)

11 Verily, verily, I say unto thee, he who longs for Him, finds Him. Go and verify this in thine own life; try for three consecutive days with genuine earnestness and thou art sure to succeed.
RAMAKRISHNA (Hindu)

12 Out of the hidden depths of my soul/To you, O hidden God, I cry—hear my prayer . . . ./Only show me Your face, let me see Your face! . . . ./I would drink of the Source of all sources, I long to bathe in the Light of all lights—/Your face, *Your* face I crave to see.
Service of the Heart (Jewish)

13 Let him who seeks cease not from seeking until he find; and when he finds he shall be astonished; astonished, he shall gain the Kingdom; and having gained the Kingdom, he shall have rest.
The Gospel of Thomas

14 Say to yourself, 'I am loved by God more than I can either conceive or understand.' Let this fill all your soul and all your prayers and never leave you. You will soon see that this is the way to find God.
HENRI DE TOURVILLE *Letters of Direction*

GOD, SERVANT OF

15 Here is my servant, whom I uphold,/my chosen one in whom I delight,/I have bestowed my spirit upon him,/and he will make justice shine on the nations.
Isa. 42.1

16 He will not break a bruised reed,/or snuff out a smouldering wick.
Isa. 42.3

1 I will make you a light to the nations,/
to be my salvation to earth's farthest
bounds.
Isa. 49.6

2 He was despised, he shrank from the
sight of men,/tormented and humbled by
suffering;/we despised him, we held him
of no account,/a thing from which men
turn away their eyes.
Isa. 53.3

3 He was pierced for our transgressions,/
tortured for our iniquities;/the chastise-
ment he bore is health for us/and by his
scourging we are healed.
Isa. 53.5

4 We had all strayed like sheep,/each of us
had gone his own way;/but the Lord
laid upon him/the guilt of us all.
Isa. 53.6

5 He was led like a sheep to the slaughter.
Isa. 53.7

GOD, SERVICE OF

6 What then, O Israel, does the Lord your
God ask of you? Only to fear the Lord
your God, to conform to all his ways, to
love him and to serve him with all your
heart and soul.
Deut. 10.12

7 O God ... whose service is perfect
freedom.
BOOK OF COMMON PRAYER From the
Collect for Peace

8 Let me offer you in sacrifice the service
of my thoughts and my tongue, but first
give me what I may offer you.
ST AUGUSTINE

9 The fact that it is God that giveth the
increase is no reason why we need not
plant and water.
ST AUGUSTINE *Sermons*

10 Father, whose bounty all creation shows,/
Christ, by whose willing sacrifice we live,/

Spirit, from whom all life in fulness flows,/
to thee with grateful hearts ourselves we
give.
ALBERT F. BAYLY *100 Hymns for Today*

11 Teach me, my God and King,/In all
things Thee to see;/And what I do in
anything,/To do it as for Thee!
A servant with this clause/Makes drud-
gery divine:/Who sweeps a room, as for
Thy laws,/Makes that and the action
fine.
GEORGE HERBERT *Hymn*

12 We give Thee but Thine own,/Whate'er
the gift may be;/All that we have is
Thine alone,/A trust, O Lord, from Thee.
WILLIAM WALSHAM HOW *Hymn*

13 Rise up, O men of God!/Have done with
lesser things;/Give heart and soul and
mind and strength/To serve the King of
kings.
WILLIAM PIERSON MERRILL *Hymn*

14 Teach me wisdom, how to expend my
blood, estate, life, and time in Thy
service for the good of all, and make all
them that are round about me wise and
holy as Thou art.
THOMAS TRAHERNE

15 Show us, O Blessed One, that though we
can recite but little of the Teaching, yet
put its Precepts into practice, ridding
ourselves of craving and delusion, and
possessed of knowledge and serenity of
mind, cleaving to nothing in this or any
other world, then we are true disciples of
Thee, O Blessed One.
Thoughts on the Way (Buddhist)

16 Lord of all being, I give you my all;/if
e'er I disown you I stumble and fall;/
But sworn in glad service your word to
obey,/I walk in your freedom to the end
of the way.
JACK C. WINSLOW *100 Hymns for Today*

GOD, SPEAKING WITH

17 At length Moses came down from Mount
Sinai with the two stone tablets of the

Tokens in his hands, and when he descended, he did not know that the skin of his face shone because he had been speaking with the Lord.
Ex. 34.29

1 There has never yet risen in Israel a prophet like Moses, whom the Lord knew face to face.
Deut. 34.10

2 Speak, Lord; thy servant hears thee.
1 Sam. 3.9

3 A great and strong wind came rending mountains and shattering rocks before him, but the Lord was not in the wind; and after the wind there was an earthquake, but the Lord was not in the earthquake; and after the earthquake fire, but the Lord was not in the fire; and after the fire a low murmuring sound.
1 Kings 19.11–12

4 If he would slay me, I should not hesitate;/I should still argue my cause to his face.
Job 13.15

5 And I know that this same man (whether in the body or out of it, I do not know—God knows) was caught up into paradise, and heard words so secret that human lips may not repeat them.
2 Cor. 12.3–4

6 Our heart oft times wakes when we sleep, and God can speak to that, either by words, by proverbs, by signs and similitudes, as well as if one was awake.
JOHN BUNYAN *The Pilgrim's Progress*

7 Lord, these are such little things for which we pray. If someone were to ask them of me, I could do them as well. But you are a hundred times more able than I and even more willing, so if we asked you for something greater, you could still give it—and the more willingly the greater it is that we ask for.
MEISTER ECKHART

8 Think oftener of God than you breathe.
EPICTETUS

9 To be straightforward with God is neither an easy nor a common grace.
FREDERICK WILLIAM FABER *Spiritual Conferences*

10 Half an hour's listening is essential except when you are very busy. Then a full hour is needed.
ST FRANCIS DE SALES

11 Lord, speak to me, that I may speak/In living echoes of Thy tone.
FRANCES RIDLEY HAVERGAL *Hymn*

12 The custom which we now use (i.e. Church music) was not instituted so much for their cause which are spiritual, as to the end that into grosser and heavier minds, whom bare words do not easily move, the sweetness of melody might make some entrance for good things.
RICHARD HOOKER *Ecclesiastical Polity*

13 The palace of my soul must have somehow two lifts—a lift which is always going up from below, and a lift which is always going down from above.
BARON F. VON HÜGEL *Selected Letters*

14 We should establish ourselves in a sense of God's Presence, by continually conversing with Him.
BROTHER LAWRENCE *The Practice of the Presence of God*

15 I am satisfied that when the Almighty wants me to do or not to do any particular thing, He finds a way of letting me know it.
ABRAHAM LINCOLN

16 If we knew how to listen to God, we should hear him speaking to us, for God does speak. He speaks in his Gospel; he speaks also through life—that new Gospel to which we ourselves add a page each day.
MICHEL QUOIST *Prayers of Life*

17 Speak to Him, thou, for He hears, and Spirit with Spirit can meet—/Closer is He than breathing, and nearer than hands and feet.
LORD TENNYSON *The Higher Pantheism*

1 The God of the Bible is indeed a universal God, but He is a God who nevertheless chooses places in which to reveal Himself to men. He is a God without frontiers, omnipresent, never the prisoner of any particular place but not an impersonal God floating everywhere and nowhere. He breaks into history and geography because He speaks to men and enters into dialogue with them; and a dialogue always takes place at a particular time and place.

PAUL TOURNIER

GOD, STRENGTH FROM

2 Nor must you say to yourselves, 'My own strength and energy have gained me this wealth', but remember the Lord your God; it is he that gives you strength to become prosperous.
Deut. 8.17–18

3 If I lift up my eyes to the hills,/where shall I find help?/Help comes only from the Lord,/maker of heaven and earth.
Ps. 121.1–2

4 Our help is in the name of the Lord,/ maker of heaven and earth.
Ps. 124.8

5 Young men may grow weary and faint,/ even in their prime they may stumble and fall;/but those who look to the Lord will win new strength.
Isa. 40.30–31

6 Give me the strength lightly to bear my joys and sorrows/Give me the strength to make my love fruitful in service/Give me the strength to raise my mind high above daily trifles./And give me the strength to surrender my strength to thy will with love.

RABINDRANATH TAGORE

GOD, SUPREMACY OF

7 In God's hand are the souls of all that live,/the spirits of all human kind.
Job 12.10

8 Source, Guide, and Goal of all that is— to him be glory for ever!
Rom. 11.36

9 The world, life, and death, the present and the future, all of them belong to you—yet you belong to Christ, and Christ to God.
1 Cor. 3.22–23

10 The sovereignty of the world has passed to our Lord and his Christ, and he shall reign for ever and ever!
Rev. 11.15

GOD, TRUST IN

11 Unto thee, O Lord my God, I lift up my heart./In thee I trust.
Ps. 25.1–2

12 My fortunes are in thy hand.
Ps. 31.15

13 In God I trust and shall not be afraid;/ what can man do to me?
Ps. 56.11

14 Trust always in God, my people,/pour out your hearts before him.
Ps. 62.8

15 Put all your trust in the Lord/and do not rely on your own understanding.
Prov. 3.5

16 Trust in the Lord for ever;/for the Lord himself is an everlasting rock.
Isa. 26.4

17 Blessed is the man who trusts in the Lord,/ and rests his confidence upon him.
Jer. 17.7

18 Set your troubled hearts at rest. Trust in God always; trust also in me.
John 14.1

19 O Lord, in thee have I trusted: let me never be confounded.
BOOK OF COMMON PRAYER From the *Te Deum*

1 Thy way, not mine, O Lord,/However
dark it be!/Lead me by Thine own hand;/
Choose out the path for me.
HORATIUS BONAR *Hymn*

2 Hold Thou my hands,—/These passionate hands too quick to smite,/These
hands so eager for delight:/Hold Thou
my hands!
And when at length/With darkened eyes
and fingers cold,/I seek some last loved
hand to hold,/Hold Thou my hands!
WILLIAM CANTON *Hymn*

3 Trust in God, and keep your powder
dry.
OLIVER CROMWELL

4 My times are in Thy hand:/My God, I
wish them there;/My life, my friends,
my soul I leave/Entirely to Thy care.
WILLIAM FREEMAN LLOYD *Hymn*

5 Courage, brother! do not stumble,/
Though thy path be dark as night;/
There's a star to guide the humble:/
'Trust in God, and do the right.'
NORMAN MACLEOD *Hymn*

6 Have faith in God, my mind,/thought of
thy light burns low;/God's mercy holds a
wiser plan/than thou canst fully know.
B. A. REES *100 Hymns for Today*

7 Be still, my soul: the Lord is on thy side;/
Bear patiently the cross of grief or pain;/
Leave to thy God to order and provide;/
In every change He faithful will remain.
KATHERINE VON SCHLEGEL *Hymn*

8 Blest is the man, O God,/That stays
himself on Thee:/Who wait for Thy
salvation, Lord,/Shall Thy salvation see.
AUGUSTUS MONTAGUE TOPLADY *Hymn*

9 O God our help in ages past,/Our hope
for years to come,/Our shelter from the
stormy blast,/And our eternal home!
ISAAC WATTS *Hymn*

GOD, UNIVERSAL

10 I am the Lord, there is no other;/I make
the light, I create darkness,/author alike
of prosperity and trouble.
Isa. 45.6–7

11 Look to me and be saved,/you peoples
from all corners of the earth.
Isa. 45.22

12 To me every knee shall bend/and by me
every tongue shall swear.
Isa. 45.23

13 There is no distinction between Jew and
Greek, because the same Lord is Lord
of all.
Rom. 10.12

14 O Thou One God, O Lord of Eternity,
how excellent are Thy designs. Thou
didst create the earth according to Thy
heart. Thou settest man in his place and
suppliest his need.
AKHNATON (Egyptian)

15 To God belongeth the east and the west;
therefore whithersoever I turn myself to
pray, there is the face of God.
The Koran (Muslim)

16 There is one; is there any other?/There
is only Thou, there is only Thou, O
God . . ./Not the regions of the sun and
the moon,/Nor the seven continents,/
Nor the seven seas, nor corn, nor wind,
shall abide./There is only Thou, there is
only Thou, O God!
GURU NANAK (Sikh)

GOD, WAITING FOR

17 Wait for the Lord; be strong, take
courage,/and wait for the Lord.
Ps. 27.14

18 My soul waits for the Lord/more eagerly
than watchmen for the morning.
Ps. 130.6

19 The Lord, I say, is all that I have;/
therefore I will wait for him patiently.
Lam. 3.24

GOD, WILL OF

1 Teach me to do thy will, for thou art my God;/in thy gracious kindness, show me the level road.
Ps. 143.10

2 Our Father in heaven,/thy name be hallowed;/thy kingdom come,/thy will be done,/on earth as in heaven.
Matt. 6.9–10

3 Not everyone who calls me 'Lord, Lord' will enter the kingdom of Heaven, but only those who do the will of my heavenly Father.
Matt. 7.21

4 What you ought to say is: 'If it be the Lord's will, we shall live to do this or that.'
Jas. 4.15

5 Lord God Almighty, I charge Thee of Thy great mercy and by the token of the holy rood that Thou guide me to Thy will and to my soul's need better than I can myself, that above all things I may inwardly love Thee with a clear mind and clean body; for Thou art my Maker, my help and my hope.
KING ALFRED THE GREAT

6 God of all goodness, grant us to desire ardently, to seek wisely, to know surely and to accomplish perfectly Thy holy will, for the glory of Thy name.
ST THOMAS AQUINAS

7 Dispose of me according to the wisdom of thy pleasure: thy will be done, though in my own undoing.
SIR THOMAS BROWNE

8 Lord, let Thy glory be my end, Thy word my rule, and then Thy will be done.
KING CHARLES I

✓9 Our wills are ours, to make them Thine.
LORD TENNYSON *In Memoriam*

10 Grant to us, O Lord, to know that which is worth knowing, to love that which is worth loving, to praise that which pleaseth thee most, to esteem that which is most precious unto thee, and to dislike whatsoever is evil in thy eyes. Grant us with true judgement to distinguish things that differ, and above all to search out and to do what is well pleasing unto thee, through Jesus Christ our Lord.
THOMAS À KEMPIS

GOD, WITHIN

11 Too late loved I Thee, O Thou Beauty of ancient days, yet ever new! too late I loved Thee! And behold Thou wert within, and I abroad, and there I searched for Thee.
ST AUGUSTINE *Confessions*

12 God is in thy heart, yet thou searchest for him in the wilderness.
The Granth (Sikh)

13 Stuff not the ear of your mind with cotton,/Take the cotton of evil suggestions from the mind's ear,/That the heavenly voice from above may enter it . . . /For what is this Divine voice but the inward voice.
JALAL-UD-DIN RUMI (Sufi)

14 I believe that God is in me as the sun is in the colour and fragrance of a flower— the Light in my darkness, the Voice in my silence.
HELEN KELLER

15 Though God be everywhere present, yet He is present to thee in the deepest and most central part of the soul.
WILLIAM LAW *The Spirit of Prayer*

16 He who is bewildered is bewildered because he sees not the creator, the holy Lord, abiding within himself.
MAITRAYANA-BRAHMANA UPANISHAD (Hindu)

17 As fragrance dwells in a flower,/And reflection in a mirror;/So does God dwell in every soul./Seek Him therefore in thy self.
GURU NANAK (Sikh)

1 Search not in distant skies;/In man's own heart God lies.
SHAO YUNG (Shinto)

2 We can find our right place in the Being that envelops us only if we experience in our individual lives the universal life which wills and rules within it. The nature of the living Being without me I can understand only through the living Being which is within me.
ALBERT SCHWEITZER *My Life and Thought*

GOD, WORD OF

3 Thy word is a lamp to guide my feet/ and a light on my path.
Ps. 119.105

4 All mankind is grass,/they last no longer than a flower of the field. . . .
The grass withers, the flowers fade,/ but the word of our God endures for evermore.
Isa. 40.6 and 8

5 Whenever I said, 'I will call him to mind no more,/nor speak in his name again',/ then his word was imprisoned in my body,/like a fire blazing in my heart,/ and I was weary with holding it under,/ and could endure no more.
Jer. 20.9

6 For the word of God is alive and active. It cuts more keenly than any two-edged sword, piercing as far as the place where life and spirit, joints and marrow, divide. It sifts the purposes and thoughts of the heart.
Heb. 4.12

GOOD AND EVIL

7 The Lord God took the man and put him in the garden of Eden to till it and care for it. He told the man, 'You may eat from every tree in the garden, but not from the tree of the knowledge of good and evil.
Gen. 2.15–17

8 Your eyes will be opened and you will be like gods knowing both good and evil.
Gen. 3.5

9 If we accept good from God, shall we not accept evil?
Job 2.10

10 Turn from evil and do good,/seek peace and pursue it.
Ps. 34.14

11 Shame on you! you who call evil good and good evil.
Isa. 5.20

12 These are the words of the Lord: Stop at the cross-roads; look for the ancient paths; ask, 'Where is the way that leads to what is good?' Then take that way, and you will find rest for yourselves. But they said, 'We will not.'
Jer. 6.16

13 Can the Nubian change his skin,/or the leopard its spots?/And you? Can you do good,/you who are schooled in evil?
Jer. 13.23

14 Do not both bad and good proceed/from the mouth of the Most High?
Lam. 3.38

15 Seek good and not evil,/that you may live,/that the Lord the God of Hosts may be firmly on your side,/as you say he is.
Amos 5.14

16 Love in all sincerity, loathing evil and clinging to the good.
Rom. 12.9

17 Never pay back evil for evil.
Rom. 12.17

18 Do not let evil conquer you, but use good to defeat evil.
Rom. 12.21

19 The existence of ethics is conditioned by that of theodicy, for if there is a distinction between good and evil, if evil exists, justification of God is inevitable.
NICHOLAS BERDYAEV *The Destiny of Man*

1 Recognize in your little fight against your avarice, or your untruthfulness, or your laziness, only one skirmish in that battle whose field covers the earth, and whose clamour rises and falls from age to age, but never wholly dies.
PHILLIPS BROOKS *Sermons*

2 'Knowledge of good and evil' means nothing else than cognizance of the opposite which the early literature of mankind designated by these two terms.
MARTIN BUBER *Images of Good and Evil*

3 All that has ever been condensed into our conception of a devil exists in human nature as a devilish element. And to cope with that the last reality has to be drawn upon.
P. T. FORSYTH

4 The main obstacle to faith in the good tidings of God which is associated with the name of Jesus is the obstinate appearance of indifference to moral considerations in material nature.
CHARLES GORE *Jesus of Nazareth*

5 Once to every man and nation comes the moment to decide,/In the strife of Truth with Falsehood, for the good or evil side.
JAMES RUSSELL LOWELL *The Present Crisis*

6 There is nothing either good or bad, but thinking makes it so.
WILLIAM SHAKESPEARE *Hamlet*

7 Man desired to know schism in the Universe. It was a knowledge reserved to God; man had been warned that he could not bear it . . . 'Ye shall be as Gods, knowing good and evil'.
CHARLES WILLIAMS *He came Down from Heaven*

GOODNESS

8 God has told you what is good;/and what is it that the Lord asks of you?/Only to act justly, to love loyalty,/to walk wisely before your God.
Micah 6.8

9 There must be no limit to your goodness, as your heavenly Father's goodness knows no bounds.
Matt. 5.48

10 Let us never tire of doing good.
Gal. 6.9

11 Let us work for the good of all, especially members of the household of the faith.
Gal. 6.10

12 Grant to us thy humble servants, that by thy holy inspiration we may think those things that be good, and by thy merciful guiding may perform the same.
BOOK OF COMMON PRAYER From the *Collect for the Fifth Sunday after Easter*

13 If a man be gracious and courteous to strangers, it shews he is a citizen of the world, and that his heart is no island cut off from other lands, but a continent that joins to them.
FRANCIS BACON *Of Goodness and Goodness of Nature*

14 Men have never been good, they are not good, they never will be good.
KARL BARTH

15 It was the highest commendation of his doctrine with all men, that he taught no otherwise than he and his followers had lived; for he neither sought nor loved anything of this world, but delighted in distributing immediately among the poor whatsoever was given him by the kings or rich men of the world.
VENERABLE BEDE *Of the Life of Bishop Aidan*

16 As resignation is the ideal of the Buddhist, and valour of the Mohammedan, so the essence of Christianity is goodness. Its Founder was the absolute personification of this characteristic quality.
E. DAPLYN Article in *Hastings' Dictionary of Christ and the Gospels*

17 He who acts out of pure love of God, not only does he not perform his actions to be seen of men, but does not do them even that God may know of them. Such

an one, if he thought it possible that his good works might escape the eye of God, would still perform them with the same joy, and in the same pureness of love.
ST JOHN OF THE CROSS *The Living Flame*

1 Hell is paved with good intentions.
SAMUEL JOHNSON

2 If I suppose that my goodness today is going to compensate for my failure yesterday, I am really supposing, as far as today is concerned, that I can be better than necessary.
LESSLIE NEWBIGIN *Christian Freedom in the Modern World*

3 And this our life exempt from public haunt/Finds tongues in trees, books in the running brooks,/Sermons in stones and good in every thing.
WILLIAM SHAKESPEARE *As You Like It*

4 I never did repent for doing good,/Nor shall not now.
WILLIAM SHAKESPEARE *The Merchant of Venice*

5 Howe'er it be, it seems to me,/'Tis only noble to be good—/Kind hearts are more than coronets,/And simple faith than Norman blood.
LORD TENNYSON *Lady Clara Vere de Vere*

6 To give our Lord a perfect hospitality, Mary and Martha must combine.
ST TERESA OF AVILA

7 Do all the good you can,/By all the means you can./In all the ways you can,/In all the places you can,/At all the times you can,/To all the people you can,/As long as ever you can.
JOHN WESLEY *John Wesley's Rule*

GOSPEL

8 I am not ashamed of the Gospel.
Rom. 1.16

9 God has made the wisdom of this world look foolish. As God in his wisdom ordained, the world failed to find him by its wisdom, and he chose to save those who have faith by the folly of the Gospel.
1 Cor. 1.21

10 Most of us read the Gospels with sealed and unwondering eyes.
DEAN CHURCH *Occasional Papers*

GRACE

11 For the man who has will always be given more, till he has enough and to spare; and the man who has not will forfeit even what he has.
Matt. 25.29

12 Grace and peace to you from God our Father and the Lord Jesus Christ.
Rom. 1.7

13 All are justified by God's free grace alone.
Rom. 3.24

14 Where sin was thus multiplied, grace immeasurably exceeded it.
Rom. 5.20

15 Shall we persist in sin, so that there may be all the more grace? No, no!
Rom. 6.1–2

16 By God's grace I am what I am, nor has his grace been given to me in vain.
1 Cor. 15.10

17 No wonder we do not lose heart! Though our outward humanity is in decay, yet day by day we are inwardly renewed.
2 Cor. 4.16

18 Thanks be to God for his gift beyond words!
2 Cor. 9.15

19 My grace is all you need; power comes to its full strength in weakness.
2 Cor. 12.9

20 The grace of the Lord Jesus Christ, and the love of God, and fellowship in the Holy Spirit, be with you all.
2 Cor. 13.14

1 It is by his grace you are saved, through trusting him: it is not your own doing. It is God's gift, not a reward for work done.
Eph. 2. 8–10

2 Prevent us, O Lord, in all our doings with thy most gracious favour, and further us with thy continual help.
BOOK OF COMMON PRAYER From the *Order for Holy Communion*

3 We humbly beseech thee, that, as by thy special grace preventing us thou dost put into our minds good desires, so by thy continual help we may bring the same to good effect.
BOOK OF COMMON PRAYER From the *Collect for Easter Day*

4 Because through the weakness of our mortal nature we can do no good thing without thee, grant us the help of thy grace.
BOOK OF COMMON PRAYER From the *Collect for the First Sunday after Trinity*

5 Lord, we pray thee that thy grace may always prevent and follow us, and make us continually to be given to all good works.
BOOK OF COMMON PRAYER From the *Collect for the Seventeenth Sunday after Trinity*

6 When I respond to God's call, the call is God's and the response is mine; and yet the response is God's too; for not only does He call me in His grace, but also by His grace brings the response to birth within my soul.
JOHN BAILLIE *Our Knowledge of God*

7 But for the grace of God there goes John Bradford.
JOHN BRADFORD (on seeing some criminals going to execution)

8 Glory is perfected grace.
MEISTER ECKHART

9 We all have secret fears to face,/our minds and motives to amend;/We seek your truth, we need your grace,/our living Lord and present Friend.
H. C. A. GAUNT *100 Hymns for Today*

10 Dependent on Thy bounteous breath,/We seek Thy grace alone,/In childhood, manhood, age, and death,/To keep us still Thine own.
REGINALD HEBER *Hymn*

11 I fancy that as we grow older, as we think longer and work harder and learn to sympathise more intelligently, the one thing we long to be able to pass on to men is a vast commanding sense of the grace of the Eternal. Compared with that, all else is but the small dust of the balance.
HUGH R. MACKINTOSH

12 To every soul, even to one ignorant of the name of God, even one reared in 'atheism, grace offers . . . that Reality of absolute goodness, which merits all our love and is able to save our life.
JACQUES MARITAIN *True Humanism*

13 All men who live with any degree of serenity live by some assurance of grace.
REINHOLD NIEBUHR *Reflections on the End of an Era*

GRIEF

14 'O, my son! Absalom my son, my son Absalom! If only I had died instead of you! O Absalom, my son, my son.'
2 Sam. 18.33

15 How long, O Lord, wilt thou quite forget me?/How long wilt thou hide thy face from me?/How long must I suffer anguish in my soul,/grief in my heart, day and night?
Ps. 13.1–2

16 Even in laughter the heart may grieve.
Prov. 14.13

GUILT

17 The wicked man runs away with no one in pursuit.
Prov. 28.1

1 The eighteen people who were killed when the tower fell on them at Siloam—do you imagine they were more guilty than all the other people living in Jerusalem? I tell you they were not.
Luke 13.4–5

2 That one of you who is faultless shall throw the first stone.
John 8.7

3 Take up your cross daily in that thing concerning which God has had a controversy with you in your conscience secretly ever since.
ALEXANDER WHYTE *Lord, Teach us to Pray*

HAPPINESS

1 Happiness lies more in giving than in receiving.
Acts 20.35

2 Lust and pride are the roots and sprouts of vice, as the desire for happiness is the root of all virtue.
ST THOMAS AQUINAS

3 We hold these truths to be self-evident: that all men are created equal; that they are endowed by their Creator with certain inalienable Rights; that among these are Life, Liberty and the pursuit of Happiness.
The Declaration of Independence

4 If I have faltered more or less/In my great task of happiness;/If I have moved among my race/And shown no glorious morning face; . . ./Lord, thy most pointed pleasure take,/And stab my spirit broad awake;/Or, Lord, if too obdurate I,/Choose thou, before that spirit die,/A piercing pain, a killing sin,/And to my dead heart run them in!
ROBERT LOUIS STEVENSON *The Celestial Surgeon*

5 You cannot read the Gospels without seeing that Jesus did not tell men how to be good in the manner of the moralists of every age, he told them how to be happy.
SIR THOMAS TAYLOR

6 How happy is he born and taught/That serveth not another's will;/Whose armour is his honest thought,/And simple truth his utmost skill!
SIR HENRY WOTTON *The Character of a Happy Life*

HEALING: HEALTH

7 There is no wealth to compare with health of body.
Ecclus. 30.16

8 Honour the doctor for his services,/for the Lord created him./His skill comes from the Most High.
Ecclus. 38.1–2

9 I have no silver or gold; but what I have I give you.
Acts 3.6

10 The prayer offered in faith will save the sick man.
Jas. 5.15

11 I cannot go to cure the body of my patient, but I forget my profession, and call unto God for his soul.
SIR THOMAS BROWNE *Religio Medici*

12 If it should ever prove possible to find some means of making men gentler and wiser than heretofore, I believe that means will be found in medicine.
RENÉ DESCARTES

13 From thee all skill and science flow,/All pity, care, and love,/All calm and courage, faith and hope;/O pour them from above.
CHARLES KINGSLEY *Hymn*

HEART

14 He knows the secrets of the heart.
Ps. 44.21

15 Create a pure heart in me, O God,/and give me a new and steadfast spirit;/do not drive me from thy presence/or take thy holy spirit from me.
Ps. 51.10–11

16 Guard your heart more than any treasure,/for it is the source of all life.
Prov. 4.23

17 A merry heart makes a cheerful face.
Prov. 15.13

18 The heart is the most deceitful of all things, desperately sick; who can fathom it?
Jer. 17.9

19 I will give them a different heart and put a new spirit into them; I will take the heart of stone out of their bodies and give

them a heart of flesh. Then they will conform to my statutes and keep my laws. They will become my people, and I will become their God.
Ezek. 11.19–20

1 The 'heart' in the biblical sense is not the inward life, but the whole man in relation to God.
DIETRICH BONHOEFFER *Letters and Papers from Prison*

2 The heart has its reasons, which reason knows not, as we feel in a thousand instances.
BLAISE PASCAL *Pensées*

3 Is thy heart right, as my heart is with thine? Dost thou love and serve God? It is enough. I give thee the right hand of fellowship.
JOHN WESLEY

4 How else but through a broken heart/May Lord Christ enter in?
OSCAR WILDE *The Ballad of Reading Gaol*

HEAVEN

5 Heaven is my throne and earth my footstool.
Isa. 66.1

6 I know a Christian man who fourteen years ago (whether in the body or out of it, I do not know—God knows) was caught up as far as the third heaven.
2 Cor. 12.2

7 O sweet and blessed country,/The home of God's elect!/O sweet and blessed country,/That eager hearts expect!
Jesus in mercy bring us/To that dear land of rest,/Who art, with God the Father/And spirit, ever blest.
BERNARD OF CLUNY *Hymn*

8 A robin redbreast in a cage/Puts all Heaven in a rage.
WILLIAM BLAKE *Auguries of Innocence*

9 A man's reach should exceed his grasp,/Or what's a heaven for?
ROBERT BROWNING *Andrea del Sarto*

10 All this, and Heaven too!
MATTHEW HENRY *Life of Philip Henry*

11 To please God . . . to be a real ingredient in the divine happiness . . . to be loved by God, not merely pitied, but delighted in as an artist delights in his work or a father in a son—it seems impossible, a weight or burden of glory which our thoughts can hardly sustain. But so it is.
C. S. LEWIS *Sermons*

12 There are more things in heaven and earth, Horatio,/Than are dreamt of in your philosophy.
WILLIAM SHAKESPEARE *Hamlet*

HOLY COMMUNION

13 Take this and eat; this is my body.
Matt. 26.26

14 Drink from it, all of you. For this is my blood, the blood of the covenant, shed for many for the forgiveness of sins.
Matt. 26.28

15 Whoever eats my flesh and drinks my blood dwells continually in me and I dwell in him.
John 6.56

16 Every time you eat this bread and drink this cup, you proclaim the death of the Lord, until he comes.
1 Cor. 11.26

17 Almighty and everliving God, we most heartily thank thee, for that thou dost vouchsafe to feed us, who have duly received these holy mysteries, with the spiritual food of the most precious Body and Blood of the Son our Saviour Jesus Christ.
BOOK OF COMMON PRAYER From the *Order for Holy Communion*

18 Thee we adore, O hidden Saviour, Thee,/Who in Thy sacrament dost deign to be:/Both flesh and spirit at Thy presence fail,/Yet here Thy presence we devoutly hail.
ST THOMAS AQUINAS *Hymn*

1 In the liturgical worship of the Eucharist the Church, in union with Christ who alone made the perfect sacrifice of obedience, offers itself as a living sacrifice for the fulfilment of the will of God and in total dependence on God and the reconciliation wrought by Christ.
F. R. BARRY *The Atonement*

2 No love that in a family dwells, no carolling in frosty air,/Nor all the steeple-shaking bells/Can with this single Truth compare—/That God was Man in Palestine/And lives to day in Bread and Wine.
SIR JOHN BETJEMAN *Collected poems*

3 And now, O Father, mindful of the love/That bought us, once for all, on Calvary's Tree,/And having with us Him that pleads above,/We here present, we here spread forth to Thee/That only offering perfect in Thine eyes,/The one true, pure, immortal sacrifice.
WILLIAM BRIGHT *Hymn*

4 Here, O my Lord, I see Thee face to face;/Here would I touch and handle things unseen,/Here grasp with firmer hand the eternal grace,/And all my weariness upon Thee lean.
HORATIUS BONAR *Hymn*

5 The sheer stupendous *quantity* of the love of God which this ever repeated action has drawn from the obscure Christian multitudes through the centuries is in itself an overwhelming thought.
GREGORY DIX *The Shape of the Liturgy*

6 Jesus, Bread of Life, I pray Thee,/Let me gladly here obey Thee;/Never to my hurt invited,/Be Thy love with love requited:/From this banquet let me measure,/Lord, how vast and deep its treasure;/Through the gifts Thou here dost give me,/As Thy guest in heaven receive me.
JOHAN FRANCK *Hymn*

7 Bread of the world, in mercy broken./Wine of the soul, in mercy shed,/By whom the words of life were spoken,/And in whose death our sins are dead:/Look on the heart by sorrow broken,/Look on the tears by sinners shed;/And be Thy feast to us the token/That by Thy grace our souls are fed.
REGINALD HEBER *Hymn*

8 Let it therefore be sufficient for me presenting myself at the Lord's Table, to know what I receive from Him, without search or enquiry of the manner how Christ performeth His promises.
RICHARD HOOKER

9 According to Thy gracious word,/In meek humility,/This will I do, my dying Lord,/I will remember Thee.
JAMES MONTGOMERY *Hymn*

10 The Eucharist is the Church at her best.
GABRIEL MORAN *Theology of Revelation*

11 If ever I had any doubts about the fundamental realities of religion, they could always be dispelled by one memory—the light upon my father's face as he came back from early communion.
ALFRED NOYES *Two Worlds for Memory*

12 The Eucharist to the Christian is the culminating point of all sacramental rites ... For this Sacrament is the constantly repeated act from which the soul draws its spiritual food. Its virtue resides in its repetition; it is repeated again and again, just because it is constantly needed to effect that contact with divine life and power which, in its aspect of communion, is all its meaning. Here the Christian believes that he takes into himself the very life which makes him one with God.
OLIVER QUICK *The Christian Sacraments*

13 Our Lord, did not say, 'Come unto me all ye faultless': neither did He say, 'Be sure you tear yourselves to pieces first.' There are only three necessities of a good Communion—Faith, Hope and Charity. To rely utterly on God and be in charity with the world—this is the essential. What you happen to be feeling at the moment, does not matter in the least.
EVELYN UNDERHILL *Letters*

1 Author of life divine,/Who hast a table spread,/Furnished with mystic wine/ And Everlasting bread,/Preserve the life Thyself hast given,/And feed and train us up for heaven.
CHARLES WESLEY *Hymn*

HOLY SPIRIT

2 The Holy Spirit whom the Father will send in my name will teach you everything.
John 14.26

3 When he comes who is the Spirit of truth, he will guide you into all the truth.
John 16.13

4 There appeared to them tongues like flames of fire, dispersed among them and resting on each one. And they were all filled with the Holy Spirit.
Acts 2.3–4

5 'Did you receive the Holy Spirit when you became believers?' 'No', they replied, 'we have not even heard that there is a Holy Spirit.'
Acts 19.2

6 If the Spirit of him who raised Jesus from the dead dwells within you, then the God who raised Christ Jesus from the dead will also give new life to your mortal bodies through his indwelling Spirit.
Rom. 8.11

7 A Spirit that makes us sons, enabling us to cry 'Abba! Father!'
Rom. 8.15

8 In everything, as we know, he co-operates for good with those who love God and are called according to his purpose.
Rom. 8.28

9 Do you not know that your body is a shrine of the indwelling Holy Spirit, and the Spirit is God's gift to you? You do not belong to yourselves; you were bought at a price. Then honour God in your body.
1 Cor. 6.19–20

10 The written law condemns to death, but the Spirit gives life.
2 Cor. 3.6

11 Where the Spirit of the Lord is, there is liberty.
2 Cor. 3.17

12 The harvest of the Spirit is love, joy, peace, patience, kindness, goodness, fidelity, gentleness, and self-control.
Gal. 5.22

13 The spirit that God gave us is no craven spirit, but one to inspire strength, love, and self-discipline.
2 Tim. 1.7

14 O God, make clean our hearts within us./ And take not thy holy Spirit from us.
BOOK OF COMMON PRAYER From the *Order for Morning Prayer*

15 O God, forasmuch as without thee we are not able to please thee; Mercifully grant, that thy Holy Spirit may in all things direct and rule our hearts.
BOOK OF COMMON PRAYER From the *Collect for the Nineteenth Sunday after Trinity*

16 Spirit of God, that moved of old/Upon the waters' darkened face,/Come, when our faithless hearts are cold,/And stir them with an inward grace.
CECIL FRANCES ALEXANDER *Hymn*

17 Our blest Redeemer, ere He breathed/ His tender last farewell,/A Guide, a Comforter bequeathed,/With us to dwell.
HARRIET AUBER *Hymn*

18 Come down, O Love Divine,/Seek Thou this soul of mine,/And visit it with Thine own ardour glowing;/O Comforter, draw near,/Within my heart appear,/And kindle it, Thy holy flame bestowing.
BIANCO DA SIENA *Hymn*

19 The primitive Church . . . confined the operation of the Holy Spirit strictly to the 'redeemed' . . . while at the same time emphasising that the eternal Christ, the *Logos* or Word, had an active relation to all men.
GREGORY DIX *The Shape of the Liturgy*

1 Breathe on me, Breath of God;/Fill me with life anew,/That I may love what Thou dost love,/And do what Thou wouldst do.
EDWIN HATCH *Hymn*

2 In the hour of my distress,/When temptations me oppress,/And when I my sins confess,/Sweet Spirit comfort me!
When I lie within my bed,/Sick in heart and sick in head,/And with doubts discomforted,/Sweet Spirit comfort me!
When the tapers now burn blue,/And the comforters are few,/And that number more than true,/Sweet Spirit comfort me!
When the Judgement is reveal'd,/And that open'd which was seal'd,/When to Thee I have appeal'd,/Sweet Spirit comfort me!
ROBERT HERRICK *Litany to the Holy Spirit*

3 The world is charged with the grandeur of God./It will flame out, like shining from shook foil;/It gathers to a greatness, like the ooze of oil/Crushed. Why do men then now not reck his rod?/Generations have trod, have trod, have trod;/And all is seared with trade; bleared, smeared with toil;/And wears man's smudge and shares man's smell: the soil/Is bare now, nor can foot feel, being shod.
And for all this, nature is never spent;/There lives the dearest freshness deep down things;/And though the last lights off the black West went/Oh, morning, at the brown brink eastward, springs—/Because the Holy Ghost over the bent/World broods with warm breast and with ah! bright wings.
GERARD MANLEY HOPKINS *God's Grandeur*

4 Holy Spirit, Truth Divine,/Dawn upon this soul of mine;/Word of God, and inward Light,/Wake my spirit, clear my sight.
SAMUEL LONGFELLOW *Hymn*

5 Come, Holy Ghost, our souls inspire/And lighten with celestial fire;/Thou the anointing Spirit art,/Who dost Thy seven-fold gifts impart.
Ninth-century hymn

6 Spirit Divine, attend our prayers,/And make this house Thy home;/Descend with all Thy gracious powers;/O Come, great Spirit, come!
ANDREW REED *Hymn*

7 Come, Holy Ghost, our hearts inspire;/Let us Thine influence prove,/Source of the old prophetic fire,/Fountain of life and love.
CHARLES WESLEY *Hymn*

HOLY TRINITY

8 Holiest Trinity, perfect in Unity,/bind in thy love every nation and race:/May we adore thee for time and eternity,/Father, Redeemer, and Spirit of grace.
PATRICK APPLEFORD *100 Hymns for Today*

9 Our doctrine, teaching, experience of the Church, must be, so to speak, in a comatose state, unless there be an active, experimental, living knowledge of the Name of the Holy Trinity, which is the living power wherewith the Church is bound together by the Holy Ghost.
R. M. BENSON *Letters*

10 Glory be to God the Father,/Glory be to God the Son,/Glory be to God the Spirit,/—/Great Jehovah, Three in One!
HORATIUS BONAR *Hymn*

11 The distinction of Persons is true only for our knowledge of God, not for his inner Being, which we cannot know.
MILLAR BURROWS *An Outline of Biblical Theology*

12 All-holy Father, Son and equal Spirit,/Trinity blessed, send us Thy salvation;/Thine is the glory, gleaming and resounding/Through all creation.
Attributed to ST GREGORY THE GREAT *Hymn*

13 Holy, holy, holy, Lord God Almighty!/All Thy works shall praise Thy Name in earth and sky and sea;/Holy, holy, holy,/merciful and mighty,/God in Three Persons, blessed Trinity!
REGINALD HEBER *Hymn*

1 I bind unto myself the Name,/The strong Name of the Trinity;/By invocation of the same,/The Three in One, and One in Three,/Of whom all nature hath creation,/Eternal Father, Spirit, Word./Praise to the Lord of my salvation:/Salvation is of Christ the Lord.
ST PATRICK *Breastplate*

HONESTY

2 You shall not steal.
Ex. 20.15

3 How shall a young man steer an honest course?/By holding to thy word.
Ps. 119.9

4 Never be ashamed to admit your mistakes.
Ecclus. 4.26

5 My duty towards my neighbour is . . . to keep my hands from picking and stealing.
BOOK OF COMMON PRAYER *The Catechism*

6 Thou shalt not steal; an empty feat,/When 'tis so lucrative to cheat.
ARTHUR HUGH CLOUGH *The Latest Decalogue*

7 The (eighth) commandment is, Thou shalt do no theft, and included in the meaning of the same all wrongful usurpation of another man's goods, either by fraud, or guile, or by usury, or by violence, or by fear.
Law of JOHN PECKHAM

8 O God, help us not to despise or oppose what we do not understand.
WILLIAM PENN

9 Ay, sir: to be honest as this world goes, is to be one man picked out of a thousand.
WILLIAM SHAKESPEARE *Hamlet*

10 Honesty is the best policy, but he who acts on that principle is not an honest man.
RICHARD WHATELEY *Apophthegms*

HOPE

11 I see a cloud no bigger than a man's hand.
1 Kings 18.44

12 Hope deferred makes the heart sick.
Prov. 13.12

13 May the God of hope fill you with all joy and peace by your faith in him, until by the power of the Holy Spirit, you overflow with hope.
Rom. 15.13

14 I have not yet reached perfection, but I press on, hoping to take hold of that for which Christ once took hold of me.
Phil. 3.12

15 The hope set before us . . . is like an anchor for our lives, an anchor safe and sure.
Heb. 6.19

16 Hope means expectancy when things are otherwise hopeless.
G. K. CHESTERTON *Heretics*

17 Say not, 'The struggle nought availeth;/The labour and the wounds are vain;/The enemy faints not nor faileth,/And as things have been they remain.'
And not by eastern windows only,/When daylight comes, comes in the light;/In front the sun climbs slow, how slowly!/But westward, look! the land is bright.
ARTHUR HUGH CLOUGH *Hymn*

18 Abandon hope, all ye who enter here.
DANTE ALIGHIERI *Inferno*

19 Let us remember, when we are inclined to be disheartened, that the private soldier is a poor judge of the fortunes of a great battle.
W. R. INGE *Personal Religion and the Life of Devotion*

20 Hope springs eternal in the human breast: Man never is, but always to be blest.
ALEXANDER POPE *Essay on Man*

1 For if you find hope in the ground of history, you are united with the great prophets who were able to look into the depth of their times, who tried to escape it, because they could not stand the horror of their visions, and who yet had the strength to look to an even deeper level and there to discover hope.
PAUL TILLICH *The Shaking of the Foundations*

HUMILITY

2 Though God himself meets the arrogant with arrogance, yet he bestows his favour on the meek.
Prov. 3.34

3 The fear of the Lord is a training in wisdom, and the way to honour is humility.
Prov. 15.33

4 The greater you are, the humbler you must be.
Ecclus. 3.18

5 At this point I will bring my work to an end. If it is found well written and aptly composed, that is what I myself hoped for; if cheap and mediocre, I could only do my best.
2 Macc. 15.38

6 Unless you turn round and become like children, you will never enter the kingdom of Heaven.
Matt. 18.3

7 Whoever exalts himself will be humbled; and whoever humbles himself will be exalted.
Matt. 23.12

8 When you receive an invitation, go and sit down in the lowest place, so that when your host comes he will say, 'Come up higher, my friend.'
Luke 14.10

9 If you feel sure that you are standing firm, beware! You may fall.
1 Cor. 10.12

10 He hath shewed strength with his arm: he hath scattered the proud in the imagination of their hearts./He hath put down the mighty from their seat; and hath exalted the humble and meek.
BOOK OF COMMON PRAYER From the *Magnificat*

11 We do not presume to come to this thy Table, O merciful Lord, trusting in our own righteousness, but in thy manifold and great mercies. We are not worthy so much as to gather up the crumbs under thy Table.
BOOK OF COMMON PRAYER From the *Order for Holy Communion*

12 Still down the ages ring/the prophet's stern commands:/To merchant, worker, king,/he brings God's high demands:/Do justly;/Love mercy;/Walk humbly with your God.
ALBERT F. BAYLY *100 Hymns for Today*

13 He that is down needs fear no fall,/He that is low, no pride;/He that is humble ever shall/Have God to be his guide.
JOHN BUNYAN *Hymn*

14 Cleanse us from ire of creed or class,/ The anger of the idle kings;/Sow in our souls, like living grass,/The laughter of all lowly things.
G. K. CHESTERTON *Hymn for the Church Militant*

15 In many things we shall do well to follow Galileo's recommendation to his readers 'to pronounce that wise, ingenious and modest sentence, "I do not know" '.
C. A. COULSON *Science and Christian Belief*

16 All the while it is open to him, the second-rater, to be first-rate in magnanimity, to honour and love those who eclipse him in every respect, and who will eclipse him to the end of the chapter.
ARCHIBALD C. CRAIG *University Sermons*

17 Let us avoid the proud speaking of the Pharisee and learn humility from the sighs of the Publican as we cry to our Saviour: Be merciful, Thou who alone art ready to absolve us.
Eastern Church

1 Hefty peasants, robust artisans, healthy athletes, aristocrats, Nazis, Fascists, Communists, and robust women in millions, neither desire nor intend to learn to be meek. For honesty's sake I ought to add to my list 'ecclesiastics'. They may be useful persons, but they are rarely meek. So Christ offends us by calling on us to be meek.
A. HERBERT GRAY *Love the One Solution*

2 Many who pray for humility would be extremely sorry if God were to grant it to them. . . . They forget that to love, desire, and ask for humility is loving, desiring, and asking for humiliations.
JEAN NICOLAS GROU *The School of Jesus Christ*

3 The submissive instinct is as truly instinctive as any other, and demands recognition in a life of perfect self-realisation. We must know how to be abased.
J. A. HADFIELD

4 I am no link of Thy great chain,/But all my company is a weed,/Lord! place me in Thy concert; give one strain/To my poor reed.
GEORGE HERBERT

5 Humble we must be, if to Heaven we go:/High is the roof there; but the gate is low:/Whene'er thou speak'st, look with a lowly eye:/Grace is increased by humility.
ROBERT HERRICK

6 Make me pure, Lord: Thou art holy: Make me meek, Lord: Thou wert lowly.
GERARD MANLEY HOPKINS *Poems*

7 The little fashions of our day/have turned in unbelief away,/and we are in the age of doubt;/Yet still with humble men of heart/and all who know their need thou art,/for such thou never wilt cast out.
DONALD WYNN HUGHES *100 Hymns for Today*

8 Whosoever therefore grounds his virtue in humility, he shall never err.
JOHN OF RUYSBROECK *The Adornment of the Spiritual Marriage*

9 Humility, that is lowliness or self-abasement, is an inward bowing down or prostrating of the heart and of the conscience before God's transcendent worth.
JOHN OF RUYSBROECK *The Fruits of Humility*

10 Because a humble state of soul is the very state of religion, because humility is the life and soul of piety, the foundation and support of every virtue and good work, the best guard and security of all holy affections; I shall recommend humility to you, as highly proper to be made the constant subject of your devotions, earnestly desiring you to think no day safe, or likely to end well, in which you have not called upon God to carry you through the day, in the exercise of a meek and lowly spirit.
WILLIAM LAW *A Serious Call to a Devout and Holy Life*

11 Humility does not mean thinking less of yourself than of other people, nor does it mean having a low opinion of your own gifts. It means freedom from thinking about yourself one way or the other at all. . . . The humility which consists in being a great deal occupied about yourself, and saying you are of little worth, is not Christian humility. It is one form of self-occupation and a very poor and futile one at that.
WILLIAM TEMPLE *Christ in his Church*

12 Let the remembrance of all the glory wherein I was created make me more serious and humble, more deep and penitent, more pure and holy before Thee.
THOMAS TRAHERNE

IDOLATRY

1 And there they will set up 'the abominable thing that causes desolation.'
Dan. 11.31

2 A God who let us prove his existence would be an idol.
DIETRICH BONHOEFFER *No Rusty Swords*

3 The dearest idol I have known,/Whate'er that idol be,/Help me to tear it from thy Throne./And worship only Thee.
WILLIAM COWPER *Hymn*

4 The worship of the false in any form is idolatry.
WILLIAM PURCELL *The Plain Man Looks at the Commandments*

IMMORTALITY

5 God created man for immortality, and made him the image of his own eternal self.
Wisd. 2.23

6 Virtue held in remembrance is a kind of immortality, because it wins recognition from God, and from men too. They follow the good man's example while it is with them, and when it is gone they mourn its loss.
Wisd. 4.1–2

7 I perceived that in kinship with wisdom lies immortality.
Wisd. 8.17

8 I will unfold a mystery: we shall not all die, but we shall all be changed in a flash, in the twinkling of an eye, at the last trumpet-call. For the trumpet will sound, and the dead will rise immortal, and we shall be changed.
1 Cor. 15.51–52

9 This perishable being must be clothed with the imperishable, and what is mortal must be clothed with immortality.
1 Cor. 15.53

10 From the unreal lead me to the real./From darkness lead me to light./From death lead me to immortality.
The Upanishads (Hindu)

11 Our birth is but a sleep and a forgetting:/The Soul that rises with us, our life's Star,/Hath had elswhere its setting,/And cometh from afar:/Not in entire forgetfulness,/And not in utter nakedness,/But trailing clouds of glory do we come/From God, who is our home.
WILLIAM WORDSWORTH *Intimations of Immortality*

THE INCARNATION

12 It is by the Holy Spirit that she has conceived this child. She will bear a son; and you shall give him the name Jesus (Saviour), for he will save his people from their sins.
Matt. 1.20–21

13 'Here am I,' said Mary; 'I am the Lord's servant; as you have spoken, so be it.'
Luke 1.38

14 God's blessing is on you above all women, and his blessing is on the fruit of your womb. Who am I, that the mother of my Lord should visit me?
Luke 1.42

15 He was rich, yet for your sake he became poor, so that through his poverty you might become rich.
2 Cor. 8.9

16 The divine nature was his from the first; yet he did not think to snatch at equality with God, but made himself nothing, assuming the nature of a slave. Bearing the human likeness, revealed in human shape, he humbled himself, and in obedience accepted even death—death on a cross.
Phil. 2.6–8

17 Hark, the glad sound! the Saviour comes,/The Saviour promised long;/Let every heart exult with joy,/And every voice be song
PHILIP DODDRIDGE *Hymn*

1 The Incarnation would be equally a miracle however Jesus entered the world.
P. T. FORSYTH

2 The highest cannot be spoken; it can only be acted.
J. W. VON GOETHE

3 The darkest time in the year,/The poorest place in the town,/Cold, and a taste of fear,/ Man and woman alone,/What can we hope for here?/More light than we can learn,/More wealth than we can treasure,/More love than we can earn,/ More peace than we can measure,/ Because one child is born.
CHRISTOPHER FRY

4 He was made what we are that He might make us what He is Himself.
ST IRENAEUS *Against Heresies*

5 Surveying the abysmal chasm between my certainty that everything human beings try to achieve was inadequate to the point of being farcical, and my equal certainty that human love was the image of God's love irradiating the whole universe, I grasped a cable-bridge, frail, swaying, but passable. And this bridge, this reconciliation between the black despair of lying bound and gagged in the tiny dungeon of the ego, and soaring upwards into the white radiance of God's universal love—this bridge was the Incarnation.
MALCOLM MUGGERIDGE *Chronicles of Wasted Time*

INDIFFERENCE

6 The righteous perish,/and no one takes it to heart,/men of good faith are swept away, but no one cares.
Isa. 57.1

7 He went past on the other side.
Luke 10.31

8 Because you are lukewarm, neither hot nor cold, I will spit you out of my mouth.
Rev. 3.16

9 When Jesus came to Birmingham they simply passed Him by,/They never hurt a hair of Him, they only let Him die;/For men had grown more tender, and they would not give Him pain,/They only just passed down the street, and left Him in the rain.
Still Jesus cried, 'Forgive them, for they/ know not what they do,'/And still it rained the wintry rain that drenched Him through and through;/The crowds went home and left the streets without a soul to see,/And Jesus crouched against a wall and cried for Calvary.
G. A. STUDDERT KENNEDY *The Unutterable Beauty*

JERUSALEM, NEW

1 Pray for the peace of Jerusalem.
Ps. 122.6

2 If I forget you, O Jerusalem,/let my right hand wither away.
Ps. 137.5

3 I saw the holy city, new Jerusalem, coming down out of heaven from God, made ready like a bride adorned for her husband.
Rev. 21.2

4 He will wipe every tear from their eyes; there shall be an end to death, and to mourning and crying and pain; for the old order has passed away!
Rev. 21.4

5 Then he who sat on the throne said, 'Behold! I am making all things new!'
Rev. 21.5

6 There shall be no more night, nor will they need the light of lamp or sun, for the Lord God will give them light; and they shall reign for evermore.
Rev. 22.5

JEWS

7 Look to the rock from which you were hewn,/to the quarry from which you were dug.
Isa. 51.1

8 In those days, when ten men from nations of every language pluck up courage, they shall pluck the robe of a Jew and say, 'We will go with you because we have heard that God is with you.'
Zech. 8.23

9 It is from the Jews that salvation comes.
John 4.22

10 The true Jew is he who is such inwardly, and the true circumcision is of the heart.
Rom. 2.29

11 The Jews were entrusted with the oracles of God.
Rom. 3.2

12 (Abraham) is the father of us all.
Rom. 4.17

13 'Can you give me one single irrefutable proof of God?'/'Yes, your Majesty, the Jews.'
MARQUIS D'ARGENS to Frederick the Great

14 How odd/Of God/To Choose/The Jews.
W. N. EWER *How Odd*

15 Spiritually we are all Semites.
POPE PIUS XI

16 Religious or secularized, the Jew remains a Jew—*malgré lui* a voluntary or involuntary witness to the truth that is symbolized in the story of God's Covenant with Abraham.
ALAN RICHARDSON *Christian Apologetics*

JOY

17 Tears may linger at nightfall,/but joy comes in the morning.
Ps. 30.5

18 Those who sow in tears/shall reap with songs of joy.
Ps. 126.5

19 Those whose sins have perished, whose doubts are destroyed, who are self-restrained, and are intent on the welfare of all other beings, these obtain God's everlasting joy.
The Bhagavad Gita (Hindu)

20 Joy is for all men. It does not depend on circumstance or condition: if it did, it could only be for the few. It is not the fruit of good luck, or of fortune, or even of outward success, which all men cannot have. It is of the soul, or the soul's character: it is the wealth of the soul's whole being when it is filled with the spirit of Jesus, which is the spirit of eternal love.
HORACE BUSHNELL, quoted in M. V. Nelsons *An Anthology of Joy*

1 My mind to me a kingdom is,/Such perfect joy therein I find,/That it excels all other bliss/That earth affords or grows by kind.
SIR EDWARD DYER *My Mind to me a Kingdom is*

2 Peace is that state in which fear of any kind is unknown. But Joy is a positive thing: in Joy one does not only feel secure, but something goes out from oneself to the universe, a warm, positive effluence of love.
RICHARD HOOKER, quoted in John Buchan: *Memory Hold the Door*

3 Joy will be ours in so far as we are genuinely interested in great ideas outside ourselves. When we have once crossed the charmed circle and got outside ourselves, we shall soon realise that all true joy has an eternal and divine source and goal ... To do our duty in our own sphere, to try to create something worth creating, as our life's work, is the way to understand what joy is in this life.
W. R. INGE

4 Dance, my heart! dance to-day with joy./ The strains of love fill the days and the nights with music, and the world is listening to its melodies:/Mad with joy, life and death dance to the rhythm of this music. The hills and the sea and the earth dance. The world of man dances in laughter and tears./Why put on the robe of the monk, and live aloof from the world in lonely pride?/Behold! my heart danceth in the delight of a hundred arts; and the Creator is well pleased.
KABIR (Indian)

5 See, this Kingdom of God is now found within us. The grace of the Holy Spirit shines forth and warms us, and, overflowing with many and varied scents into the air around us, regales our senses with heavenly delight, as it fills our hearts with joy inexpressible.
ST SERAPHIN OF SAROR

6 Joy is everywhere; it is in the earth's green covering of grass: in the blue serenity of the sky: in the reckless exuberance of spring: in the severe abstinence of grey winter: in the living flesh that animates our bodily frame: in the perfect poise of the human figure, noble and upright: in living, in the exercise of all our powers: in the acquisition of knowledge: in fighting evils: in dying for gains we never can share. Joy is there everywhere.
RABINDRANATH TAGORE *Sadhana*

7 This is the secret of joy. We shall no longer strive for our own way; but commit ourselves, easily and simply, to God's way, acquiesce in his will and in so doing find our peace.
EVELYN UNDERHILL

JUDGEMENT

8 The Lord does not see as man sees; men judge by appearances but the Lord judges by the heart.
1 Sam. 16.7

9 You have been weighed in the balance and found wanting.
Dan. 5.27

10 Trust your own judgement,/for it is your most reliable counsellor.
Ecclus. 37.13

11 Pass no judgement, and you will not be judged.
Matt. 7.1

12 Why do you look at the speck of sawdust in your brother's eye, with never a thought for the great plank in your own?
Matt. 7.3

JUDGEMENT, LAST

13 The day of reckoning is no secret to the Almighty, though those who know him have no hint of its date.
Job 24.1

14 Multitudes, in the Valley of Decision!
Joel 3.14

1 Prepare to meet your God.
Amos 4.12

2 The day of the Lord is indeed darkness, not light,/a day of gloom with no dawn.
Amos 5.20

3 The small man may find pity and forgiveness, but the powerful will be called powerfully to account.
Wisd. 6.6

4 Hold yourselves ready, therefore, because the Son of Man will come at the time you least expect him.
Matt. 24.44

5 We shall all stand before God's tribunal.
Rom. 14.10

6 Don't wait for the last Judgement. It takes place every day.
ALBERT CAMUS *The Fall*

7 Mine eyes have seen the glory of the coming of the Lord;/He is trampling out the vintage where the grapes of wrath are stored;/He hath loosed the fatal lightning of His terrible swift sword:/His truth is marching on.
JULIA WARD HOWE *Hymn*

8 Truly at the day of judgement we shall not be examined on what we have read, but what we have done; not how well we have spoken, but how religiously we have lived.
THOMAS À KEMPIS *The Imitation of Christ*

JUSTICE: INJUSTICE

9 We are given no straw, yet they keep on telling us to make bricks.
Ex. 5.16

10 Why do the wicked enjoy long life,/hale in old age, and great and powerful?
Job 21.7

11 One man, I tell you, dies crowned with success,/lapped in security and comfort,/his loins full of vigour/and the marrow juicy in his bones;/another dies in bitterness of soul/and never tastes prosperity;/side by side they are laid in earth,/and worms are the shroud of both.
Job 21.23–26

12 If a man shuts his ears to the cry of the helpless,/he will cry for help himself and not be heard.
Prov. 21.13

13 I have seen slaves on horseback and men of high rank going on foot like slaves.
Eccl. 10.7

14 Is not this what I require of you as a fast:/to loose the fetters of injustice,/to untie the knots of the yoke,/to snap every yoke/and set free those who have been crushed?/Is it not sharing your food with the hungry,/taking the homeless poor into your house,/clothing the naked when you meet them/and never evading a duty to your kinsfolk?
Isa. 58.6–7

15 Why do the wicked prosper/and traitors live at ease?
Jer. 12.1

16 For crime after crime of Israel/I will grant them no reprieve,/because they sell the innocent for silver/and the destitute for a pair of shoes.
Amos 2.6

17 Spare me the sound of your songs;/I cannot endure the music of your lutes./Let justice roll on like a river/and righteousness like an ever-flowing stream.
Amos 5.23–24

18 Grant unto all that are put in authority …that they may truly and indifferently minister justice, to the punishment of wickedness and vice, and to the maintenance of thy true religion, and virtue.
BOOK OF COMMON PRAYER From the *Order for Holy Communion*

19 There are no fêtes, no bazaars, no balls given *for Justice*. The usage of society does not allow fairs to be held for the payment of one's debts or making good one's petty thefts.
JACQUES DEBOUT *My Sins of Omission*

1 He calls us to revolt and fight/with him
for what is just and right,/to sing and live
Magnificat/in crowded street and council
flat.
FRED KAAN *100 Hymns for Today*

2 When two human beings have to settle
something and neither has the power to
impose anything on the other, they have
to come to an understanding. Then
justice is consulted, for justice alone has
the power to make wills coincide.
SIMONE WEIL *Waiting on God*

KINDNESS

1 If your enemy is hungry, give him bread to eat;/if he is thirsty, give him water to drink;/so you will heap glowing coals on his head,/and the Lord will reward you.
Prov. 25.21–22

2 Remember to show hospitality. There are some who, by so doing, have entertained angels without knowing it.
Heb. 13.2

3 Have you had a kindness shown?/Pass it on;/'Twas not given for thee alone,/Pass it on;/Let it travel down the years,/Let it wipe another's tears,/'Till in Heaven the deed appears—/Pass it on.
HENRY BURTON *Pass It On*

4 Humanitarianism is a grand-sounding word, but it can sometimes mean something very much thinner than human kindness.
A. C. CRAIG *University Sermons*

5 There is a grace of kind listening, as well as a grace of kind speaking.
FREDERICK WILLIAM FABER *Spiritual Conferences*

6 Does it never come into your mind to fear lest He should demand of you why you had not exercised towards your brother a little of that mercy which He, who is your Master, so abundantly bestows on you?
F. DE LA M. FÉNELON *Letters and Reflections*

7 I shall pass through this world but once. Any good thing therefore, that I can do, or any kindness that I can show to any human being, let me do it now. Let me not defer it or neglect it, for I shall not pass this way again.
Attributed to STEPHEN GRELLET, American Quaker.

8 Getting money is not all a man's business: to cultivate kindness is a valuable part of the business of life.
SAMUEL JOHNSON Boswell's *Life of Johnson*

9 Simeon the Righteous declared that the world is based upon these things . . . the Law, worship, and the imparting of kindnesses.
T. W. MANSON *Ethics and the Gospel*

10 That best portion of a good man's life,/His little, nameless, unremembered acts of kindness and of love.
WILLIAM WORDSWORTH *Lines above Tintern Abbey*

LAW

1 In those days there was no king in Israel and every man did what was right in his own eyes.
Judg. 17.6

2 The law of the Medes and Persians stands for ever.
Dan. 6.12

3 Do not suppose that I have come to abolish the Law and the prophets; I did not come to abolish, but to complete.
Matt. 5.17

4 When Gentiles who do not possess the law carry out its precepts by the light of nature, then, although they have no law, they are their own law, for they display the effect of the law inscribed in their hearts.
Rom. 2.14–15

5 Law brings only the consciousness of sin.
Rom. 3.20

6 The law was a kind of tutor in charge of us until Christ should come.
Gal. 3.24

7 Though the sovereign good is desired naturally, its fulfilment by natural means is made impossible by the Fall. By God's grace we are given the Divine Law, to rectify obliquity withal.
RICHARD HOOKER *Ecclesiastical Polity*

8 The Ten Commandments, when written on tablets of stone and given to man did not then first begin to belong to him; they had their existence in man and lay as a seed hidden in the form and make of his soul.
WILLIAM LAW *The Spirit of Love*

9 There is a universal moral law, as distinct from a moral code, which consists of certain statements of fact about the nature of man; and by behaving in conformity with which, man enjoys his true freedom.
DOROTHY L. SAYERS *The Mind of the Maker*

10 The enlargements and explications made by our blessed Lord, together with the repetition of the old, that is the Christian Law: it is the perfect code and digest of the Natural Law.
JEREMY TAYLOR *Ductor Dubitantium*

LIFE

11 That a man should eat and drink and enjoy himself, in return for all his labours, is a gift of God.
Eccl. 3.13

12 For a man who is counted among the living there is still hope: remember, a live dog is better than a dead lion.
Eccl. 9.4

13 He said to me, 'Man, can these bones live again?' I answered, 'Only thou knowest that, Lord God.' He said to me, 'Prophesy over these bones and say to them, O dry bones, hear the word of the Lord. This is the word of the Lord God to these bones: I will put breath into you, and you shall live.'
Ezek. 37.3–5

14 Man in his wickedness may kill, but he cannot bring back the breath of life that has gone forth nor release a soul that death has arrested.
Wisd. 16.14

15 Do not miss a day's enjoyment/or forgo your share of innocent pleasure.
Ecclus. 14.14

16 The gate is wide that leads to perdition, there is plenty of room on the road, and many go that way; but the gate that leads to life is small and the road is narrow, and those who find it are few.
Matt. 7.13–14

17 By gaining his life a man will lose it; by losing his life for my sake, he will gain it.
Matt. 10.39

18 I have come that men may have life, and may have it in all its fullness.
John 10.10

1 A godly, righteous, and sober life.
BOOK OF COMMON PRAYER From the *General Confession*

2 The preservation of life should be only a secondary concern, and the direction of it our principal.
JOSEPH ADDISON *The Spectator*

3 Live unto the Dignity of thy Nature, and leave it not disputable at last, whether thou hast been a Man.
SIR THOMAS BROWNE

4 If a man would live well, let him fetch his last day to him, and make it always his company-keeper.
JOHN BUNYAN *The Pilgrim's Progress*

5 A life of pleasure is the most unpleasing life in the world.
OLIVER GOLDSMITH

6 Man knowes where first he ships him-selfe;/But he never can tell, where shall his landing be.
ROBERT HERRICK *Hesperides*

7 I have life before me still/And thy purpose to fulfil;/Yea a debt to pay thee yet:/Help me, Sir, and so I will.
GERARD MANLEY HOPKINS

8 Creative life is always on the yonder side of convention.
C. G. JUNG *The Integration of the Personality*

9 'Tis all a checker-board of Nights and Days/Where Destiny with Men for Pieces plays.
OMAR KHAYYAM *The Rubaiyat*

10 But helpless Pieces of the Game He plays/Upon this Checker-board of Nights and Days;/Hither and thither moves, and checks, and slays,/And one by one back in the Closet lays.
OMAR KHAYYAM *The Rubaiyat*

11 Preparation for becoming attentive to Christianity does not consist in reading many books . . . but in fuller immersion in existence.
SÖREN KIERKEGAARD

12 And in the wreck of noble lives/Something immortal still survives.
HENRY WADSWORTH LONGFELLOW *The Building of the Ship*

13 Life is real! Life is earnest!/And the grave is not its goal.
HENRY WADSWORTH LONGFELLOW *A Psalm of Life*

14 Having gained a human body/It is thy opportunity to meet the Lord . . ./Learn to adore the Divine Spirit/And fulfil life's purpose.
GURU NANAK (Sikh)

15 Real life is meeting.
J. H. OLDHAM

16 If one way of life is no better than another, then no way of life is valuable at all.
MICHAEL ROBERTS *The Recovery of the West*

17 He only is advancing in life whose heart is getting softer, whose blood warmer, whose brain quicker, whose spirit is entering into living peace.
JOHN RUSKIN *Sesame and Lilies*

18 Life . . . is a tale/Told by an idiot, full of sound and fury,/Signifying nothing.
WILLIAM SHAKESPEARE *Macbeth*

19 We are such stuff/As dreams are made on, and our little life/Is rounded with a sleep.
WILLIAM SHAKESPEARE *The Tempest*

20 Life is a watch or a vision/Between a sleep and a sleep.
A. C. SWINBURNE *Atalanta in Calydon*

21 To be able to live peaceably with hard and perverse persons, or with the disorderly or with such as go contrary to us, is a great grace, and a most commendable and manly thing.
THOMAS À KEMPIS *The Imitation of Christ*

22 Attraction, desire, and union as the fulfilment of desire; this is the way Life works, in the highest as in the lowest things.
EVELYN UNDERHILL *Mysticism*

1 I believe in life after birth.
Untraced

2 Take care of your life; and the Lord will take care of your death.
GEORGE WHITEFIELD

LIFE AFTER DEATH

3 The souls of the just are in God's hand, and torment shall not touch them. In the eyes of foolish men they seemed to be dead; their departure was reckoned as defeat, and their going from us as disaster. But they are at peace.
Wisd. 3.1–3

4 Those who have put their trust in him shall understand that he is true, and the faithful shall attend upon him in love; they are his chosen, and grace and mercy shall be theirs.
Wisd. 3.9

5 Now we see only puzzling reflections in a mirror, but then we shall see face to face. My knowledge now is partial; then it will be whole, like God's knowledge of me.
1 Cor. 13.12

6 If it is for this life only that Christ has given us hope, we of all men are most to be pitied.
1 Cor. 15.19

7 Here we have no permanent home, but we are seekers after the city which is to come.
Heb. 13.14

8 To him who is victorious I will give the right to eat from the tree of life that stands in the Garden of God.
Rev. 2.7

9 Only be faithful till death, and I will give you the crown of life.
Rev. 2.10

10 I have formerly lived by hear-say and faith, but now I go where I shall live by sight, and shall be with him in whose company I delight myself.
JOHN BUNYAN *The Pilgrim's Progress*

11 One short sleep past, we wake eternally,/ And Death shall be no more: Death, thou shalt die!
JOHN DONNE *Death*

12 Oh may I join the choir invisible/Of those immortal dead who live again/In lives made better by their presence.
GEORGE ELIOT *Poems*

13 You'll get pie in the sky when you die.
JOE HILL *Folk Songs of North America*

14 If a beast can be changed into a man, then death can change the sinner into a saint—but not else.
CHARLES KINGSLEY *Village Sermons*

15 When once our heav'nly-guided soul shall climb,/Then all this earthly gross-ness quit,/Attir'd with stars, we shall for ever sit,/Triumphing over death, and chance, and thee, O Time.
JOHN MILTON *On Time*

16 Who can imagine by a stretch of fancy the feelings of those who, having died in faith, wake up to enjoyment!
CARDINAL NEWMAN *Sermons*

17 There is nothing in the world of which I feel so certain. I have no idea what it will be like, and I am glad that I have not, as I am sure it would be wrong. I do not want it for myself as mere continuance, but I want it for my understanding of life. And moreover 'God is love' appears to me nonsense in view of the world He has made, if there is no other.
WILLIAM TEMPLE

LIFE, BREVITY OF

18 My days are swifter than a shuttle/and come to an end as the thread runs out.
Job 7.6

19 Is not my life short and fleeting?/Let me be, that I may be happy for a moment,/

before I depart to a land of gloom,/a land of deep darkness, never to return,/ a land of gathering shadows, of deepening darkness,/lit by no ray of light, dark upon dark.
Job 10.20–22

1 Man born of woman is short-lived and full of disquiet./He blossoms like a flower and then he withers;/he slips away like a shadow and does not stay.
Job 14.1–2

2 For there are but few years to come/ before I take the road from which I shall not return.
Job 16.22

3 Lord, let me know my end/and the number of my days;/tell me how short my life must be.
Ps. 39.4

4 Seventy years is the span of our life,/ eighty if our strength holds.
Ps. 90.10

5 Man's days are like the grass;/he blossoms like the flowers of the field:/a wind passes over them, and they cease to be,/ and their place knows them no more./ But the Lord's love never fails those who fear him.
Ps. 103.15–17

6 What is man and what use is he?.../ His span of life is at the most a hundred years;/compared with endless time, his few years/are like one drop of sea-water or a single grain of sand.
Ecclus 18.8,9–10

7 Your life, what is it? You are no more than a mist, seen for a little while and then dispersing.
Jas. 4.14

8 The present life of man upon earth, O King, seems to me, in comparison to the time which is unknown to us, like to the swift flight of a sparrow through that house wherein you sit at supper in winter with your ealdormen and thegns, while the fire blazes in the midst, and the

hall is warmed, but the wintry storms of rain or snow are raging abroad without. The sparrow, flying in at one door and immediately out at another, whilst he is within is safe from the wintry tempest; but after a short space of fair weather he immediately vanishes out of your sight, passing from winter into winter again. So this life of man appears for a little while, but of what is to follow or what before we know nothing at all. If therefore this new doctrine tells us something more certain, it seems justly to deserve to be followed.
VENERABLE BEDE *Historia ecclesiastica gentis anglorum*

9 On the pedestal these words appear:/ 'My name is Ozymandias, king of kings:/ Look on my works, ye Mighty, and despair!'/Nothing beside remains. Round the decay/Of that colossal wreck, boundless and bare/The lone and level sands stretch far away.
PERCY BYSSHE SHELLEY *Ozymandias*

LIFE ETERNAL

10 Yet I am always with thee,/thou holdest my right hand;/thou dost guide me by thy counsel/and afterwards wilt receive me with glory.
Ps. 73.23–24

11 Whom have I in heaven but thee?/And having thee, I desire nothing else on earth./Though heart and body fail,/yet God is my possession for ever.
Ps. 73.25–26

12 God loved the world so much that he gave his only Son, that everyone who has faith in him may not die but have eternal life.
John 3.16

13 Anyone who gives heed to what I say and puts his trust in him who sent me has hold of eternal life, and does not come up for judgement, but has already passed from death to life.
John 5.24

1 I am the resurrection and I am life. If a man has faith in me, even though he die, he shall come to life; and no one who is alive and has faith shall ever die.
John 11.25–26

2 This is eternal life: to know thee who alone art truly God, and Jesus Christ whom thou hast sent.
John 17.3

3 Sin pays a wage, and the wage is death, but God gives freely, and his gift is eternal life.
Rom. 6.23

4 And this is the promise that he himself gave us, the promise of eternal life.
I John 2.25

5 Only an eternal life already begun and truly known in part here, though fully to be achieved and completely to be understood hereafter, corresponds to the deepest longings of man's spirit as touched by the prevenient Spirit, God.
BARON F. VON HÜGEL *Eternal Life*

LIFE, RACE OF

6 Every athlete goes into strict training. They do it to win a fading wreath; we, a wreath that never fades.
1 Cor. 9.25

7 Run the great race of faith and take hold of eternal life.
1 Tim. 6.12

8 I have run the great race, I have finished the course, I have kept faith.
2 Tim. 4.7

LOVE

9 So Jacob worked seven years for Rachel, and they seemed like a few days because he loved her.
Gen. 29.20

10 Love and fidelity have come together;/ justice and peace join hands.
Ps. 85.10

11 Love turns a blind eye to every fault.
Prov. 10.12

12 Better a dish of vegetables if love go with it/than a fat ox eaten in hatred.
Prov. 15.17

13 Love is strong as death.
S. of S. 8.6

14 Many waters cannot quench love.
S. of S. 8.7

15 If you love only those who love you, what reward can you expect?
Matt. 5.46

16 The whole law is summed up in love.
Rom. 13.10

17 I may speak in tongues of men or of angels, but if I am without love, I am a sounding gong or a clanging cymbal.
1 Cor. 13.1

18 I may have faith strong enough to move mountains; but if I have no love, I am nothing.
1 Cor. 13.2

19 Love is patient; love is kind and envies no one. Love is never boastful, nor conceited, nor rude; never selfish, not quick to take offence.
1 Cor. 13.4–5

20 Love will never come to an end.
1 Cor. 13.8

21 There are three things that last for ever: faith, hope, and love; but the greatest of them all is love.
1 Cor. 13.13

22 Never cease to love your fellow-Christians.
Heb. 13.1

23 Love cancels innumerable sins.
1 Pet. 4.8

1 Dear friends, let us love one another, because love is from God. Everyone who loves is a child of God and knows God.
1 John 4.7

2 The unloving know nothing of God.
1 John 4.8

3 God himself dwells in us if we love one another.
1 John 4.12

4 Perfect loves banishes fear.
1 John 4.18

5 We love because he loved us first.
1 John 4.19

6 Love all God's creation, both the whole and every grain of sand. Love every leaf, every ray of light. Love the animals, love the plants, love each separate thing. If thou love each thing then thou wilt perceive the mystery of God in all; and when thou perceive this, then thou wilt thenceforward grow every day to a fuller understanding of it.
F. DOSTOEVSKY *The Brothers Karamazov*

7 'God is Love' is not the whole gospel. Love is not evangelical till it has dealt with holy law. In the midst of the rainbow is a throne.
P. T. FORSYTH

8 Thou art my life, my love, my heart,/ The very eyes of me:/And hast command of every part/To live and die for thee.
ROBERT HERRICK *To Anthea*

9 When the evening of this life comes, we shall be judged on love.
ST JOHN OF THE CROSS

10 Wouldst thou learn thy Lord's meaning in this thing? Learn it well: Love was His meaning. Who shewed it thee? Love. What shewed He thee? Love. Wherefore shewed it He? For Love. Hold thee therein and thou shalt learn and know more in the same.
MOTHER JULIAN OF NORWICH *Revelations of Divine Love*

11 God is Love, and a three times divorced cinema actor is the perfect Lover, and heaven gets mixed up with hell.
G. A. STUDDERT KENNEDY *The New Man in Christ*

12 I hold it true, what'er befall,/I feel it, when I sorrow most;/'Tis better to have loved and lost/Than never to have loved at all.
LORD TENNYSON *In Memoriam*

13 Love feels no burden, thinks nothing of trouble, attempts what is above its strength, pleads no excuse of impossibility; for it thinks all things lawful for itself, and all things possible. It is therefore able to undertake all things, and warrants them to take effect, where he who does not love, would faint and lie down.
THOMAS À KEMPIS

14 Show love to all creatures, and thou wilt be happy; for when thou lovest all things, thou lovest the Lord, for he is all in all.
TULSI DAS (Hindu)

15 In this death and life game of high stakes God has already, as it were, declared what are trumps. They are not clubs (sheer blind force), diamonds (the power of wealth) or even spades (dogged hard work and ingenuity) but hearts.
R. C. WALLS in *Asking Them Questions*

MAN

1 So God created man in his own image;
in the image of God he created him; male
and female he created them.
Gen. 1.27

2 Then the Lord God formed a man from
the dust of the ground and breathed into
his nostrils the breath of life. Thus the
man became a living creature.
Gen. 2.7

3 When the Lord saw that man had done
much evil on earth and that his thoughts
and inclinations were always evil, he was
sorry that he had made man on earth, and
he was grieved at heart.
Gen. 6. 5–6

4 Can mortal man be more righteous than
God,/or the creature purer than his
Maker?
Job 4.17

5 Yet thou hast made him little less than a
god,/crowning him with glory and honour.
Thou makest him master over all thy
creatures;/thou hast put everything under
his feet.
Ps. 8.5–6

6 Not one does anything good,/no, not
even one.
Ps. 14.3

7 In very truth men are a puff of wind,/all
men are faithless;/put them in the
balance and they can only rise,/all of
them lighter than wind.
Ps. 62.9

8 God, when he made man, made him
straightforward, but man invents endless subtleties of his own.
Eccl. 7.29

9 I know, O Lord,/that man's ways are not
of his own choosing;/nor is it for a man
to determine his course in life.
Jer. 10.23

10 A curse on the man who trusts in man/
and leans for support on human kind,/
while his heart is far from the Lord!
Jer. 17.5

11 What creature is worthy of honour? Man.
What men? Those who fear the Lord./
What creature is worthy of contempt?
Man./What men? Those who break the
commandments.
Ecclus 10.19

12 We humbly beseech thee for all sorts and
conditions of men.
BOOK OF COMMON PRAYER From the
Prayer for all Conditions of Men

13 The floodstream of the love of man
passes through the heart of God. I must
first have God before I can have man.
God is the way to man.
KARL ADAM *Two Essays*

14 Where there is no God there is no man.
Man without God is no longer man.
NICHOLAS BERDYAEV *The End of our
Time*

15 Man found his form and his identity
under the action of religious principles and
energies; the confusion in which he is
losing them cannot be re-ordered by
purely human efforts.
NICHOLAS BERDYAEV *The End of the
Renaissance*

16 To Mercy, Pity, Peace, and Love/All
pray in their distress;/And to these
virtues of delight/Return their thankful-
ness,
For Mercy, Pity, Peace, and Love/Is
God, our Father dear/, And Mercy, Pity,
Peace, and Love/Is man, His child and
care.
For Mercy has a human heart,/Pity a
human face,/And love, the human form
divine,/And Peace, the human dress.
Then every man, of every clime,/That
prays in his distress,/Prays to the human
form divine,/Love, Mercy, Pity, Peace.
And all must love the human form,/In
heathen, Turk or Jew;/Where Mercy,
Love, and Pity dwell/There God is
dwelling too.
WILLIAM BLAKE *Songs of Innocence*

17 Man's inhumanity to man/Makes countless thousands mourn.
ROBERT BURNS *Man was made to Mourn*

1 I am a little world made cunningly/Of elements, and an angelic sprite.
JOHN DONNE *Holy Sonnets*

2 If all hearts were open and all desires known—as they would be if people showed their souls—how many gapings, sighings, clenched fists, knotted brows, broad grins, and red eyes would we see in the market place!
THOMAS HARDY *Diary*

3 So far as Auschwitz is concerned, I have never known or heard of a single person being found alive when the gas chambers were opened half an hour after the gas had been inducted.
RUDOLF HOESS, Commandant of Auschwitz

4 I can make a Lord, but only the Almighty can make a gentleman.
JAMES I

5 To regard man . . . as the final and unsurpassable achievement of creation, especially at his present-day particularly dangerous and disagreeable state of development, is certainly the most arrogant and dangerous of all untenable doctrines. If I thought of man as the final image of God, I should not know what to think of God.
KONRAD LORENZ *On Aggression*

6 The soil of human nature, though many spots are certainly better weeded, planted, and manured than others, is everywhere the same, universally bad.
JOHN NEWTON *Cardiphonia*

7 There are only two kinds of men: the righteous who believe themselves sinners; the rest, sinners who believe themselves righteous.
BLAISE PASCAL

8 An honest man's the noblest work of God.
ALEXANDER POPE *Essay on Man*

9 What a piece of work is man!/How noble in reason!/How infinite in faculty!/In form and moving/How express and admirable!/In action how like an angel!/In apprehension how like a god!
WILLIAM SHAKESPEARE *Hamlet*

10 False of heart, light of ear, bloody of hand: hog in sloth, fox in stealth, wolf in greediness, dog in madness, lion in prey.
WILLIAM SHAKESPEARE *King Lear*

11 God does not require that each individual shall have capacity for everything.
RICHARD ROTHE *Still Hours*

12 Glory to Man in the highest! For Man is the master of things.
A. C. SWINBURNE *Hymn of Man*

13 I am greater than the stars for I know that they are up there and they do not know that I am down here.
WILLIAM TEMPLE

14 I am a man: and nothing that bears upon human nature can be a matter of indifference to me.
TERENCE *Heauton Timoroumenos*

15 In short, the Man Jesus Christ has the decisive place in man's ageless relationship with God. He is what God means by 'Man', He is what man means by God.
J. S. WHALE

MARRIAGE

16 Then the Lord God said, 'It is not good for the man to be alone. I will provide a partner for him.'
Gen. 2.18

17 There are three sights which warm my heart/and are beautiful in the eyes of the Lord and of men:/concord among brothers, friendship among neighbours,/and a man and wife who are inseparable.
Ecclus 25.1

18 In the beginning, at the creation, God made them male and female. For this reason a man shall leave his father and mother, and be made one with his wife; and the two shall become one flesh.
Mark 10.6–8

1 The wife cannot claim her body as her own; it is her husband's. Equally, the husband cannot claim his body as his own; it is his wife's. Do not deny yourselves to one another.
1 Cor. 7.4–5

2 As a wife you may be your husband's salvation; as a husband you may be your wife's salvation.
1 Cor. 7.16

3 A wife is bound to her husband as long as he lives.
1 Cor. 7.39

4 Husbands, love your wives, as Christ also loved the church and gave himself up for it.
Eph. 5.25

5 In loving his wife a man loves himself.
Eph. 5.28

6 I take thee to my wedded wife, to have and to hold from this day forward, for better for worse, for richer for poorer, in sickness and in health, to love and to cherish, till death us do part, according to God's holy ordinance; and thereto I plight thee my troth.
BOOK OF COMMON PRAYER From the *Marriage Service*

7 With this Ring I thee wed, with my body I thee worship, and with all my worldly goods I thee endow.
BOOK OF COMMON PRAYER From the *Marriage Service*

8 Those whom God hath joined together let no man put asunder.
BOOK OF COMMON PRAYER From the *Marriage Service*

9 The greater the friendship the more permanent it should be. The greatest friendship is that between man and wife, who are coupled not only by physical intercourse, which even among animals conduces to a certain sweet friendship, but also for the sharing of domestic life.
ST THOMAS AQUINAS

10 We break the line with stroke and luck,/ The arrows run like rain,/If you be struck, or I be struck/There's one to strike again./If you befriend, or I befriend,/The strength is in us twain/And good things end, and bad things end/And you and I remain.
G. K. CHESTERTON *A Marriage Song*

11 O perfect Love, all human thought transcending,/Lowly we kneel in prayer before Thy throne,/That theirs may be the love which knows no ending/Whom Thou for evermore dost join in one.
DOROTHY FRANCES GURNEY *Hymn*

12 There are three kinds of love; false, natural and married. False love is that which seeks its own, just as one loves gold, goods, honour or women outside of matrimony contrary to God's command. Natural love is between father and children, brother and sister. But above them all is married love. It burns as fire, and seeks nothing more than the mate. It says, 'I wish not yours; I wish neither gold nor silver, neither this nor that. I want only you.'
MARTIN LUTHER

13 Ah, dear God, marriage is not a thing of nature but a gift of God: the sweetest, the dearest, and the purest life above all celibacy and all singleness, when it turns out well, though the very devil if it does not.
MARTIN LUTHER

14 There is no surprise more magical than the surprise of being loved. It is the finger of God on a man's shoulder.
CHARLES MORGAN

15 None can be eternally united who have not died for each other.
COVENTRY PATMORE

MARTYRDOM

16 So they stoned Stephen, and as they did so, he called out, 'Lord Jesus, receive my spirit.'
Acts 7.59

1 A martyrdom is never the design of men; for the true martyr is he who has become the instrument of God, who has lost his will in the will of God, not lost it but found it, for he has found freedom in submission to God.
T. S. ELIOT

2 Play the man, Master Ridley: we shall this day light such a candle, by God's grace, in England, as I trust shall never be put out.
BISHOP LATIMER, last words of

3 The blood of the martyrs is the seed of the Church.
TERTULLIAN *Apologeticus*

MEDITATION

4 Observe for thyself what place best agrees with thy spirit; whether within doors, or without. Isaac's example in 'going out to meditate in the field' will, I believe, best suit with most.
RICHARD BAXTER *The Saints' Everlasting Rest*

5 A devotee should devote himself to abstraction, alone with his mind, and self restrained. Fixing his seat firmly not too high nor too low. There, fixing his mind on one point, with the working of the mind and senses restrained, he should practise devotion for purity of self, in silence before the One. Holding his body, head, and neck erect, even and unmoved, remaining steady. Eyes resting before the tip of his own nose (for closing of the eyes leads to sleep) and not looking about in all directions, he should concentrate on God. Thus he attains that tranquillity which finally brings freedom and one-ness with God.

As a flame standing in a windless place flickers not, so is the mind restrained in infinite happiness. This happiness comes to one whose mind is fully tranquil and who has become one with God.
The Bhagavad Gita (Hindu)

6 Not covetous with heart benevolent/ A man should dwell, with concentrated thought,/With mind one-pointed, inwardly controlled.
Book of the Numerical Sayings (Buddhist)

7 Meditation is the concentration of the mind on God and his qualities ... It integrates the mind, stills its turbulence, cleanses it, strengthens it. Just as a body that has been cleansed of its toxic waste becomes healthier and stronger, so a mind emptied of its encumbering dross becomes purer and nobler ...

If you meditate in the morning the inner serenity achieved will be carried into the working day. If you meditate before going to bed you will sleep like a child and awake wonderfully refreshed.
K. T. LALVANI *Beyond No One's Reach* (Sikh)

8 One ought to meditate upon the syllable OM ... It is the most approximate name for God, and when this name is used He becomes pleased, just as a man is pleased when addressed by a name dear to him.
SANKARA'S commentary on *Chandogya Upanishad* (Hindu)

9 The first lesson is to sit for some time and let the mind run on. The mind is bubbling up all the time. It is like the monkey jumping about. Let that monkey jump as much as he can—you simply wait and watch ... you will find that each day the mind's vagaries are becoming less and less violent.
VIVEKANANDA (Hindu)

10 Meditation frees man from the animal nature; discerns the reality of things; puts man in touch with God ...

The meditative faculty is akin to the mirror; if you put it before earthly objects it will reflect them ... But if you turn the mirror of your spirit heavenwards ... the rays of the Sun of Reality will be reflected in your heart, and the virtues of the kingdom will be obtained.
Wisdom of Abdu'l-Baha (Bahai)

MESSIAH

1 Therefore the Lord himself shall give you a sign: A young woman is with child, and she will bear a son, and will call him Immanuel.
Isa. 7.14

2 For a boy has been born for us, a son given to us/to bear the symbol of dominion on his shoulder;/and he shall be called/in purpose wonderful, in battle God-like,/Father for all time, Prince of peace.
Isa. 9.6

3 The spirit of the Lord shall rest upon him,/a spirit of wisdom and understanding,/a spirit of counsel and power,/a spirit of knowledge and the fear of the Lord.
Isa. 11.2

4 The spirit of the Lord God is upon me/because the Lord has anointed me;/he has sent me to bring good news to the humble,/to bind up the broken-hearted,/to proclaim liberty to captives/and release to those in prison.
Isa. 61.1

5 'And you', he asked, 'who do you say I am?' Peter replied: 'You are the Messiah.'
Mark 8.29

MESSIANIC AGE

6 They shall beat their swords into mattocks/and their spears into pruning-knives;/nation shall not lift sword against nation/nor ever again be trained for war.
Isa. 2.4

7 Then the wolf shall live with the sheep,/and the leopard lie down with the kid;/and calf and the young lion shall grow up together,/and a little child shall lead them.
Isa. 11.6

8 They shall not hurt or destroy in all my holy mountain;/for as the waters fill the sea,/so shall the land be filled with the knowledge of the Lord.
Isa. 11.9

9 They shall enter Zion with shouts of triumph,/crowned with everlasting gladness./Gladness and joy shall be their escort,/and suffering and weariness shall flee away.
Isa. 35.10

10 Before they call to me, I will answer,/and while they are still speaking I will listen.
Isa. 65.24

11 Thereafter the day shall come/when I will pour out my spirit on all mankind;/your sons and your daughters shall prophesy,/your old men shall dream dreams/and your young men see visions.
Joel 2.28

MIDDLE AGE

12 When I was a child, my speech, my outlook, and my thoughts were all childish. When I grew up, I had finished with childish things.
1 Cor. 13.11

13 The long, dull, monotonous years of middle-aged prosperity or middle-aged adversity are excellent campaigning weather (for the Devil).
C. S. LEWIS *The Screwtape Letters*

14 Select, select: make an anthology/Of what's been given you by bold casual time./Revise, omit; keep what's significant./Fill, fill deserted time.
EDWIN MUIR *Soliloquy*

15 There's a watershed in human life,/A natural mountain that we have to scale;/And once at the top, our journey all lies downward,/Down the long slope to age and sleep and the end.
EDWIN MUIR *Soliloquy*

1 My glass is half unspent; forbear t'arrest/
My thriftless day too soon: my poor
request/Is, that my glass may run but out
the rest.
I have a world of sins to be lamented;/
I have a sea of tears that must be vented:/
O spare till then; and then I die conten-
ted.
FRANCIS QUARLES *My glass is half un-
spent*

2 Manhood in the Christian life is a better
thing than boyhood, because it is a riper
thing; and old age ought to be a brighter
and a calmer, and a more serene thing
than manhood.
F. W. ROBERTSON *Sermons*

3 Middle age is attended, for all of us, with
grave danger of moral stagnation.
A. E. TAYLOR *The Faith of a Moralist*

MONEY

4 What use is money in the hands of a
stupid man?/Can he buy wisdom if he
has no sense?
Prov. 17.16

5 Better have wisdom behind you than
money.
Eccl. 7.12

6 The table has its pleasures, and wine
makes a cheerful life; and money is
behind it all.
Eccl. 10.19

7 No servant can be the slave of two
masters . . . You cannot serve God and
Money.
Matt. 6.24

8 I will say to myself, 'Man, you have
plenty of good things laid by, enough for
many years: take life easy, eat, drink, and
enjoy yourself.' But God said to him,
'You fool, this very night you must
surrender your life; you have made your
money—who will get it now?'
Luke 12.19–20

9 The love of money is the root of all evil
things.
1 Tim. 6.10

10 Silly people think that money commands
the bodily goods most worth having.
ST THOMAS AQUINAS

11 Money never made any man rich, but his
mind.
BEN JONSON *Discourses*

12 We can hardly respect money enough
for the blood and toil it represents.
Money is frightening. It can serve or
destroy man.
MICHEL QUOIST *Prayers of Life*

13 Make all you can, save all you can, give
all you can.
JOHN WESLEY

MORALITY

14 Love and *then* what you will, do.
ST AUGUSTINE *Commentaries*

15 The probability is that moral advance
moves in a spiral rather than a straight
line, and no generation, involved in its
own present, can be sure whether the
curve is rising or falling.
F. R. BARRY *Christian Ethics and Secular
Society*

16 No society has yet solved the problem of
how to teach morality without religion.
So the law must base itself on Christian
morals and to the best of its ability
enforce them, not simply because they
are the morals of most of us, nor simply
because they are the morals taught by the
established Church—on these points the
law recognises the right to dissent—but
for the compelling reason that without
the help of Christian teaching the law
will fail.
LORD DEVLIN *The Enforcement of Morals*

17 Nothing can of itself always be labelled
as 'wrong'.
J. A. T. ROBINSON *Honest to God*

1 There are many religions, but there is only one morality.
JOHN RUSKIN *Lectures on Art*

MOTHER

2 The man called his wife Eve because she was the mother of all who live.
Gen. 3.20

3 A mother in Israel.
Judg. 5.7

4 Do not despise your mother when she is old.
Prov. 23.22

5 Like mother, like daughter.
Ezek. 16.44

6 God could not be everywhere, so He made mothers.
Jewish proverb

MURDER

7 He that sheds the blood of a man,/for that man his blood shall be shed;/for in the image of God/has God made man.
Gen. 9.6

8 You shall not commit murder.
Ex. 20.13

9 You have learned that our forefathers were told, 'Do not commit murder; anyone who commits murder must be brought to judgement.' But what I tell you is this: Anyone who nurses anger against his brother must be brought to judgement.
Matt. 5.21–22

10 Thou shalt not kill; but need'st not strive/ Officiously to keep alive.
ARTHUR H. CLOUGH *The Latest Decalogue*

NEIGHBOUR

1 You shall love your neighbour as a man like yourself.
Lev. 19.18

2 Be sparing in visits to your neighbour's house,/if he sees too much of you, he will dislike you.
Prov. 25.17

3 A neighbour at hand is better than a brother far away.
Prov. 27.10

4 Always treat others as you would like them to treat you.
Matt. 7.12

5 'Which of these three do you think was neighbour to the man who fell into the hands of the robbers?' He answered, 'The one who showed him kindness.' Jesus said, 'Go and do as he did.'
Luke 10.36–37

6 Care as much about each other as about yourselves.
Rom. 12.16

7 The whole law can be summed up in a single commandment: 'Love your neighbour as yourself.'
Gal. 5.14

8 When I needed a neighbour, were you there, were you there?/When I needed a neighbour, were you there?
And the creed and the colour and the name won't matter,/Were you there?
SYDNEY CARTER *100 Hymns for Today*

9 Although I am far from Thee, may no one else be far from Thee.
HAFIZ (Persian)

10 Love your neighbour, yet pull not down your hedge.
GEORGE HERBERT *Jacula Prudentium*

11 In love to the neighbour, God is the middle term; if you love God above all else, then you may also love your neighbour and in your neighbour every man.
SÖREN KIERKEGAARD *Works of Love*

12 Love of God is the root, love of our neighbour the fruit of the Tree of Life. Neither can exist without the other, but the one is cause and the other effect.
WILLIAM TEMPLE *Readings in St John's Gospel*

13 We cannot know whether we love God, although there may be strong reasons for thinking so, but there can be no doubt about whether we love our neighbour or no.
ST TERESA OF AVILA

OLD AGE

1 There is wisdom, remember, in age,/and long life brings understanding.
Job 12.12

2 It is not only the old who are wise/or the aged who understand what is right.
Job 32.9

3 Grey hair is a crown of glory.
Prov. 16.31

4 And when youth's gone/As men count going, twixt us two alone/Still let me be/ Thy little child, left learning at Thy knee.
ANON.

5 Lord, hear our prayer for those who, growing old,/Feel all their time of usefulness is told,/Let them still find some little part to play,/Nor feel unwanted at the close of day.
ANON.

6 Now hath my life across a stormy sea/ Like a frail bark reached that wide port where all/Are bidden, ere the final reckoning fall/Of good and evil for eternity.
MICHELANGELO BUONARROTI

7 If I cannot work or rise from my chair or my bed, love remains to me; I can pray.
FATHER CONGREVE

8 It is not years that make souls grow old, but having nothing to love, nothing to hope for.
FATHER CONGREVE

9 I've wrestled on towards heaven,/'Gainst storm and wind and tide;/Now, like a weary traveller/That leaneth on his guide,/ Amid the shades of evening,/While sinks life's lingering sand,/I hail the glory dawning/In Immanuel's land.
ANNE ROSS COUSIN *Hymn*

10 Stronger by weakness, wiser men become/As they draw near to their eternal home./Leaving the old, both worlds at once they view/That stand upon the threshold of the new.
EDMUND WALLER *Old Age*

PALM SUNDAY

1 Rejoice, rejoice, daughter of Zion,/shout aloud, daughter of Jerusalem;/for see, your king is coming to you,/his cause won, his victory gained,/humble and mounted on an ass.
Zech. 9.9

2 Hosanna to the Son of David! Blessings on him who comes in the name of the lord! Hosanna in the heavens!
Matt. 21.9

3 Fools! For I also had my hour;/One far fierce hour, and sweet:/There was a shout about my ears,/And palms before my feet.
G. K. CHESTERTON *The Donkey*

PARENTS

4 Honour your father and your mother.
Ex. 20.12

5 Attend, my son, to your father's instruction/and do not reject the teaching of your mother.
Prov. 1.8

6 The religion of a child depends on what its mother and father are, and not on what they say.
H.-F. AMIEL *Journal intime*

7 The joys of parents are secret; and so are their griefs and fears.
FRANCIS BACON *Of Parents and Children*

8 A man should never hesitate to alleviate a father's or a mother's grief, even at the risk of his life.
Buddhist saying

9 The Duty of Parents to their children. . . is to be tender-hearted, pitiful, and gentle.
JEREMY TAYLOR

PATIENCE

10 To be patient shows great understanding;/quick temper is the height of folly.
Prov. 14.29

11 Possess your soul with patience.
JOHN DRYDEN *The Hind and the Panther*

12 It is difficult to be long-suffering with falsity, untrustworthiness. One is tempted to feel sick with people who are false and unreliable, but we must first find out the truth about it.
G. A. STUDDERT KENNEDY *The New Man in Christ*

13 They also serve who only stand and wait.
JOHN MILTON *On his Blindness*

14 'Rest in the Lord, wait patiently on Him, and He shall give thee thy heart's desire.' The more central this thought becomes, the less difficult you will find its outward expression, that is to say, long-suffering and gentleness, in all the encounters of everyday life.
EVELYN UNDERHILL

PEACE

15 Now I will lie down in peace, and sleep;/for thou alone, O Lord, makest me live unafraid.
Ps. 4.8

16 To wink at a fault causes trouble;/a frank rebuke leads to peace.
Prov. 10.10

17 Thou dost keep in peace men of constant mind,/in peace because they trust in thee.
Isa. 26.3

18 There is no peace for the wicked,/says the Lord.
Isa. 48.22

19 You must not think that I have come to bring peace to the earth; I have not come to bring peace, but a sword.
Matt. 10.34

1 Peace to this house.
Luke 10.5

2 Those who live on the level of the spirit have the spiritual outlook, and that is life and peace.
Rom. 8.6

3 If possible, so far as it lies with you, live at peace with all men.
Rom. 12.18

4 The peace of God, which is beyond our utmost understanding, will keep guard over your hearts and your thoughts, in Christ Jesus.
Phil. 4.7

5 Give peace in our time, O Lord./Because there is none other that fighteth for us, but only thou, O God.
BOOK OF COMMON PRAYER From the *Order for Morning Prayer*

6 Lord, now lettest thou thy servant depart in peace according to thy word.
BOOK OF COMMON PRAYER From the *Nunc Dimittis*

7 O God, from whom all holy desires, all good counsels, and all just works do proceed; Give unto thy servants that peace which the world cannot give.
BOOK OF COMMON PRAYER From the *Order for Evening Prayer*

8 Calm soul of all things, make it mine/To feel amid the city's jar/That there exists a peace of thine/Man did not make and cannot mar.
MATTHEW ARNOLD *Lines written in Kensington Gardens*

9 Peace between man and God is the well ordered obedience of faith to eternal law. Peace between man and man is well ordered concord.
ST AUGUSTINE *City of God*

10 O God of love, O King of peace,/Make wars throughout the world to cease.
HENRY WILLIAMS BAKER *Hymn*

11 We should hardly remain within the limits of Biblical promise if we expected that within this sinful world the nations of the earth could ever be a perfectly harmonious family of nations, entirely governed by the spirit of love.
EMIL BRUNNER

12 God the All-wise! by the fire of Thy chastening,/Earth shall be freedom and truth be restored;/Through the thick darkness Thy Kingdom is hastening;/Thou wilt give peace in Thy time, O Lord.
HENRY FOTHERGILL CHORLEY *Hymn*

13 O God, make us children of quietness, and heirs of peace.
ST CLEMENT

14 Does it seem strange to you that the angels should have announced Peace, when ceaselessly the world has been stricken with War and the fear of War?
T. S. ELIOT *Murder in the Cathedral*

15 I am a man of peace. I believe in peace. But I do not want peace at any price. I do not want peace that you find in stone; I do not want the peace that you find in the grave; but I do want the peace which you find embedded in the human breast, which is exposed to the arrows of the whole world, but which is protected from all harm by the power of Almighty God.
MAHATMA GANDHI

16 To thee, O God, we turn for peace . . . but grant us too the blessed assurance that nothing shall deprive us of that peace, neither ourselves, nor our foolish earthly desires, nor my wild longings, nor the anxious cravings of my heart.
SÖREN KIERKEGAARD

17 The time of business does not differ from the time of prayer; and in the noise and clutter of my kitchen, while several persons are at the same time calling for different things, I possess God in as great tranquillity as if I were upon my knees at the Blessed Sacrament.
BROTHER LAWRENCE *Practice of the Presence of God*

1 My son, now will I teach thee the way of peace and inward liberty. Be desirous to do the will of another rather than thine own. Choose always to have less rather than more. Seek always the lowest place, and to be inferior to everyone. Wish always, and pray, that the will of God· may be wholly fulfilled in thee.

THOMAS À KEMPIS *The Imitation of Christ*

PENITENCE

2 I will set off and go to my father, and say to him, 'Father, I have sinned, against God and against you; I am no longer fit to be called your son; treat me as one of your paid servants.'
Luke 15.18–19

3 Just as I am, without one plea/But that Thy blood was shed for me,/And that Thou bidd'st me come to Thee,/O Lamb of God, I come.
CHARLOTTE ELLIOTT *Hymn*

4 Once I turned from thee and hid,/Bound on what thou hadst forbid;/Sow the wind I would; I sinned:/I repent of what I did. Bad I am, but yet thy child./Father, be thou reconciled,/Spare thou me, since I see/With thy might that thou art mild.
GERARD MANLEY HOPKINS *Poems*

5 It is not finished, Lord./There is not one thing done,/There is no battle of my life,/That I have really won./And now I come to tell Thee/How I fought to fail,/My human, all too human, tale/Of weakness and futility./And yet there is a faith in me, That thou wilt find in it/One word that Thou canst take/And make/The centre of a sentence/In thy book of poetry.
G. A. STUDDERT KENNEDY *The Unutterable Beauty*

6 Oh, I cannot say what thy chosen servant says: that he filled up that which is behind of the afflictions of Christ in his flesh; no, I can only say that I increased thy sufferings, added new ones to those which thou didst once suffer in order to save me.
SÖREN KIERKEGAARD

7 O Lord, turn not away Thy face/From him that lies prostrate,/Lamenting sore his sinful life,/Before Thy mercy gate; Mercy, good Lord, mercy I ask,/This is the total sum;/For mercy, Lord, is all my suit:/Lord, let Thy mercy come.
JOHN MARCKANT *Hymn*

8 Come, let us to the Lord our God/With contrite hearts return;/Our God, is gracious, nor will leave/The desolate to mourn.
JOHN MORISON *Hymn*

9 One who is all unfit to count/As scholar in Thy school,/Thou of Thy love hast named a friend—/O kindness wonderful! From the Marathi of NARAYAN VAMAN TILAK *Hymn*

10 Yea, though I sin each day times seven,/And dare not lift the fearfullest eyes to Heaven,/Thanks must I give/Because that seven times are not eight or nine,/And that my darkness is all mine,/And that I live/Within this oak-shade one more minute even,/Hearing the winds their Maker magnify.
COVENTRY PATMORE *Faint yet pursuing*

11 Lord, Thou art Life, though I be dead;/Love's Fire Thou art, however cold I be:/Nor heaven have I, nor place to lay my head,/Nor home, but Thee.
CHRISTINA G. ROSSETTI *Hymn*

12 O Jesus, full of pardoning grace,/More full of grace than I of sin,/Yet once again I seek Thy face;/Open Thine arms and take me in,/And freely my backslidings heal,/And love the faithless sinner still.
CHARLES WESLEY *Hymn*

PHARISEES

13 I tell you, unless you show yourselves far better men than the Pharisees and the doctors of the law, you can never enter the kingdom of Heaven.
Matt. 5.20

1 They are blind guides, and if one blind man guides another they will both fall into the ditch.
Matt. 15.14

2 You strain off a midge, yet gulp down a camel!
Matt. 23.24

3 I thank thee, O God, that I am not like the rest of men.
Luke 18.11

4 To their zeal for God I can testify; but it is an ill-informed zeal.
Rom. 10.2

5 The Pharisee is that extremely admirable man who subordinates his entire life to his knowledge of good and evil, and is as severe a judge of himself as of his neighbour to the honour of God, whom he humbly thanks for this knowledge.
DIETRICH BONHOEFFER *Ethics*

6 O ye wha are sae guid yoursel,/Sae pious and sae holy,/Ye've nought to do but mark and tell/Your neebours' fauts and folly!
ROBERT BURNS *Address to the Unco Guid or the Rigidly Righteous*

PIETY

7 There must be something farcical and fraudulent in the kind of pietism which preaches from villas in the West End to slums in the East End about mansions in heaven.
A. C. CRAIG *Warrack Lectures*

8 That man is little to be envied whose patriotism would not upon gain force the plain of Marathon, or whose piety would not grow warmer among the ruins of Iona!
SAMUEL JOHNSON Boswell's *Journal of a Tour to the Hebrides*

9 The Moving Finger writes; and, having writ,/Moves on: nor all your Piety nor Wit/Shall lure it back to cancel half a Line,/Nor all your Tears wash out a Word of it.
OMAR KHAYYAM *The Rubaiyat*

10 Do not, therefore, please yourself with thinking how piously you would act and submit to God in a plague, a famine, or persecution, but be intent upon the perfection of the present day, and be assured that the best way of showing a true zeal is to make little things the occasion of great piety.
WILLIAM LAW *A Serious Call to a Devout and Holy Life*

11 The consciousness that the human spirit is derived and responsible, that all its functions are heritages and trusts, involves a sentiment of gratitude and duty we may call piety.
GEORGE SANTAYANA *Reason in Religions*

12 The Child is father of the Man;/And I could wish my days to be/Bound each to each by natural piety.
WILLIAM WORDSWORTH *My Heart Leaps up when I Behold*

PILGRIMAGE

13 Happy the men whose refuge is in thee,/ whose hearts are set on the pilgrim ways!
Ps. 84.5

14 Who would true valour see,/Let him come hither;/One here will constant be,/Come wind, come weather;/There's no discouragement/Shall make him once relent/His first avowed intent/To be a pilgrim.
JOHN BUNYAN *Hymn*

15 They went then till they came to the 'Delectable Mountains'; which Mountains belong to the Lord of that hill of which we have spoken before; so they went up to the Mountains to behold the gardens and orchards, the vineyards and fountains of water; where also they drank and washed themselves and did freely eat of the vineyards.
JOHN BUNYAN *The Pilgrim's Progress*

16 Never weather-beaten Sail more willing bent to shore,/Never tired Pilgrim's limbs

affected slumber more,/Than my wearied sprite now longs to fly out of my toubled breast./O come quickly, sweetest Lord, and take my soul to rest.
THOMAS CAMPION *Book of Airs*

1 Alone with none but Thee, my God,/I journey on my way;/What need I fear when Thou art near,/Oh King of night and day—/More safe am I within Thy hand/Than if a host did round me stand.
Attributed to ST COLUMBA

2 Through each perplexing path of life/ Our wandering footsteps guide;/Give us each day our daily bread,/And raiment fit provide.
O spread Thy covering wings around,/ Till all our wanderings cease,/And at our Father's loved abode/Our souls arrive in peace.
PHILIP DODDRIDGE *Hymn*

3 So with all our inconsistencies and weaknesses and sins we are kept in the one Way, the one Truth, and the one Life; and each step that we take brings us nearer to the one Father above.
F. J. A. HORT *The Way, The Truth, the Life*

4 Through the night of doubt and sorrow/ Onward goes the pilgrim band,/Singing songs of expectation,/Marching to the promised land.
BERNHARDT SEVERIS INGEMANN *Hymn*

5 Then give us courage, Father God,/ to choose again the pilgrim way,/And help us to accept with joy/the challenge of tomorrow's day.
FRED KAAN *100 Hymns for Today*

6 Lead, kindly Light, amid the encircling gloom,/Lead Thou me on;/The night is dark, and I am far from home;/Lead Thou me on./Keep Thou my feet; I do not ask to see/The distant scene,—one step enough for me.
CARDINAL NEWMAN *Hymn*

7 Give me my scallop shell of quiet,/My staff of faith to walk upon,/My scrip of joy, immortal diet,/My bottle of salvation:

My gown of glory, hope's true gage,/ And thus I'll take my pilgrimage.
SIR WALTER RALEIGH *The Passionate Man's Pilgrimage*

8 God made the moon as well as the sun: and when he does not see fit to grant us the sunlight, he means us to guide our steps as well as we can by moonlight.
RICHARD WHATELY

9 It is therefore the opinion of the present writer that even in this age there are no supersonic flights to the Celestial City or even to the Palace Beautiful. Increased awareness can be obtained only by a journey on foot by way of the Slough of Despond, the Hill of Difficulty, Doubting Castle, and the rest.
H. A. WILLIAMS *Soundings*

10 Guide me, O Thou great Jehovah,/ Pilgrim through this barren land;/I am weak, but Thou art mighty;/Hold me with Thy powerful hand:/Bread of heaven,/Feed me till my want is o'er.
WILLIAM WILLIAMS *Hymn*

11 Jesus still lead on,/Till our rest be won,/ And, although the way be cheerless,/ We will follow, calm and fearless;/Guide us by Thy hand/To our fatherland.
NICOLAUS LUDWIG VON ZINZENDORF *Hymn*

POVERTY

12 But the poor shall not always be unheeded/nor the hope of the destitute be always vain.
Ps. 9.18

13 Better a dry crust and concord with it/ than a house full of feasting and strife.
Prov. 17.1

14 A man who sneers at the poor insults his Maker.
Prov. 17.5

15 Give me neither poverty nor wealth.
Prov. 30.8

1 Is it nothing to you that you crush my people/and grind the faces of the poor?
Isa. 3.15

2 You have the poor among you always; but you will not always have me.
Matt. 26.11

PRAISE

3 Let us now sing the praises of famous men,/the heroes of our nation's history.
Ecclus. 44.1

4 Out of the same mouth come praises and curses.
Jas. 3.10

5 It is a sure sign of mediocrity to be niggardly with praise.
MARQUIS DE VAUVENARGUES *Reflections and Maxims*

PRAYER

6 O God, hear my prayer,/listen to my supplication.
Ps. 54.2

7 Lord, hear my prayer/and let my cry for help reach thee./Hide not thy face from me/when I am in distress.
Ps. 102.1–2

8 I love the Lord, for he has heard me/and listens to my prayer;/for he has given me a hearing/whenever I have cried to him.
Ps. 116.1–2

9 Let my prayer be like incense duly set before thee/and my raised hands like the evening sacrifice.
Ps. 141.2

10 God grant that I may speak according to his will, and that my own thoughts may be worthy of his gifts.
Wisd. 7.15

11 Do not grow weary of praying.
Ecclus. 7.10

12 Your Father knows what your needs are before you ask him.
Matt. 6.8

13 Ask, and you will receive; seek and you will find; knock, and the door will be opened.
Matt. 7.7

14 Whatever you ask for in prayer, believe that you have received it and it will be yours.
Mark 11.24

15 Lord, teach us to pray.
Luke 11.1

16 Keep on praying and never lose heart.
Luke 18.1

17 We do not even know how we ought to pray, but through our inarticulate groans the Spirit himself is pleading for us.
Rom. 8.26

18 Pray continually.
1 Thess. 5.17

19 A good man's prayer is powerful and effective.
Jas. 5.16

20 Often I have heard people say that they could pray to God while they were walking about and doing their chores, but that as soon as they knelt down they were plagued with distracting thoughts. The truth about that is that they prayed best when they were least conscious of themselves.
FATHER ANDREW

21 The apostle saith 'Pray with all manner of Prayer': therefore it is meet we should take notice how many kinds of prayer there are: wherein the apostle guides us when he says 'Let Supplications, Prayers, Thanksgivings and Intercessions be made.'
LANCELOT ANDREWES *Preces Privatae*

1 Prayer is evoked by the need to feel oneself not entirely dependent upon the necessity which reigns in the world and upon the power of fate which belongs to this world. Prayer is conversation with the Existent One who is exalted above the world cycle, above the falsity and wrongness in which the world is submerged.
NICHOLAS BERDYAEV *The Divine and the Human*

2 O God, early in the morning do I cry unto Thee./Help me to pray and to think only of Thee./I cannot pray alone./In me there is darkness./But with Thee there is light.
DIETRICH BONHOEFFER *Letters and Papers from Prison*

3 When thou prayest, rather let thy heart be without words than thy words without heart.
JOHN BUNYAN

4 Lord, we know not what we ought to ask of Thee; Thou only knowest what we need.
F. DE LA M. FÉNELON

5 Many p sons distract themselves, first by their fear of distraction, and then by their regret of such distraction.
F. DE LA M. FÉNELON *Letters*

6 The greatest element in life is not what occupies most of its time, else sleep would stand high in the scale. Nor is it what engrosses most of its thought, else money would be very high . . . The two or three hours of worship and preaching weekly has perhaps been the greatest single influence on English life. Half an hour of prayer, morning or evening, every day, may be a greater element in shaping our course than all our conduct and all our thought.
P. T. FORSYTH

7 Fools, who came to scoff, remain'd to pray.
OLIVER GOLDSMITH *The Deserted Village*

8 My spirit bare before Thee stands;/I bring no gift, I ask no sign,/I come to Thee with empty hands,/The surer to be filled from Thine.
DORA GREENWELL

9 One thing is certain: as long as you only pray to God for yourselves, your prayers will not be as perfect as He wishes them to be.
JEAN NICOLAS GROU *The School of Jesus Christ*

10 Speaking generally, it is true to say that the necessities and accidents of life form the main subject and the actuating motive of the prayers of the ordinary Christian.
JEAN NICOLAS GROU *The School of Jesus Christ*

11 Lord—Thine the day, And I the day's.
DAG HAMMARSKJÖLD

12 'Necessity teaches man to pray.' But if once through necessity the intercourse with higher beings is opened up and help and deliverance follow on the prayer, man is thereafter led to pray, not only by the menace to his bare existence, but by the desire for an intensification, enhancement, and enrichment of life.
F. HEILER *Prayer*

13 Prayer is the central phenomenon of religion, the very hearthstone of all piety.
F. HEILER *Prayer*

14 Religion and Prayer are not identical, but are related to one another as life and breathing, as thought and speech. Just as there can be no true religion without the idea of God, and of the eternal, so there can be no genuine religious life without the life of prayer.
F. HEILER *Prayer*

15 Pray as if everything depended on God and act as if everything depended on oneself.
ST IGNATIUS OF LOYOLA

16 Why has our sincere prayer for each other such great power over others? Because of the fact that by cleaving to God during prayer I become one spirit with Him, and unite with myself by faith, and love, those for whom I pray; for the Holy Ghost acting in me also acts at the same time in them, for He accomplishes all things. 'We, being many, are one bread, one body.' 'There is one body and one spirit.'
JOHN OF CRONSTADT

1 I am the Ground of thy beseeching.
MOTHER JULIAN OF NORWICH *Revelations of Divine Love*

2 So too with prayer in the name of Jesus, Jesus assumes the responsibility and all the consequences, He steps forward for us, steps into the place of the person praying.
SÖREN KIERKEGAARD *Journals*

3 There is nothing that makes us love a man so much as praying for him.
WILLIAM LAW *A Serious Call to a Devout and Holy Life*

4 When one says to the great Thinker: 'Here is one of thy thoughts: I am thinking it now,' that is a prayer—a word to the big heart from one of its own little hearts.
GEORGE MACDONALD

5 Prayer is a fundamental style of thinking, passionate and compassionate, responsible and thankful, that is deeply rooted in our humanity and that manifests itself not only among believers but also among serious-minded people who do not profess any religious faith.
JOHN MACQUARRIE *Paths in Spirituality*

6 Make us, O Lord, to flourish like pure lilies in the courts of Thine house, and to show forth to the faithful the fragrance of good works, and the example of a godly life.
The Mozarabic Liturgy

7 Come, my soul, thy suit prepare;/Jesus loves to answer prayer;/He himself has bid thee pray,/Therefore will not say thee nay.
JOHN NEWTON *Hymn*

8 Approach, my soul, the mercy-seat,/Where Jesus answers prayer;/There humbly fall before His feet,/For none can perish there.
JOHN NEWTON *Hymn*

9 The people think that they pray before God. But it is not so. For the prayer itself is the essence of the Godhead.
RABBI PINHAS OF KOREZ

10 If your heart is truly turned towards God in prayer, be assured that He will hear you.
Rabbinic saying

11 The way through to the vision of the Son of man and the knowledge of God, which is the heart of contemplative prayer, is by unconditional love of the neighbour, of 'the nearest *Thou* to hand'.
J. A. T. ROBINSON *Honest to God*

12 Prayer is no other but the revelation of the will or mind of God.
JOHN SALTMARSH

13 God is perfect love and perfect wisdom. We do not pray in order to change His Will, but to bring our wills into harmony with His.
WILLIAM TEMPLE

14 More things are wrought by prayer than this world dreams of.
LORD TENNYSON *Idylls of the King*

15 Remember what St Augustine tells us . . . how he sought God in many places and at last found the Almighty within himself. It is of no slight importance for a soul given to wandering thoughts to realize this truth, and to see it has no need to go to heaven in order to speak to the eternal Father or to enjoy His company.
ST TERESA OF AVILA

16 I offer up unto Thee my prayers and intercessions, for those especially who have in any matter hurt, grieved, or found fault with me, or who have done me any damage or displeasure.

For all those also whom, at any time, I have vexed, troubled, burdened, and scandalised, by words or deeds, knowingly or in ignorance: that Thou wouldst grant us all equally pardon for our sins, and for our offences against each other.

Take away from our hearts, O Lord, all suspiciousness, indignation, wrath and contention, and whatsoever may hurt charity, and lessen brotherly love. Have mercy, O Lord, have mercy on those that

crave Thy mercy, give grace unto them that stand in need thereof, and make us such that we may be worthy to enjoy Thy grace, and go forward to life eternal.
THOMAS À KEMPIS

1 Prayer is/The world in tune.
HENRY VAUGHAN

PRAYER, EVENING

2 The night is come like to the day,/Depart not Thou, great God, away;/Let not my sins, black as the night,/Eclipse the lustre of Thy light./Keep still in my horizon, for to me/The sun makes not the day, but Thee./Thou whose nature cannot sleep,/On my temples sentry keep;/Guard me 'gainst those watchful foes,/Whose eyes are open while mine close.
SIR THOMAS BROWNE *Evening Hymn*

3 Now God be with us, for the night is closing;/The light and darkness are of His disposing,/And 'neath His shadow here to rest we yield us,/For He will shield us.
PETRUS HERBERT *Hymn*

4 Abide with me; fast falls the eventide;/The darkness deepens; Lord, with me abide:/When other helpers fail, and comforts flee,/Help of the helpless, O abide with me.
HENRY FRANCIS LYTE *Hymn*

5 Now may He who from the dead/Brought the Shepherd of the sheep,/Jesus Christ, our King and Head,/All our souls in safety keep.
JOHN NEWTON *Hymn*

6 Now cheer our hearts this eventide,/Lord Jesus Christ, and with us bide;/Thou that canst never set in night,/Our heavenly Sun, our glorious Light.
Yattendon Hymnal

PRAYER: GRACE BEFORE MEALS

7 Some ha'e meat, and canna eat,/And some wad eat that want it;/But we ha'e meat, and we can eat,/And sae the Lord be thankit.
ROBERT BURNS

8 Here a little child I stand,/Heaving up my either hand;/Cold as paddocks though they be,/Here I lift them up to thee,/For a benison to fall/On our meat, and on us all.
ROBERT HERRICK *Noble Numbers*

9 What God gives, and what we take,/'Tis a gift for Christ his sake:/Be the meal of beans and peas,/God be thank'd for those, and these./Have we flesh, or have we fish./All are fragments from his dish.
ROBERT HERRICK *Noble Numbers*

PRAYER, METHODS OF

10 When you pray, go into a room by yourself, shut the door, and pray to your Father who is there in the secret place.
Matt. 6.6

11 One should gather a little nosegay of devotion. My meaning is as follows: Those who have been walking in a beautiful garden do not leave it willingly without taking away with them four or five flowers, in order to inhale their perfume and carry them about during the day: even so, when we have considered some mystery in meditation, we should choose one or two or three points in which we have found most relish, and which are specially proper to our advancement, in order to remember them throughout the day, and to inhale their perfume spiritually. Now we should do this in the place where we have made our meditation, either staying where we are, or walking about alone for a little while afterwards.
ST FRANCIS DE SALES *Introduction to the Devout Life*

12 The first thing that you are to do when you are upon your knees is to shut your eyes, and with a short silence let your soul place itself in the presence of God: that is, you are to use this, or some other better method, to separate yourself from

all common thoughts, and make your heart as sensible as you can of the Divine presence.

WILLIAM LAW *A Serious Call to a Devout and Holy Life*

1 Lift up your heart to Him, sometimes even at your meals, and when you are in company: the least little remembrance will always be acceptable to Him. You need not cry very loud, He is nearer to us than we are aware of.

BROTHER LAWRENCE *The Practice of the Presence of God*

2 Pray unto Him in any way you like. He is sure to hear you, for He can hear even the footfall of an ant.

RAMAKRISHNA (Hindu)

3 If Christ Himself needed to retire from time to time to the mountain-top to pray, lesser men need not be ashamed to acknowledge that necessity.

B. H. STREETER *Concerning Prayer*

PRAYER, MORNING

4 In the morning, when I say my prayers,/ thou wilt hear me.
Ps. 5.3

5 Now that the daylight fills the sky,/We lift our hearts to God on high,/That He, in all we do or say,/Would keep us free from harm to-day.
Eighth-century hymn

6 O Lord, Thou knowest how busy I must be this day. If I forget Thee, do not forget me.
SIR JACOB ASTLEY

7 Wish us good morning when we wake/ And light us, Lord, with Thy daybreak./ Beat from our brains the thicky night/ And fill the world up with delight.
Attributed to ST BERNARD OF CLAIRVAUX

8 Teach us, good Lord, to serve Thee as Thou deservest; to give and not to count the cost, to fight and not to heed the wounds, to toil and not to seek for rest,

to labour and not to ask for any reward, save that of knowing that we do Thy will.
ST IGNATIUS OF LOYOLA

9 Direct, control, suggest, this day,/All I design, or do, or say,/That all my powers with all their might,/In Thy sole glory may unite.
THOMAS KEN *Hymn*

10 Lord, let me live and will this day—/ Keep rising from the dead;/Lord, make my spirit good and gay—/Give me my daily bread.
GEORGE MACDONALD *Hymn*

11 Help us this day, O God, to serve Thee devoutly, and the world busily.
Traditional

12 Forth in Thy Name, O Lord, I go,/My daily labour to pursue,/Thee, only Thee, resolved to know/In all I think, or speak, or do.
CHARLES WESLEY *Hymn*

PREACHERS: PREACHING

13 Moses said, 'O Lord, I have never been a man of ready speech'.
Ex. 4.10

14 We cannot possibly give up speaking of things we have seen and heard.
Acts 4.20

15 Keep clear of these men, I tell you; leave them alone. For if this idea of theirs or its execution is of human origin, it will collapse; but if it is from God, you will never be able to put them down.
Acts 5.38–39

16 Keep watch over yourselves and over all the flock of which the Holy Spirit has given you charge, as shepherds of the church of the Lord, which he won for himself by his own blood.
Acts 20.28

16 Paul, you are raving; too much study is driving you mad.
Acts 26.24

1 Agrippa said to Paul, 'You think it will not take much to win me over and make a Christian of me.'
Acts 26.28

2 I have become eveything in turn to men of every sort, so that in one way or another I may save some.
1 Cor. 9.22

3 Proclaim the message, press it home on all occasions, convenient or inconvenient, use argument, reproof, and appeal, with all the patience that the work of teaching requires.
2 Tim. 4.2

4 Every man is a priest, even involuntarily; his conduct is an unspoken sermon, which is for ever preaching to others.
H.-F. AMIEL *Journal intime*

5 Almighty God, Thy word is cast/Like seed into the ground;/Now let the dew of heaven descend,/And righteous fruits abound.
JOHN CAWOOD *Hymn*

6 Christ's lore and His apostles twelve,/ He taught, but first he practised it himself.
GEOFFREY CHAUCER *The Canterbury Tales*

7 God calleth preaching folly. Do not grudge/To pick out treasures from an earthen pot./The worst speaks something good: if all want sense,/God takes a text, and preacheth patience.
GEORGE HERBERT *The Temple*

8 Sir, a woman preaching is like a dog's walking on his hinder legs. It is not done well: but you are surprised to find it done at all.
SAMUEL JOHNSON Boswell's *Life of Johnson*

9 A good, honest, and painful sermon.
SAMUEL PEPYS *Diary*

10 So into a pew there and heard Dr. Ball make a very good sermon, though short of what I expected, as for the most part it do fall out.
SAMUEL PEPYS *Diary*

11 The duty of the clergyman is to remind people in an eloquent manner of the existence of God.
JOHN RUSKIN *Unto This Last*

12 As the French say, there are three sexes, —men, women, and clergymen.
SYDNEY SMITH in Lady Holland's *Memoirs*

13 A Curate—there is something which excites compassion in the very name of a Curate!
SYDNEY SMITH *Peter Plymly's Letters*

14 For their tender minds he served up half a Christ.
A. C. SWINBURNE

15 Preach not because you have to say something, but because you have something to say.
RICHARD WHATELY *Apophthegms*

PRIDE

16 Pride comes before disaster,/and arrogance before a fall.
Prov. 16.18

17 Pride will bring a man low;/a man lowly in spirit wins honour.
Prov. 29.23

18 Be not too proud to listen,/for it is the Lord who speaks.
Jer. 13.15

19 So they were filled,/and, being filled, grew proud;/and so they forgot me.
Hos. 13.6

20 Arrogance is hateful to God and man.
Ecclus. 10.7

21 The origin of pride is to forsake the Lord,/man's heart revolting against his Maker.
Ecclus. 10.12

22 I am the master of my fate:/I am the captain of my soul.
W. E. HENLEY *Invictus*

1 The proud will not enter the Blissful Abode.
MUHAMMAD *Hadith* (Muslim)

PROGRESS

2 The only specific Christian politics are the politics of the world to come.
CHRISTOPHER DAWSON

3 It is no good dreaming dreams of utopia if one cannot draft the appropriate legislation.
LORD KILMUIR *Political Adventure*

4 I consider that the way of life in urbanised, rich countries, as it exists today, and as it is likely to go on developing, is probably the most degraded and unillumined ever to come to pass on earth.
MALCOLM MUGGERIDGE *Jesus Rediscovered*

5 The world, as you can very well see, has not noticeably changed since the Incarnation.
CHARLES PÉGUY

PROPHETS

6 'I wish that all the Lord's people were prophets and that the Lord would confer his spirit on them all!'
Num. 11.29

7 Is Saul also among the prophets?
1 Sam. 10.11

8 As soon as Ahab saw Elijah, he said to him, 'Is it you, you troubler of Israel?'
1 Kings 18.17

9 Elijah was carried up in the whirlwind to heaven. When Elisha saw it, he cried, 'My father, my father, the chariots and the horsemen of Israel!'
2 Kings 2.11–12

10 'Do not be afraid, for those who are on our side are more than those on theirs.' Then Elisha offered this prayer: 'O Lord, open his eyes and let him see.' And the Lord opened the young man's eyes, and he saw the hills covered with horses and chariots of fire all round Elisha.
2 Kings 6.16–17

11 The word of the Lord came to me: 'Before I formed you in the womb I knew you for my own; before you were born I consecrated you, I appointed you a prophet to the nations.'
Jer. 1.4–5

12 They have denied the Lord,/saying, 'He does not exist./No evil shall come upon us;/we shall never see sword or famine./ The prophets will prove mere wind,/the word not in them.'
Jer. 5.12–13

13 Prophets and priests are frauds,/every one of them;/they dress my people's wound, but skin-deep only,/with their saying, 'All is well.'/All well? Nothing is well!
Jer. 6.13–14

14 I have been made a laughing-stock all the day long,/everyone mocks me./Whenever I speak I must needs cry out/and proclaim violence and destruction./I am reproached and mocked all the time/ for uttering the word of the Lord.
Jer. 20.7–8

15 Oh, those prophets who say, 'It is the very word of the Lord', when it is not the Lord who has sent them.
Ezek. 13.6

16 But when it comes, as come it will, they will know that there has been a prophet in their midst.
Ezek. 33.33

17 The lion has roared; who is not terrified?/ The Lord God has spoken; who will not prophesy?
Amos 3.8

18 'I am no prophet,' Amos replied to Amaziah, 'nor am I a prophet's son; I am a herdsman and a dresser of sycomore-figs. But the Lord took me as I followed the flock and said to me, "Go and prophesy to my people Israel." '
Amos 7.14–15

1 No one can interpret any prophecy of Scripture by himself. For it was not through any human whim that men prophesied of old; men they were, but, impelled by the Holy Spirit, they spoke the words of God.
2 Pet. 1.20–21

2 If we do not listen to the prophets we shall have to listen to Providence.
A. C. CRAIG

PROVIDENCE

3 For God is judge;/he puts one man down and raises up another.
Ps. 75.7

4 The rich man in his castle,/The poor man at his gate,/God made them, high or lowly,/And ordered their estate.
CECIL FRANCES ALEXANDER *Hymn*

5 There's a divinity that shapes our ends,/Rough-hew them how we will.
WILLIAM SHAKESPEARE *Hamlet*

6 A greater power than we can contradict/Hath thwarted our intents.
WILLIAM SHAKESPEARE *Romeo and Juliet*

PURITY

7 Who may go up the mountain of the Lord?/And who may stand in his holy place?/He who has clean hands and a pure heart,/who has not set his mind on falsehood,/and has not committed perjury.
Ps. 24.3–4

8 I am absolutely convinced, as a Christian, that nothing is impure in itself; only, if a man considers a particular thing impure, then to him it is impure.
Rom. 14.14

9 To the pure all things are pure.
Titus 1.15

10 Our eyes may see some uncleanness, but let not our mind see things that are not clean. Our ears may hear some uncleanness, but let not our mind hear things that are not clean.
Shinto prayer

RECONCILIATION

1 A fool is too arrogant to make amends;/
upright men know what reconciliation
means.
Prov. 14.9

2 If someone slaps you on the right cheek,
turn and offer him your left.
Matt. 5.39

3 (God) has entrusted us with the message
of reconciliation.
2 Cor. 5.19

RELIGION

4 Great beyond all question is the mystery
of our religion.
1 Tim. 3.16

5 The kind of religion which is without
stain or fault in the sight of God our
Father is this: to go to the help of orphans
and widows in their distress and keep
oneself untarnished by the world.
Jas. 1.27

6 It were better to have no religion than
a religion which did not conform to
reason.
ABDU'L-BAHA (Bahai)

7 Children of men! the unseen Power, whose
eye/For ever doth accompany mankind,/
Hath look'd on no religion scornfully/
That men did ever find.
MATTHEW ARNOLD *Progress*

8 Religious veneration is inconsistent with
what is called impartiality, which means
that as you see some good and some evil
on both sides, you identify yourself with
neither, and are able to judge of both.
DR THOMAS ARNOLD *Life*

9 A religion that is small enough for our
understanding is not great enough for
our need.
A. J. BALFOUR

10 Religion that is not embedded in the
common life too soon degenerates into
religiosity, and an inward-looking Church
is a dying Church.
F. R. BARRY *Christian Ethics and Secular
Society*

11 Perhaps few among you have so many
dealings with men of different races,
different religions, different beliefs and
different cultures as I—unworthily—
have. In all these dealings I have always
found that a great love, a wide-open
heart, always opens the hearts of others.
This great love must be not mere diplom-
acy but the result of an inner conviction
that we are all children of one God, who
has created mankind, who has created
each one of us, and whose children we
all are.
CARDINAL BEA

12 The proper food of all inward religion is
the forms we give it outwardly.
STOPFORD A. BROOKE *Religion in Literature
and Religion in Life*

13 Let your religion be less of a theory and
more of a love affair.
G. K. CHESTERTON

14 'When I mention religion I mean the
Christian religion, and not only the Christian religion, but the Protestant religion;
and not only the Protestant religion, but
the Church of England.'
HENRY FIELDING *Tom Jones* (Parson
Thwackum)

15 If one wishes to feel the very pulse beat of
any religion, it must as a rule be sought
in its liturgy.
FREDERICK C. GRANT *Introduction to New
Testament Thought*

16 True religion is betting one's life that
there is a God.
DONALD HANKEY *A Student in Arms*

17 During the past thirty years people from
all the civilized countries of the earth
have consulted me ... Among all my
patients in the second half of life—that
is to say over thirty-five—there has not
been one whose problem in the last resort

was not that of finding a religious outlook on life. It is safe to say that every one of them fell ill because he had lost that which the living religions of every age have given to their followers, and none of them has been really healed who did not regain his religious outlook.
C. G. JUNG

1 The great contribution of the Hebrew to religion was that he did away with it.
JOHN MACMURRAY *The Clue to History*

2 Religion is the opium of the people.
KARL MARX *Criticism of Hegel's Philosophy of Right*

3 Things are coming to a pretty pass when religion is allowed to invade private life.
Attributed to LORD MELBOURNE

4 We are generally the better persuaded by the reasons we discover than by those given to us by others.
BLAISE PASCAL

5 The capacity for religious or mystical awareness, as for aesthetic or psychic awareness, is largely a question of natural endowment.
J. A. T. ROBINSON *Honest to God*

6 The pleasure of the religious man is an easy and a portable pleasure, such a one as he carries about in his bosom without alarming either the eye or envy of the world.
ROBERT SOUTH *Sermons*

7 There is one plan which you might at least try. I should recommend you to be crucified and to rise again on the third day.
C. M. DE TALLEYRAND (on being asked how to found a new religion)

8 It is a mistake to assume that God is interested only, or even chiefly, in religion.
WILLIAM TEMPLE

9 Orthodoxy is my doxy; heterodoxy is another man's doxy.
WILLIAM WARBURTON (Remark to Lord Sandwich)

10 Religion begins in knowledge, proceeds in practice, and ends in happiness.
BENJAMIN WHICHCOTE *Moral and Religious Aphorisms*

11 For over two centuries religion has been on the defensive, and on a weak defensive.
A. N. WHITEHEAD *Science and the Modern World*

12 The worship of God is not a rule of safety—it is an adventure of the spirit, a flight after the unattainable. The death of religion comes with the repression of the high hope of adventure.
A. N. WHITEHEAD *Science and the Modern World*

13 Of the one light of Truth teach us to see in every religion a several ray.
Zoroastrian

REMEMBRANCE

14 Then a new king ascended the throne of Egypt, one who knew nothing of Joseph.
Ex. 1.8

15 Some there are who have left a name behind them/to be commemorated in story./There are others who are unremembered;/they are dead, and it is as though they had never existed.
Ecclus 44.8–9

16 Their bodies are buried in peace,/but their name lives for ever.
Ecclus 44.14

17 The tumult and the shouting dies;/The captains and the kings depart;/ Still stands Thine ancient sacrifice,/An humble and a contrite heart./Lord God of hosts, be with us yet,/Lest we forget—lest we forget!
RUDYARD KIPLING *Recessional*

REPENTANCE

18 When you are in distress and all these things come upon you, you will in days to

come turn back to the Lord your God and obey him. The Lord your God is a merciful God; he will never fail you nor destroy you, nor will he forget the covenant guaranteed by oath with your forefathers.
Deut. 4.30–31

1 I repent in dust and ashes.
Job 42.6

2 Turn back all of you by God's help;/ practise loyalty and justice/and wait always upon your God.
Hos. 12.6

3 There will be greater joy in heaven over one sinner who repents than over ninety-nine righteous people who do not need to repent.
Luke 15.7

4 'Here and now, sir, I give half my possessions to charity; and if I have cheated anyone, I am ready to repay him four times over.' Jesus said to him, 'Salvation has come to this house today!'
Luke 19.8–9

5 Repent then and turn to God, so that your sins may be wiped out.
Acts 3.19

6 For right as by the courtesy of God He forgets our sins when we repent, right so will He that we forget our sin, and all our heaviness, and all our doubtful dreads.
MOTHER JULIAN OF NORWICH *Revelations*

7 Repentance, I suppose, is nothing else than the sight, for a moment, of sin as God sees it.
W. M. MACGREGOR *Jesus Christ the Son of God*

RESURRECTION

8 Many of those who sleep in the dust of the earth will wake,/some to everlasting life/and some to the reproach of eternal abhorrence.
Dan. 12.2

9 Since we die for his laws, the King of the universe will raise us up to a life everlastingly made new.
2 Macc. 7.9

10 For if he had not been expecting the fallen to rise again, it would have been foolish and superfluous to pray for the dead.
2 Macc. 12.44

11 When they rise from the dead, men and women do not marry; they are like angels in heaven.
Mark 12.25

12 Our Lord has written the promise of the resurrection not in books alone, but in every leaf in springtime.
MARTIN LUTHER

13 The resurrection that awaits us beyond physical death will be but the glorious consummation of the risen life which already we have in Christ.
D. T. NILES

RESURRECTION OF CHRIST

14 If they do not listen to Moses and the prophets they will pay no heed even if someone should rise from the dead.
Luke 16.31

15 The story appeared to them to be nonsense, and they would not believe them.
Luke 24.11

16 Did we not feel our hearts on fire as he talked with us on the road and explained the scriptures to us?
Luke 24.32

17 He had been recognized by them at the breaking of the bread.
Luke 24.35

18 God raised him to life again, setting him free from the pangs of death, because it could not be that death should keep him in its grip.
Acts 2.24

1 Why is it considered incredible among you that God should raise dead men to life?
Acts 26.8

2 If Christ was not raised, then our gospel is null and void, and so is your faith.
1 Cor. 15.14

3 You believe in the resurrection, not because it is reported by the apostles, but because the resurrected One himself encounters you, the living Mediator.
EMIL BRUNNER *I Believe in the Living God*

4 I danced on a Friday/when the sky turned black;/It's hard to dance/with the devil on your back./They buried my body/and they thought I'd gone;/But I am the dance and I still go on:
Dance, then, wherever you may be;/I am the Lord of the Dance, said he,/And I'll lead you all, wherever you may be,/And I'll lead you all in the dance, said he.
SYDNEY CARTER *100 Hymns for Today*

5 Christ has turned all our sunsets into dawns.
CLEMENT OF ALEXANDRIA

6 Jesus Christ is risen today,/Our triumphant holy day,/Who did once, upon the Cross,/Suffer to redeem our loss.
LYRA DAVIDICA *Hymn*

7 Everywhere in the time process a principle of redemption is at work; but only in one cycle of events does the principle receive full expression. The death and Resurrection of Christ bring the inner principle of his whole career into focus and form the unique symbol of the redemption and sanctification of all time.
F. W. DILLISTONE *Christianity and Symbolism*

8 Shakespeare is dust, and will not come/To question from his Avon tomb,/And Socrates and Shelley keep/An Attic and Italian sleep . . . .
They see not. But, O Christians, who/Throng Holborn and Fifth Avenue,/May you not meet, in spite of death,/A traveller from Nazareth?
JOHN DRINKWATER *To and Fro about the City*

9 Jesus lives! thy terrors now/Can, O Death, no more appal us;/Jesus lives! by this we know/Thou, O grave, canst not enthral us.
CHRISTIAN FURCHTEGOTT GELLERT *Hymn*

10 The New Testament throbs and rings with the sense that the line between expectation and fulfilment has been crossed.
WILLIAM MANSON *Jesus and the Christian*

11 The birth and rapid rise of the Christian Church therefore remain an unsolved enigma for any historian who refuses to take seriously the only explanation offered by the Church itself.
C. F. D. MOULE *The Phenomenon of the New Testament*

12 It has never at any time been possible to fit the resurrection of Jesus into any world view except a world view of which it is the basis.
LESSLIE NEWBIGIN *Honest Religion for Secular Man*

13 The strife is o'er, the battle done;/Now is the Victor's triumph won;/O let the song of praise be sung,—/'Alleluia!'
G. P. DA PALESTRINA *Hymn*

14 Christian theology has never suggested that the 'fact' of Christ's resurrection could be known apart from faith.
ALAN RICHARDSON *History Sacred and Profane*

15 God raised up Jesus, not simply to give credence to man's immemorial hopes of life beyond the grave, but to shatter history and remake it by a cosmic, creative event, ushering in a new age and a new dimension of existence.
J. S. STEWART in *Asking Them Questions*

16 Blest morning, whose first dawning rays/Beheld the Son of God/Arise triumphant from the grave,/And leave His dark abode!
ISAAC WATTS *Hymn*

1 'Christ the Lord is risen today,'/Songs of men and angels say;/Raise your joys and triumphs high;/Sing, ye heavens, and, earth, reply./Love's redeeming work is done,/Fought the fight, the battle won;Lo! our Sun's eclipse is o'er;/Lo! He sets in blood no more.
CHARLES WESLEY *Hymn*

RETRIBUTION

2 Wherever hurt is done, you shall give life for life, eye for eye, tooth for tooth.
Ex. 21.23–24

3 Then Samson leaned forward with all his might, and the temple fell on the lords and on all the people who were in it. So the dead whom he killed at his death were more than those he had killed in his life.
Judg. 16.30

4 Israel sows the wind and reaps the whirlwind.
Hos. 8.7

5 Dig a pit and you will fall into it;/set a trap and you will be caught by it.
Ecclus. 27.26

6 We see divine retribution revealed from heaven and falling upon all the godless wickedness of men.
Rom. 1.18

7 Make no mistake about this: God is not to be fooled; a man reaps what he sows.
Gal. 6.7

REVELATION

8 We are no better than pots of earthenware to contain this treasure, and this proves that such transcendent power does not come from us, but is God's alone.
2 Cor. 4.7

9 To see a World in a grain of sand,/And a Heaven in a wild flower,/Hold Infinity in the palm of your hand,/And eternity in an hour.
WILLIAM BLAKE *Auguries of Innocence*

10 The first and most important thing we know about God is that we know nothing about him except what he himself makes known.
EMIL BRUNNER *Our Faith*

11 Blessed art Thou, O Lord, who hast revealed thyself in music, and granted me the love of it.
Contemporary Hebrew

12 Thus Man by his own strength to Heaven would soar;/And would not be obliged to God for more./Vain, wretched creature, how art thou misled/To think thy wit these God-like notions bred!/These truths are not the product of thy mind,/But dropped from heaven, and of a nobler kind./Reveal'd religion first inform'd thy sight,/And reason saw not till faith sprung the light.
JOHN DRYDEN *Religio Laici*

13 It is our revelation we have to preach, and not our religion.
P. T. FORSYTH

14 Every act formed by charity is a revelation of God. Every word of truth and love, every hand extended in kindness, echoes the inner life of the Trinity.
GABRIEL MORAN *Theology of Revelation*

15 It is Christ Himself, rather than any of the things which He did, who is the supreme miracle and the chief attestation of the truth of the biblical revelation.
ALAN RICHARDSON *Christian Apologetics*

16 The events of history as such do not themselves constitute a revelation; it is the prophetic interpretation of historical events which is the vehicle of special revelation in the sense in which the biblical and Christian tradition understands that conception. Where there are no prophets, there can be no special revelation.
ALAN RICHARDSON *Christian Apologetics*

1 We affirm, then, that unless all existence is a medium of Revelation, no particular Revelation is possible.
WILLIAM TEMPLE *Nature, Man and God*

2 The essential condition of effectual revelation is the coincidence of divinely controlled event and minds divinely illumined to read it aright.
WILLIAM TEMPLE Essay in *Revelation*

RICHES

3 Man, though he stands upright, is but a puff of wind,/he moves like a phantom;/ the riches he piles up are no more than vapour,/he does not know who will enjoy them.
Ps. 39.5–6

4 The rich have friends in plenty.
Prov. 14.20

5 Better a pittance with the fear of the Lord/than great treasure and trouble in its train.
Prov. 15.16

6 A good name is more to be desired than great riches.
Prov. 22.1

7 Do not store up for yourselves treasure on earth.
Matt. 6.19

8 Where your treasure is, there will your heart be also.
Matt. 6.21

9 It is easier for a camel to pass through the eye of a needle than for a rich man to enter the kingdom of God.
Matt. 19.24

10 What do superfluous riches profit in this world, when you find in them neither a succour in birth nor a defence against death? For without a covering are we born into the world, without provision we depart hence, and in the grave we have no inheritance.
ST AMBROSE *Epistles*

11 I cannot call riches better than the baggage of virtue; for as the baggage is to an army, so is riches to virtue; it cannot be spared nor left behind, but it hindereth the march.
FRANCIS BACON *Of Riches*

12 Theirs is an endless road, a hopeless maze, who seek for goods before they seek for God.
ST BERNARD OF CLAIRVAUX *De diligendo deo*

13 Ill fares the land, to hastening ills a prey,/ Where wealth accumulates, and men decay.
OLIVER GOLDSMITH *The Deserted Village*

14 Avarice breeds anger and blind desires, and is the fruitful mother of a countless spawn of sin.
Hindu saying

15 The evils of riches, to the Christian, are the evils of distraction (the distraction that keeps men from thinking about God), the evils of a false dependence on the created order, and a would-be security that fails to take account of the inevitable fragility of human destiny on this earth.
D. L. MUNBY *God and the Rich Society*

16 What does it matter how much you have? What you do not have amounts to far more.
SENECA

17 The assumption is that the attainment of material riches is the supreme object of human endeavour and the final criterion of human success. Such a philosophy, plausible, militant, and not indisposed, when hard pressed, to silence criticism by persecution, may triumph or may decline. What is certain is that it is the negation of any system of thought or morals which can, except by a metaphor, be described as Christian.
R. H. TAWNEY

18 I wonder'd much to see/That all my wealth should be/Confin'd in such a little room,/Yet hope for more I scarcely durst presume./It griev'd me sore/That such a scanty store/Should be my all:/

For I forgot my ease and health,/Nor did I think of hands or eyes,/Nor soul nor body prize;/I neither thought the sun,/Nor moon, nor stars, nor people, mine,/Though they did round about me shine;/And therefore was I quite undone.
THOMAS TRAHERNE

RIGHT: RIGHTEOUS

1 I will maintain the rightness of my cause, I will never give up;/so long as I live, I will not change.
Job 27.6

2 For thou, O Lord, wilt bless the righteous;/thou wilt hedge him round with favour as with a shield.
Ps. 5.12

3 O Lord, who may lodge in thy tabernacle?/Who may dwell on thy holy mountain?/The man of blameless life, who does what is right/and speaks the truth from his heart.
Ps. 15.1–2

4 I have been young and am now grown old,/and never have I seen a righteous man forsaken.
Ps. 37.25

5 The course of the righteous is like morning light, growing brighter till it is broad day.
Prov. 4.18

6 Righteousness raises a people to honour;/to do wrong is a disgrace to any nation.
Prov. 14.34

7 For right is right, since God is God,/And right the day must win;/To doubt would be disloyalty,/To falter would be sin.
FREDERICK WILLIAM FABER   *Hymn*

8 Lord, give us faith that right makes might.
ABRAHAM LINCOLN *Speeches and Letters*

SABBATH: SUNDAY

1 God blessed the seventh day and made it holy, because on that day he ceased from all the work he had set himself to do.
Gen. 2.3

2 The Sabbath was made for the sake of man and not man for the Sabbath.
Mark 2.27

3 Sunday clears away the rust of the whole week.
JOSEPH ADDISON *The Spectator*

4 What made these Sundays, the observance of which was absolutely uniform, so peculiarly trying was that I was not permitted the indulgence of any secular respite. I might not open a scientific book, or make a drawing, nor examine a specimen. I was not allowed to go into the road, except to proceed with my parents to the Room, nor to discuss worldly subjects at meals, nor to enter the little chamber where I kept my treasures. I was hotly and tightly dressed in black, all day long, as though ready at any moment to attend a funeral with decorum.
EDMUND GOSSE *Father and Son*

5 On the 13th of the same month he (Johnson) wrote in his journal the following scheme of life for Sunday:
'Having lived' (as he with tenderness of conscience expresses himself), 'not without an habitual reverence for the Sabbath yet without that attention to its religious duties which Christianity requires:
1. To rise early, and in order to do it, to go to sleep early on Saturday.
2. To use some extraordinary devotion in the morning.
3. To examine the tenour of my life, and particularly the last week; and to mark my advances in religion, or recession from it.
4. To read the scriptures methodically with such helps as are at hand.
5. To go to Church twice.
6. To read books of Divinity, either speculative or practical.
7. To instruct my family.

8. To wear off by meditation any worldly soil contracted in the week.'
SAMUEL JOHNSON Boswell's *Life of Johnson*

6 He said, he would not have Sunday kept with rigid severity and gloom, but with a gravity and simplicity of behaviour.
SAMUEL JOHNSON Boswell's *Life of Johnson*

7 Rest and success are fellows.
Proverb

8 As the heavy is the foundation of the light, so is repose the foundation of action.
Taoist saying

9 It is better to plough upon holy days, than to do nothing, or to do viciously.
JEREMY TAYLOR

10 Bright shadows of true rest! some shoots of bliss; Heaven once a week.
HENRY VAUGHAN *Sundays*

SACRAMENTS

11 The symbolic actions of former and present times, which because of their pertaining to divine things are called sacraments.
ST AUGUSTINE *Letters*

12 Whatever we see, wherever we look, whether we recognize it as true or not, we cannot touch or handle the things of earth and not, in that very moment, be confronted with the sacraments of heaven.
C. A. COULSON *Science and Christian Belief*

13 For mankind there are two unique sacraments which disclose the meaning and convey the experience of reality: they are the created universe and the person of Jesus Christ.
C. E. RAVEN

14 No ordinary meal—a sacrament awaits us/ On our tables daily spread,/For men are risking lives on sea and land/That we may dwell in safety and be fed.
Scottish prayer

1 When psalmist or prophet calls Israel to lift their eyes to the hills, or to behold how the heavens declare the glory of God, or to listen to that unbroken tradition which day passes to day and night to night, of the knowledge of the Creator, it is not proofs to doubting minds which he offers: it is spiritual nourishment to hungry souls. These are not arguments— they are sacraments.
SIR GEORGE ADAM SMITH *The Book of Isaiah*

SACRIFICE

2 The heroic three made their way through the Philistine lines and drew water from the well by the gate of Bethlehem and brought it to David. But David refused to drink it; he poured it out to the Lord and said. 'God forbid that I should do such a thing! Can I drink the blood of these men who risked their lives for it?'
2 Sam. 23.16–17

3 I will not offer to the Lord my God whole-offerings that have cost me nothing.
2 Sam. 24.24

4 I tell you this: there is no one who has given up home, or wife, brothers, parents, or children, for the sake of the kingdom of God, who will not be repaid many times over in this age, and in the age to come have eternal life.
Luke 18.29–30

5 Here we offer and present unto thee, O Lord, ourselves, our souls and bodies, to be a reasonable, holy, and lively sacrifice unto thee.
BOOK OF COMMON PRAYER From the *Order for Holy Communion*

SAINTS

6 A saint abroad, and a devil at home.
JOHN BUNYAN *The Pilgrim's Progress*

7 And Satan trembles when he sees/The weakest saint upon his knees.
WILLIAM COWPER and JOHN NEWTON *Olney Hymns*

8 For wherever a saint has dwelt, wherever a martyr has given his blood for the blood of Christ,/There is holy ground, and the sanctity shall not depart from it.
T. S. ELIOT *Murder in the Cathedral*

9 The tears of Saints more sweet by far/ Than all the songs of sinners are.
ROBERT HERRICK *Tears*

10 God creates out of *nothing.* Wonderful, you say. Yes, to be sure, but He does what is still more wonderful: He makes saints out of sinners.
SÖREN KIERKEGAARD *Journals*

11 The Blessed Francis, fearing that the people might take too much notice of this astonishing miracle, began saying funny things to make them laugh.
JOHN R. H. MOORMAN *The New Fioretti*

12 At times I have seen him (St Francis of Assisi) with my own eyes draw a stick across his arm in the guise of one playing the viol and sing in French praises of the Lord.
THOMAS OF CELANO

13 God deliver us from sullen saints!
ST TERESA OF AVILA

SALVATION

14 How can I repay the Lord/for all his gifts to me?/I will take in my hands the cup of salvation/and invoke the Lord by name./I will pay my vows to the Lord/ in the presence of all his people.
Ps. 116.12–14

15 If on your lips is the confession, 'Jesus is Lord', and in your heart the faith that God raised him from the dead, then you will find salvation.
Rom. 10.9

1 You must work out your own salvation in fear and trembling.
Phil. 2.12

2 May the strength of God pilot us./May the power of God preserve us./May the wisdom of God instruct us./May the hand of God protect us./May the way of God direct us./May the shield of God defend us./May the host of God guard us against the snares of evil and the temptations of the world./May Christ be with us./Christ before us./Christ in us./Christ over us./May Thy salvation, O Lord, be always ours this day and forever more.
ST PATRICK *Breastplate*

3 There is no expeditious road/To pack and label men for God,/And save them by the barrel-load.
FRANCIS THOMPSON *A Judgement in Heaven*

SCIENCE

4 When science has discovered something more/We shall be happier than we were before.
HILAIRE BELLOC *On the Benefit of the Electric Light*

5 Now the history of scientific advances has shown us clearly that any appeal to Divine Purpose, or any supernatural agency, to explain any phenomenon, is in fact only a concealed confession of ignorance, and a bar to genuine research.
J. D. BERNAL *Science and Ethics*

6 In science, we sometimes have convictions which we cherish, but cannot justify; we are influenced by some innate sense of the fitness of things.
SIR ARTHUR EDDINGTON

7 Most people say that it is the intellect which makes a great scientist. They are wrong: it is the character.
ALBERT EINSTEIN

8 Science without religion is lame, religion without science is blind.
ALBERT EINSTEIN *The World as I see it*

9 Science is not to be regarded merely as a store-house of facts to be used for material purposes, but as one of the great human endeavours to be ranked with arts and religion as the guide and expression of man's fearless quest for truth.
SIR RICHARD GREGORY

10 The over-witty notion of a Fool, who would fain turn topsy-turvy the whole Art of Astronomy.
MARTIN LUTHER on Copernicus

11 The Christmas message—which is also the Christian message—is 'Gloria in excelsis Deo' . . . . Glory to God in the highest and on earth peace among men of goodwill. This is not a bad definition of the aim of all true science; the aim of rejoicing in the splendid mysteries of the world and universe we live in, and of attempting so to understand those mysteries that we can improve our command over nature, improve our conditions of life and so ensure peace.
E. A. MILNE *Modern Cosmology and the Christian Idea of God*

12 At the present time only science has the vigour, and the authority of achievement, which is necessary to give them that fresh vivacious *joie de vivre* which captivates men's hearts and minds.
C. H. WADDINGTON *The Scientific Attitude*

SELF

13 What will a man gain by winning the whole world, at the cost of his true self?
Matt. 16.26

14 They valued their reputation with men rather than the honour which comes from God.
John 12.43

15 'I'm a self-made man, you know,' explained a certain magnate of modern business to Dr. Joseph Parker, 'who immediately replied, 'Sir, you have lifted a great load of responsibility from the Almighty.'
JOHN BAILLIE *Invitation to Pilgrimage*

1 God helps them that helps themselves.
BENJAMIN FRANKLIN *Poor Richard's Almanac*

2 We can destroy ourselves indeed, but we can destroy nothing but ourselves.
DENIS DE ROUGEMONT *La Part du Diable*

SELF-DISCIPLINE

3 Watch your step and save your life.
Prov. 16.17

4 (Temperance is) that action whereby the soul extricates itself from the love of lower beauty and wings its way to true stability and finds security in God!
ST AUGUSTINE

5 Where is temperance to be found if not in the life of Christ? Those alone are temperate who strive to imitate his life . . . whose life is the mirror of temperance.
ST BERNARD OF CLAIRVAUX

6 'All things are lawful for me, but I will not be brought under the power of anything,' saith St Paul; and to be perpetually longing and impatiently desirous of anything, so that a man cannot abstain from it, is to lose a man's liberty.
JEREMY TAYLOR *Holy Living*

7 Propound to thyself (if thou beest in a capacity) a constant rule of living, of eating, and drinking: which though it may not be fit to observe scrupulously, lest it become a snare to thy conscience, or endanger thy health upon every accidental violence: yet let not thy rule be broken often nor much, but upon great necessity and in small degrees.
JEREMY TAYLOR *Holy Living*

8 Where temperance, self-control, is perfect, no impulse, however assertive, no feeling , however strong, no endowment, however conspicuous, finds play without the sanction of that central ruling power, throned in the soul, which represents the true self.
B. F. WESTCOTT

9 The Christian is a competitor in a life-long struggle for an eternal prize.
B. F. WESTCOTT *Lessons from Work*

10 He that commands others is not so much as free, if he doth not govern himself. The greatest performance in the life of man is the government of his spirit.
BENJAMIN WHICHCOTE *Moral and Religious Aphorisms*

SELFISHNESS

11 Satan answered the Lord, 'Skin for skin! There is nothing the man will grudge to save himself. But stretch out your hand and touch his bone and his flesh, and see if he will not curse you to your face.'
Job 2.4–5

12 Pluck out self-love as with the hand you pluck the autumn water-lily, and you will set your heart on the perfect path of peace.
Buddhist saying

13 The foolish man is full of selfishness; he toils day and night, greedy for wealth, as if he will never grow old, or die.
Jainist saying

14 The region of man's life is a spiritual region. God, his friends, his neighbours, his brothers all, is the wide world in which alone his spirit can find room. Himself is his dungeon.
GEORGE MACDONALD *Unspoken Sermons*

15 He who hates not in himself his self-love and that instinct which leads him to make himself a God, is indeed blinded.
BLAISE PASCAL

16 There is no room for God in him who is full of himself.
Service of the Heart (Jewish)

17 One suffers most who is most selfish.
Taoist saying

SELF-KNOWLEDGE

1 What use do I put my Soul to? It is a very serviceable question this, and should frequently be put.
MARCUS AURELIUS

2 I thank Thee, Lord, for knowing me better than I know myself, and for letting me know myself better than others know me.
ABU BEKR (Muslim)

3 Be ye islands unto yourselves, be a refuge unto yourselves, seek not for refuge in others.
Parinibbana Sutta (Buddhist)

4 Know then thyself, presume not God to scan;/The proper study of mankind is Man.
ALEXANDER POPE *Essay on Man*

5 Self-reverence, self-knowledge, self-control,/These three alone lead life to sovereign power.
LORD TENNYSON *Oenone*

6 An humble knowledge of thyself is a surer way to God than a deep search after learning.
THOMAS À KEMPIS *The Imitation of Christ*

7 Christ will come unto thee, and show thee his own consolation, if thou prepare for him a worthy mansion within thee.
THOMAS À KEMPIS *The Imitation of Christ*

8 The highest and most profitable reading is the true knowledge and consideration of ourselves.
THOMAS À KEMPIS *The Imitation of Christ*

SELF-PITY

9 Hezekiah turned his face to the wall and offered this prayer to the Lord: 'O Lord, remember how I have lived before thee, faithful and loyal in thy service, always doing what was good in thine eyes.'
2 Kings 20.2–3

10 Pity me, pity me, you that are my friends;/ for the hand of God has touched me.
Job. 19.21

11 I now have come to feel that there is hardly anything more radically mean and deteriorating than, as it were, *sulking through the inevitable*, and just simply counting the hours till it passes.
BARON F. VON HÜGEL *Selected Letters*

SENSE

12 A blessing on your good sense.
1 Sam. 25.33

13 Does my sense not warn me when my words are wild?
Job 6.30

14 A man without sense despises others,/ but a man of understanding holds his peace.
Prov. 11.12

15 Like a gold ring in a pig's snout/is a beautiful woman without good sense.
Prov. 11.22

16 If a man is wise in the conduct of his own life,/his good sense can be trusted when he speaks.
Ecclus. 37.22

SERVICE

17 When you have carried out all your orders, you should say, 'We are servants and deserve no credit; we have only done our duty.'
Luke 17.10

18 Whatever you are doing, put your whole heart into it, as if you were doing it for the Lord, and not for men.
Col. 3.23

19 Vocation is not the exceptional prerogative of a few specially good or gifted people . . . All men and women are called to serve God.
F. R. BARRY *Vocation and Ministry*

1 In Jesus the service of God and the service of the least of the brethren were one.
DIETRICH BONHOEFFER *The Cost of Discipleship*

2 When a man turns to God desiring to serve Him, God directs his attention to the world and its need.
EMIL BRUNNER *The Divine Imperative*

3 Lord, make me an instrument of Thy peace. Where there is hatred, let me sow love. Where there is injury, pardon. Where there is doubt, faith. Where there is despair, hope. Where there is darkness, light. Where there is sadness, joy.

O Divine Master, grant that I may not so much seek to be consoled as to console; to be understood, as to understand; to be loved, as to love; for it is in giving that we receive, it is in pardoning that we are pardoned, and it is in dying that we are born to Eternal Life.
ST FRANCIS OF ASSISI

4 Great works do not always lie in our way, but every moment we may do little ones excellently, that is, with great love.
ST FRANCIS DE SALES *On the Love of God*

5 Not with the hope of gaining aught,/Not seeking a reward;/But as thyself hast loved me,/O ever-loving Lord.
ST FRANCIS XAVIER

6 Through our calling closely knitted,/daily to your praise committed,/for a life of service fitted,/let us now your love proclaim.
FRED KAAN *100 Hymns for Today*

7 There came to me as I awoke, the thought that I must not accept this happiness as a matter of course, but must give something in return for it . . . I settled with myself before I got up, that I would consider myself justified in living till I was thirty for science and art, in order to devote myself from that time forward to the direct service of humanity.
ALBERT SCHWEITZER *My Life and Thought*

8 O good old man! how well in thee appears/The constant service of the antique world,/ When service sweat for duty, not for meed!/Thou art not for the fashion of these times,/Where none will sweat but for promotion,/And having that, do choke their service up/Even with the having: it is not so with thee.
WILLIAM SHAKESPEARE *As You Like It*

9 If she (Martha) had been like the Magdalene, rapt in contemplation, there would have been no-one to give to eat to this divine Guest.
ST TERESA OF AVILA *The Way of Perfection*

10 When thou seest thy brother, thou seest thy Lord.
TERTULLIAN *De Oratione*

11 What is service?—the rent we pay for our room on earth.
TOC H

SEX

12 Give me chastity . . . but not yet.
ST AUGUSTINE *Confessions*

13 In the earlier periods of sexual obsession a lot of its force lay just in the fact that sexual enjoyment is fun, and gains a zest from the prohibitions of its indiscriminate exercise by a tradition of customs and morals. Departures from the tradition were dashing, daring and naughty escapades. Now, this is no longer so. Venereal experiences outside marriage are either casual, or invested with a solemn prophylactic significance, on the grounds that suppression produces mental disease.
V. A. DEMANT *Christian Sex Ethics*

14 The practice of Christian sex ethics is not to be recovered by preaching the ethics. . . . A renewed, creative and fully personal fulfilment of sexuality will only come from people who are aware of the pressure of a debilitated civilisation and, without contracting out of it, can put down roots in an alternative culture. Christianity is such a culture.
V. A. DEMANT *Christian Sex Ethics*

1 At a time when a large part of mankind is beginning to discard Christianity, it is worth while to understand clearly why it was originally accepted. It was accepted in order to escape at last from the brutality of antiquity. As soon as we discard it, licentiousness returns, as is impressively exemplified by life in our modern cities.
C. G. JUNG

SILENCE

2 Even a fool, if he holds his peace, is thought wise;/keep your mouth shut and show your good sense.
Prov. 17.28

3 Never remain silent when a word might put things right.
Ecclus. 4.23

4 There was silence in heaven.
Rev. 8.1

5 For the most part we are much too busy living and thinking to have leisure to be silent and see.
AUROBINDO (Hindu)

6 To forbear replying to an unjust reproach, and overlook it with a generous or, if possible, with an entire neglect of it, is one of the most heroic acts of a great mind.
JOSEPH ADDISON *The Tatler*

7 Lord, the Scripture says: 'There is a time for silence and a time for speech'. Saviour, teach me the silence of humility, the silence of wisdom, the silence of love, the silence of perfection, the silence that speaks without words, the silence of faith.

Lord, teach me to silence my own heart that I may listen to the gentle movement of the Holy Spirit within me and sense the depths which are of God.
Frankfurt prayer (Sixteenth century)

8 For thy great gift, O Father,/We thank Thee today—/The gift of Silence:/For the rich, warm, generous silence/We thank Thee,/Wherein our souls,/Stunted and shrivelled and starved/In the arid desert of everyday hurry and strain,/May rest, and quietly grow, and expand/Upward to Thee.
JOHN S. HOYLAND

9 Much silence and a good disposition, there are no two works better than these.
MUHAMMAD *Hadith* (Muslim)

SIMPLICITY

10 Simple and sincere minds are never more than half mistaken.
JOSEPH JOUBERT

11 Pray God, keep us simple.
W. M. THACKERAY

12 Seek simplicity; and distrust it.
A. N. WHITEHEAD *Process and Reality*

SIN

13 Your sin will find you out.
Num. 32.23

14 Who is aware of his unwitting sins?/ Cleanse me of any secret fault./Hold back thy servant also from sins of self-will,/lest they get the better of me.
Ps. 19.12–13

15 Against thee, thee only, I have sinned/ and done what displeases thee.
Ps. 51.4

16 O God, thou knowest how foolish I am,/ and my guilty deeds are not hidden from thee.
Ps. 69.5

17 Let none of those who look to thee be shamed on my account,/O Lord God of Hosts;/Let none who seek thee be humbled through my fault.
Ps. 69.6

1 If thou, Lord, shouldest keep account of sins,/who, O Lord, could hold up his head?
Ps. 130.3

2 Six things the Lord hates,/seven things are detestable to him:/a proud eye, a false tongue,/hands that shed innocent blood,/a heart that forges thoughts of mischief,/and feet that run swiftly to do evil,/a false witness telling a pack of lies,/and one who stirs up quarrels between brothers.
Prov. 6.16–19

3 Who can say, 'I have a clear conscience'?
Prov. 20.9

4 Though your sins are scarlet,/they may become white as snow;/though they are dyed crimson,/they may yet be like wool.
Isa. 1.18

5 We all became like a man who is unclean/and all our righteous deeds like a filthy rag.
Isa. 64.6

6 The fathers have eaten sour grapes/and the children's teeth are set on edge.
Jer. 31.29

7 The soul that sins shall die.
Ezek. 18.4

8 Heavier than the darkness was the burden each was to himself.
Wisd. 17.21

9 Handle pitch and it will make you dirty.
Ecclus. 13.1

10 'Why is it that your master eats with tax-gatherers and sinners?' Jesus heard it and said, 'It is not the healthy that need a doctor, but the sick.'
Matt. 9.11–12

11 Out of a man's heart come evil thoughts, acts of fornication, of theft, murder, adultery, ruthless greed, and malice; fraud, indecency, envy, slander, arrogance, and folly; these evil things all come from inside, and they defile the man.
Mark 7.21–23

12 O God, have mercy on me, sinner that I am.
Luke 18.13

13 Because they have not seen fit to acknowledge God, he has given them up to their own depraved reason.
Rom. 1.28

14 All alike have sinned, and are deprived of the divine splendour.
Rom. 3.23

15 What I do is not what I want to do, but what I detest.
Rom. 7.15

16 The good which I want to do, I fail to do; but what I do is the wrong which is against my will.
Rom. 7.19

17 In my inmost self I delight in the law of God, but I perceive that there is in my bodily members a different law.
Rom. 7.22–23

18 Miserable creature that I am, who is there to rescue me out of this body doomed to death?
Rom. 7.24

19 I myself, subject to God's law as a rational being, am yet, in my unspiritual nature, a slave to the law of sin.
Rom. 7.25

20 Bad company is the ruin of a good character.
1 Cor. 15.33

21 Christ Jesus came into the world to save sinners.
1 Tim. 1.15

22 He who has not felt what *sin* is in the Old Testament knows little what *grace* is in the New. He who has not trembled in Moses, and wept in David, and wondered in Isaiah, will rejoice little in Matthew, rest little in John.
R. W. BARBOUR *Thoughts*

1 It will immediately appear that vice cannot be the happiness, but must upon the whole be the misery, of such a creature as man; a moral, an accountable agent.
JOSEPH BUTLER *Sermons*

2 What history does is to uncover Man's universal sin.
HERBERT BUTTERFIELD *Christianity and History*

3 We should strengthen ourselves against these failings: neglect of godliness; study without understanding; failure to act up to what we believe to be right; inability to change bad habits.
CONFUCIUS

4 A dreadful matter is sin, and disorder of life is the soul's worst sickness ... sin is evil of man's own choosing, springing from free-will.
CYRIL OF JERUSALEM *Catechetical Lectures*

5 How many men sin over the sins of their youth again in their age, by a sinful delight in remembering those sins, and a sinful desire that their bodies were not past them?
JOHN DONNE *Fifty Sermons*

6 Let us remember for our consolation that we never perceive our sins till we begin to cure them.
F. DE LA M. FÉNELON *Letters and Reflections*

7 It is not the sins that damn but the sin into which sins settle down.
P. T. FORSYTH

8 History ... is indeed little more than the register of the crimes, follies and misfortunes of mankind.
EDWARD GIBBON *Decline and Fall of the Roman Empire*

9 For if we never fell, we should not know how feeble and how wretched we are of our self, and also we should not fully know that marvellous love of our Maker.
MOTHER JULIAN OF NORWICH *Revelations of Divine Love*

10 In conversation be sincere;/Keep conscience as the noontide clear;/Think how all-seeing God thy ways/And all thy secret thoughts surveys.
THOMAS KEN *Hymn*

11 If you follow an earthly will, every step you take is a departure from God, till you become as incapable of God and the life of God as the animals of this world.
WILLIAM LAW *The Way to Divine Knowledge*

12 As Chesterton pointed out, the Fall of Man is only the banana-skin joke carried to cosmic proportions.
MALCOLM MUGGERIDGE *Jesus Rediscovered*

13 *If* there be a God, *since* there is a God, the human race is implicated in some terrible aboriginal calamity. It is out of joint with the purposes of its Creator.
CARDINAL NEWMAN *Apologia pro Vita Sua*

14 O Thou who man of baser earth didst make/And who with Eden didst devise the snake,/For all the sin wherewith the face of Man/Is blackened, Man's forgiveness give—and take!
OMAR KHAYYAM *The Rubaiyat*

15 It is no disgrace that the soiling of the day's life affects our souls; it is disgrace if we suffer it to remain uncleansed and accept the defilement. So we ask God for cleansing from 'the dust of the way'.
GEORGE S. STEWART *The Lower Levels of Prayer*

16 My sins are not scarlet, they are grey—all grey.
WILLIAM TEMPLE

17 I never heard any speak ill of me but I saw plainly it came short of what was true; for though not in those very particulars, I have offended God in many others.
ST TERESA OF AVILA *The Way of Perfection*

SLANDER

18 I tell you this: no sin, no slander, is beyond forgiveness for men; but whoever

slanders the Holy Spirit can never be forgiven.
Mark 3.28–29

1 My duty towards my neighbour is . . . to keep my tongue from evil-speaking, lying and slandering.
BOOK OF COMMON PRAYER *The Catechism*

2 Whispered insinuations are the rhetoric of the devil.
J. W. VON GOETHE

3 It is unworthy of a Muslim to injure another's reputation, to curse anyone, to abuse anyone, or to talk vainly.
The Sayings of Muhammad

4 Who steals my purse steals trash; 'tis something, nothing;/'Twas mine, 'tis his, and has been slave to thousands/But he that filches from me my good name/Robs me of that which not enriches him/And makes me poor indeed.
WILLIAM SHAKESPEARE *Othello*

5 The slanderous tongue kills three; the slandered, the slanderer, and him who listens to the slander.
The Talmud

6 Slander, meanest spawn of hell—/And women's slander is the worst.
LORD TENNYSON *The Letters*

SLEEP

7 Sweet is the sleep of the labourer.
Eccles. 5.12

8 Oh sleep! it is a gentle thing,/Beloved from pole to pole./To Mary Queen the praise be given!/She sent the gentle sleep from Heaven,/That slid into my soul.
S. T. COLERIDGE *The Ancient Mariner*

9 I don't like the man who doesn't sleep, says God./Sleep is the friend of man./Sleep is the friend of God./Sleep is perhaps the most beautiful thing I have created./And I myself rested on the seventh day./ He whose heart is pure,

sleeps. And he who sleeps has a pure heart.
CHARLES PÉGUY *Basic Verities*

SON OF MAN

10 I was still watching in visions of the night and I saw one like a man coming with the clouds of heaven; he approached the Ancient in Years and was presented to him. Sovereignty and glory and kingly power were given to him, so that all people and nations of every language should serve him.
Dan. 7.13–14

11 Foxes have their holes, the birds their roosts; but the Son of Man has nowhere to lay his head.
Matt. 8.20

12 When the Son of Man comes, will he find faith on earth?
Luke 18.8

13 I can see the Son of Man standing at God's right hand.
Acts 7.56

14 'Hereafter ye shall see the Son of man seated at the right hand of power.' The hereafter refers to their seeing. He Himself sees now. He is conscious of being in a very real sense at the right hand of power now. He is with God now; the victory is His now.
H. H. FARMER *The Healing Cross*

SORROW

15 You will bring down my grey hairs in sorrow to the grave.
Gen. 42.38

16 When he heard the woman's story, the king rent his clothes. He was walking along the wall at the time, and when the people looked, they saw that he had sackcloth underneath, next to his skin.
2 Kings 6.30

1 Turn to me and show me thy favour,/ for I am lonely and oppressed./Relieve the sorrows of my heart/and bring me out of my distress.
Ps. 25.16–17

2 By the rivers of Babylon we sat down and wept/when we remembered Zion.
Ps. 137.1

3 Why did I come forth from the womb/to know only sorrow and toil,/to end my days in shame?
Jer. 20.18

SPIRIT

4 A man's spirit may sustain him in sickness,/but if the spirit is wounded, who can mend it?
Prov. 18.14

5 The wind blows where it wills; you hear the sound of it, but you do not know where it comes from, or where it is going. So with everyone who is born from spirit.
John 3.8

6 God is spirit, and those who worship him must worship in spirit and in truth.
John 4.24

7 The spirit cannot die—in no circumstances, under no torment, despite whatever calumnies, in no bleak places.
FRANZ MARC

STARS

8 The stars fought from heaven,/the stars in their courses fought against Sisera.
Judg. 5.20

9 When the stars threw down their spears,/ And water'd heaven with their tears,/ Did he smile his work to see?/Did he who made the lamb make thee?
WILLIAM BLAKE *Songs of Experience: The Tiger*

10 Two things fill the mind with ever new and increasing wonder and awe—the starry heavens above me and the moral law within me.
IMMANUEL KANT *Critique of Practical Reason*

11 Men at some time are masters of their fates:/The fault, dear Brutus, is not in our stars,/But in ourselves, that we are underlings.
WILLIAM SHAKESPEARE *Julius Caesar*

STRENGTH

12 The Lord will give strength to his people;/ the Lord will bless his people with peace.
Ps. 29.11

13 If your strength fails on a lucky day,/how helpless will you be on a day of disaster!
Prov. 24.10

14 In stillness and in staying quiet, there lies your strength.
Isa. 30.15

15 Victory does not depend on numbers; strength comes from Heaven alone.
1 Macc. 3.19

16 I am well content, for Christ's sake, with weakness, contempt, persecution, hardship, and frustration; for when I am weak, then I am strong.
2 Cor. 12.10

17 I have strength for anything through him who gives me power.
Phil. 4.13

18 The Lord stood by me and lent me strength.
2 Tim. 4.17

19 I count life just a stuff/To try the soul's strength on.
ROBERT BROWNING *In a Balcony*

SUFFERING

1 For seven days and seven nights they sat beside him on the ground, and none of them said a word to him; for they saw that his suffering was very great.
Job 2.13

2 Why should the sufferer be born to see the light?/Why is life given to men who find it so bitter?
Job 3.20

3 The arrows of the Almighty find their mark in me,/and their poison soaks into my spirit.
Job 6.4

4 I reckon that the sufferings we now endure bear no comparison with the splendour, as yet unrevealed, which is in store for us.
Rom. 8.18

5 For the wound which is borne in God's way brings a change of heart too salutary to regret.
2 Cor. 7.10

6 What credit is there in fortitude when you have done wrong and are beaten for it? But when you have behaved well and suffer for it, your fortitude is a fine thing in the sight of God.
1 Pet. 2.20

7 It is better to suffer for well-doing if such should be the will of God, than for doing wrong. For Christ also died for our sins once and for all. He, the just, suffered for the unjust, to bring us to God.
1 Pet. 3.17–18

8 We commend to thy fatherly goodness all those, who are any ways afflicted, or distressed, in mind, body, or estate.
BOOK OF COMMON PRAYER From the *Prayer for all Conditions of Men*

9 Watch Thou, dear Lord, with those who wake, or watch, or weep to-night, and give Thine angels charge over those who sleep.

Tend Thy sick ones, O Lord Christ; rest Thy weary ones; bless Thy dying ones; soothe Thy suffering ones; shield Thy joyous ones; and all for Thy love's sake.
ST AUGUSTINE

10 It is infinitely easier to suffer with others than to suffer alone. It is infinitely easier to suffer as public heroes than to suffer apart and in ignominy. It is infinitely easier to suffer physical death than to endure spiritual suffering.
DIETRICH BONHOEFFER *Letters and Papers from Prison*

11 To love sufferings and afflictions for the love of God is the highest point of most holy charity; for in this there is nothing lovable save the love of God only.
ST FRANCIS DE SALES *On the Love of God*

12 Whenever pain is so borne as to be prevented from breeding bitterness or any other evil fruit, a contribution is made to rescuing God's creation from the devil's grip.
LEONARD HODGSON *The Doctrine of Atonement*

13 But men at whiles are sober/And think by fits and starts,/And if they think, they fasten/Their hands upon their hearts.
A. E. HOUSMAN *A Shropshire Lad*

14 I wish you could convince yourself that God is often nearer to us, and more effectually present with us, in sickness than in health.
BROTHER LAWRENCE *The Practice of the Presence of God*

15 Christ has given us an example, that we may follow in His steps. He went through far more, infinitely more, than we can be called to suffer. Our brethren have gone through much more; and they seem to encourage us by their success, and to sympathize in our essay. Now it is our turn.
CARDINAL NEWMAN *Sermons*

16 Shut out suffering, and you see only one side of this strange and fearful thing, the

life of man. Brightness and happiness and rest—that is not life. It is only one side of life. Christ saw both sides.

F. W. ROBERTSON *Sermons*

1 It is remarkable with what Christian fortitude and resignation we can bear the suffering of other folks.

JONATHAN SWIFT

2 Grant that I may suffer like a Christian and not grieve like an unbeliever;—that I may receive troubles as a punishment due to my past offences, as an exercise of my faith and patience and humility,—and as a trial of my obedience;—and that I may improve all my afflictions to the good of my soul and Thy glory.

BISHOP THOMAS WILSON

TAUNTS

1 (Goliath) said to David, 'Am I a dog that you come out against me with sticks?'
1 Sam. 17.43

2 Who has the king of Israel come out against? What are you pursuing? A dead dog, a mere flea.
1 Sam. 24.14

3 'Is it peace, you Zimri, you murderer of your master?'
2 Kings 9.31

4 No doubt you are perfect men/and absolute wisdom is yours!
Job 12.2

TEMPTATION

5 God keeps faith, and he will not allow you to be tested above your powers, but when the test comes he will at the same time provide a way out, by enabling you to sustain it.
1 Cor. 10.13

6 Lord, we beseech thee, grant thy people grace to withstand the temptations of the world, the flesh, and the devil, and with pure hearts and minds to follow thee the only God; through Jesus Christ our Lord.
BOOK OF COMMON PRAYER *Collect for the Eighteenth Sunday after Trinity*

7 Christian life means a walking; it goes by steps. There is a straight fence run for us between right and wrong. There is no sitting on that fence. No; only walking, one side or other. You can hardly look across without stepping through.
ROBERT W. BARBOUR *Thoughts*

8 Lord, often have I thought with myself, I will sin but this one sin more, and then I will repent of it, and of all the rest of my sins together. So foolish was I and ignorant. As if I should be more able to pay my debts when I owe more; or as if I should say, I will wound my friend once again, and then I will lovingly shake hands with him: but what if my friend will not shake hands with me?
THOMAS FULLER

9 It is one thing to be tempted, another thing to fall.
WILLIAM SHAKESPEARE *Measure for Measure*

10 We must not be surprised that we are tempted. We are placed here to be proved by temptations. Everything is temptation to us.
F. DE LA M. FÉNELON *Letters and Reflections*

11 I can resist everything except temptation.
OSCAR WILDE *Lady Windermere's Fan*

THANKSGIVING

12 Offer to God the sacrifice of thanksgiving/ and pay your vows to the Most High.
Ps. 50.14

13 Give thanks whatever happens.
1 Thess. 5.18

14 We bless thee for our creation, preservation, and all the blessings of this life; but above all, for thine inestimable love in the redemption of the world by our Lord Jesus Christ; for the means of grace, and for the hope of glory.
BOOK OF COMMON PRAYER From the *General Thanksgiving*

15 Some people always sigh in thanking God.
ELIZABETH BARRETT BROWNING *Aurora Leigh*

16 And still, O Lord, to me impart/An innocent and grateful heart.
S. T. COLERIDGE

17 Praised be thou, O Lord, that our spirits are comfortable, though our present condition is as it is.
OLIVER CROMWELL

1 Now thank we all our God,/With heart and hands and voices,/Who wondrous things hath done,/In whom His world rejoices,—/Who, from our mothers' arms,/Hath blessed us on our way/With countless gifts of love,/And still is ours to-day.
MARTIN RINKART *Hymn*

2 We ought all to make an effort to act on our first thoughts and let our unspoken gratitude find expression. Then there will be more sunshine in the world, and more power to work for what is good.
ALBERT SCHWEITZER *Memories of Childhood and Youth*

3 It is not sight a jewel? Is not hearing a treasure? Is not speech a glory? O my Lord pardon my ingratitude, and pity my dullness who am not sensible of these gifts.
THOMAS TRAHERNE

4 Some persons grumble because God placed thorns among roses. Why not thank God he placed roses among thorns?
Untraced

5 Let us, therefore, be thankful for health and a competence and, above all, for a quiet conscience.
ISAAK WALTON *The Compleat Angler*

THOUGHTS

6 May all that I say and think be acceptable to thee,/O Lord, my rock and my reedeemer!
Ps. 19.14

7 A perishable body weighs down the soul, and its frame of clay burdens the mind so full of thoughts.
Wisd. 9.15

8 All that is true, all that is noble, all that is just and pure, all that is lovable and gracious, whatever is excellent and admirable—fill all your thoughts with these things.
Phil. 4.8

9 Whether he walk or stand or sit or lie,/Whoso thinks thoughts of ill or worldly things,/He, gone astray and by delusion blinded,/Can never reach Supreme Enlightenment.
Whether he walk or stand or sit or lie,/Whoso, controlling thought, doth take delight/In ceasing from all thought, that brother sure/Is fit to win Supreme Enlightenement.
Book of the Numerical Sayings (Buddhist)

10 This mind of mine went formerly wandering about as it liked, but now I hold it in, as a rider who holds the hook holds in the furious elephant.
Dhammapada (Buddhist)

11 Art is the expression of the profoundest thoughts in the simplest way.
ALBERT EINSTEIN

12 It is thoughts of God's thinking which we need to set us right and, remember, they are not as our thoughts.
W. M. MACGREGOR *Jesus Christ the Son of God*

13 When the first spark of thought appeared on the earth, life found it had brought into the world a power capable of criticizing it and judging it.
P. TEILHARD DE CHARDIN *The Phenomenon of Man*

TIME

14 For everything its season, and for every activity under heaven its time: /a time to be born and a time to die;/a time to plant and a time to uproot;/a time to kill and a time to heal;/a time to pull down and a time to build up;/a time to weep and a time to laugh;/a time for mourning and a time for dancing;/a time to scatter stones and a time to gather them;/a time to embrace and a time to refrain from embracing;/a time to seek and a time to lose;/a time to keep and a time to throw away;/a time to tear and a time to mend;/a time for silence and a time for speech;/a time to love and a time to hate;/a time for war and a time for peace.
Eccl. 3.1–8

1 What then is time? If no one asks of me, I know; if I wish to explain to him who asks, I know not.
ST AUGUSTINE *Confessions*

2 Lives of great men all remind us/We can make our lives sublime,/And, departing, leave behind us/Footprints on the sands of time.
HENRY WADSWORTH LONGFELLOW *A Psalm of Life*

3 O! call back yesterday, bid time return.
WILLIAM SHAKESPEARE *Richard II*

4 Time, like an ever-rolling stream,/Bears all its sons away.
ISAAC WATTS *Hymn*

TROUBLE

5 Man is born to trouble, as surely as birds fly upwards.
Job 5.7

6 When I lie down, I think,/'When will it be day that I may rise?'
Job 7.4

7 My thoughts today are resentful,/for God's hand is heavy on me in my trouble.
Job 23.2

8 Here was a poor wretch who cried to the Lord;/he heard him and saved him from all his troubles.
Ps. 34.6

9 The good man's misfortunes may be many,/the Lord delivers him out of them all.
Ps. 34.19

10 Oh that I had the wings of a dove/to fly away and be at rest!
Ps. 55.6

11 I shall remain at Ephesus until Whitsuntide, for a great opportunity has opened for effective work, and there is much opposition.
1 Cor. 16.8–9

12 The Arlanzon had to be crossed. The bridges had been carried away by the flood and there were only makeshift footbridges. The horrified innkeeper begged Teresa to wait a few days until the crossing should be feasible, but she was determined to go on . . . .

God had said to her: 'When have I failed thee?' He did not fail her in the midst of these perils.

Those who were on the bank saw her carriage swerve and stop as it hung over the torrent: the Foundress jumped out into the water which came half-way up her legs, she was not very agile and hurt herself. As always, her cry was a calling upon God: this time she complained: 'Lord, amid so many ills this comes on top of all the rest!'

The Voice answered her: 'Teresa, that is how I treat my friends.'

'Ah my God! That is why you have so few of them.'
M. AUCLAIR *St Teresa of Avila*

13 I never knew any man in my life who could not bear another's misfortunes perfectly like a Christian.
ALEXANDER POPE *Thoughts on Various Subjects*

TRUTH

14 Truth spoken stands firm for ever,/but lies live only for a moment.
Prov. 12.19

15 Buy truth, never sell it.
Prov. 23.23

16 Truth stumbles in the market-place.
Isa. 59.14

17 Speak the truth to each other, administer true and sound justice in the city gate.
Zech. 8.16

18 Truth conquers all.
1 Esd. 3.12

1 Fight to the death for truth,/and the Lord God will fight on your side.
Ecclus. 4.28

2 Refuse ever to tell a lie.
Ecclus. 7.13

3 You shall know the truth, and the truth will set you free.
John 8.32

4 Pilate said, 'What is truth?'
John 18.38

5 God must be true though every man living were a liar.
Rom. 3.4

6 Let us speak the truth in love.
Eph. 4.15

7 Fulfil now, O Lord, the desires and petitions of thy servants, as may be most expedient for them; granting us in this world knowledge of thy truth, and in the world to come life everlasting.
BOOK OF COMMON PRAYER From the *Prayer of St Chrysostom*

8 'What is truth?' said jesting Pilate, and would not stay for an answer.
FRANCIS BACON *Of Truth*

9 The commandment of absolute truthfulness is really only another name for the fullness of discipleship.
DIETRICH BONHOEFFER *The Cost of Discipleship*

10 To the question, 'what is a primrose?' several valid answers may be given. One person says:/'A primrose by the river's brim/A yellow primrose was to him,/And it was nothing more.'/Just that, and no more. Another person, the scientist, says 'a primrose is a delicately balanced biochemical mechanism, requiring potash, phosphates, nitrogen and water in definite proportions.' A third person says 'a primrose is God's promise of spring.' All three descriptions are correct.
C. A. COULSON *Science and Christian Belief*

11 It is more from carelessness about truth than from intentional lying, that there is so much falsehood in the world.
SAMUEL JOHNSON Boswell's *Life of Johnson*

12 What is true in the lamplight is not always true in the sunlight.
JOSEPH JOUBERT

13 'Beauty is truth, truth beauty,'—that is all/Ye know on earth, and all ye need to know.
JOHN KEATS *Ode on a Grecian Urn*

14 Truth is given, not to be contemplated, but to be done. Life is an action, not a thought.
F. W. ROBERTSON *Sermons*

15 To thine own self be true,/And it must follow, as the night the day,/Thou canst not then be false to any man.
WILLIAM SHAKESPEARE *Hamlet*

16 Lie not at all, neither in a little thing nor a great, neither in the substance nor in the circumstance, neither in word nor deed: that is, pretend not what is false, cover not what is true.
JEREMY TAYLOR

UNBELIEF

1 Mock on, mock on, Voltaire, Rousseau;/
Mock on, mock on; 'tis all in vain!/You
throw the sand against the wind,/And the
wind blows it back again.
WILLIAM BLAKE *Mock on*

2 Just when we're safest, there's a sunset-
touch,/A fancy from a flower-bell, some
one's death,/A chorus-ending from Euri-
pides,—/And that's enough for fifty
hopes and fears . . . /The grand Perhaps!
ROBERT BROWNING *Bishop Blougram's
Apology*

3 My head is with Spinoza but my heart is
with Paul and John.
S. T. COLERIDGE

4 Blind unbelief is sure to err,/And scan his
work in vain;/God is his own interpreter,/
And he will make it plain.
WILLIAM COWPER *Light Shining out of
Darkness*

UNDERSTANDING

5 But the spirit of God himself is in man,/
and the breath of the Almighty gives him
understanding.
Job 32.8

6 I will light a lamp of understanding in
your mind, which will not go out until
you have finished all that you are to
write.
2 Esd. 14.25

7 For it is not length of life and number of
years which bring the honour due to
age; if men have understanding, they have
grey hairs enough.
Wisd. 4.8–9

8 Understanding is the reward of faith.
Therefore seek not to understand that
thou mayest believe, but believe that
thou mayest understand.
ST AUGUSTINE in *St Julius Gospel*

UNIVERSALISM

9 Surely what God has originated, God
can destroy, be it spirit or matter. Yet I
cannot get rid of a feeling that men never
are annihilated.
F. J. A. HORT *Life and Letters*

10 What will God say to us, if some of us
go to him without the others?
CHARLES PÉGUY

11 The wish that of the living whole/No life
may fail beyond the grave,/Derives it not
from what we have/The likest-God within
the soul?
LORD TENNYSON *In Memoriam*

THE UNIVERSE

12 Upon the whole, there is a kind of moral
government implied in God's natural
government: virtue and vice are naturally
rewarded and punished as beneficial and
mischievous to society, and rewarded
and punished directly as virtue and vice.
The notion then of a moral scheme of
government is not fictitious, but natural;
for it is suggested to our thoughts by the
constitution and course of nature.
JOSEPH BUTLER

13 You will hardly find one among the
profounder sort of scientific minds,
without peculiar religious feelings of
his own . . . His religious feeling takes
the form of rapturous amazement at the
harmony of the natural law.
ALBERT EINSTEIN

14 All things are open to these two events,/
All to Rewards, or else to Punishments.
ROBERT HERRICK *Hesperides*

15 We may be in the universe as dogs and
cats are in our libraries, seeing the
books and hearing the conversation, but
having no inkling of the meaning of it
all.
WILLIAM JAMES *A Pluralistic Universe*

16 The scientist has a faith . . . which is
reflected in the fact that he would never

consider that an experiment begun on a Wednesday would yield entirely different results from one undertaken on a Friday. He believes in the orderliness of the universe. He stakes his shirt on his faith that everything happens in such a reasonable and well ordered fashion that the same experiment will give the same result . . . If the contents of our universe did not behave in so regular and predictable a fashion no real scientific research would be possible.

ROBERT PILKINGTON *World without End*

1 One God, one law, one element,/ And one far-off divine event,/To which the whole creation moves.

LORD TENNYSON *In Memoriam*

VIOLENCE

1 The Lord weighs just and unjust/and hates with all his soul the lover of violence.
Ps. 11.5

2 Better be slow to anger than a fighter,/ better govern one's temper than capture a city.
Prov. 16.32

3 Neither by force of arms nor by brute strength, but by my spirit! says the Lord of Hosts.
Zech. 4.6

4 The modern choice is between Non-Violence or Non-Existence.
MARTIN LUTHER KING

5 'Jesus and no quarter.'
Scottish Covenanters' battle-cry

VIRGIN MARY

6 My soul doth magnify the Lord: and my spirit hath rejoiced in God my Saviour./ For he hath regarded the lowliness of his hand-maiden./For behold, from henceforth: all generations shall call me blessed.
BOOK OF COMMON PRAYER From the *Magnificat*

7 Be thou then, O thou dear/Mother, my atmosphere;/My happier world, wherein/ To wend and meet no sin;/Above me, round me lie/Fronting my froward eye/ With sweet and scarless sky;/Stir in my ears, speak there/Of God's love, O live air,/Of patience, penance, prayer:/World-mothering air, air wild,/Wound with thee, in thee isled,/Fold home, fast fold thy child.
GERARD MANLEY HOPKINS

8 Mother of the Fair Delight,/Thou handmaid perfect in God's sight,/Now sitting fourth beside the Three,/Thyself a woman-Trinity,—/Being a daughter borne to God,/Mother of Christ from stall to rood,/And wife unto the Holy Ghost:—/Oh when our need is uttermost,/Think that to such as death may strike/Thou once wert sister sisterlike!/ Thou headstone of humanity,/Groundstone of the great Mystery,/Fashioned like us, yet more than we!
DANTE GABRIEL ROSSETTI *Ave*

9 At the Cross, her station keeping,/Stood the mournful Mother weeping,/Where He hung, the dying Lord;/For her soul, of joy bereaved,/ Bowed with anguish, deeply grieved,/Felt the sharp and piercing sword.
Thirteenth-century hymn

WAR

1 Like Nimrod, a mighty hunter before the Lord.
Gen. 10.9

2 A sword for the Lord and for Gideon!
Judg. 7.20

3 All who take the sword die by the sword.
Matt. 26.52

4 If the trumpet-call is not clear, who will prepare for battle?
1 Cor. 14.8

5 For a war to be just, three conditions are necessary: public authority, just cause, right motive . . . Augustine declares that the decision and authority of declaring war lies with rulers, if the moral order is to be peacefully composed . . . Those who are attacked should deserve to be attacked . . . Those who go to war should fight to achieve some good or avoid some evil.
ST THOMAS AQUINAS

6 The Church knows nothing of a sacredness of war. The Church which prays the 'Our Father' asks God only for peace.
DIETRICH BONHOEFFER *No Rusty Swords*

7 There never was a good war or a bad peace.
BENJAMIN FRANKLIN *Letter to Quincy*

8 It is impossible to reject wholesale the doctrine of a just war, since it contains an important element of truth, that might become relevant even today in particular limited situations, where a non-atomic conflict was concerned . . . But . . . the change brought about by the new weapons is that a war involving their use is no longer feasible as a means of defence. It inevitably destroys what it is supposed to defend. It is sheer nonsense to attempt to justify nuclear weapons and nuclear warfare on the basis of the traditional evaluation of arms and military protection and to deny the novelty of the problem presented by this technical development in warfare.
HELMUT GOLLWITZER

It is the business of the Church to make my business impossible.
EARL HAIG

9 War is kinder than a Godless peace.
G. A. STUDDERT KENNEDY *The Unutterable Beauty*

10 Waste of Muscle, waste of Brain,/Waste of Patience, waste of Pain,/Waste of Manhood, waste of Health,/Waste of Beauty, waste of Wealth,/Waste of Blood, and waste of Tears,/Waste of Youth's most precious years,/Waste of ways the Saints have trod,/Waste of Glory, waste of God,—/War!
G. A. STUDDERT KENNEDY *The Unutterable Beauty*

11 Weapons of war are tools of evil; those who truly admire them are murderers at heart.
Taiost saying

WIFE

12 A capable wife is her husband's crown.
Prov. 12.4

13 Find a wife, and you find a good thing.
Prov. 18.22

14 A nagging wife is like water dripping endlessly.
Prov. 19.13

15 An intelligent wife is a gift from the Lord.
Prov. 19.14

16 Better to live in a corner of the house-top/ than have a nagging wife and a brawling household.
Prov. 21.9

17 Who can find a capable wife?/Her worth is far beyond coral.
Prov. 31.10

18 Charm is a delusion and beauty fleeting;/ it is the God-fearing woman who is honoured.
Prov. 31.30

1 Do not lose the chance of a wise and good wife.
Ecclus 7.19

2 A good wife means a good life.
Ecclus 26.3

3 Teacher tender, comrade, wife,/A fellow-farer true through life,/Heart-whole and soul-free,/The august Father/Gave to me.
R. L. STEVENSON *A Husband to a Wife*

WINE

4 Wine to gladden men's hearts.
Ps. 104.15

5 Wine brings gaiety and high spirits,/if a man knows when to drink and when to stop.
Ecclus 31.28

6 Stop drinking nothing but water; take a little wine for your digestion.
1 Tim. 5.23

WISDOM

7 But where can wisdom be found?/And where is the source of understanding?/No man knows the way to it;/it is not found in the land of living men.
Job 28.12–13

8 But God understands the way to it,/he alone knows its source.
Job 28.23

9 And he said to man:/The fear of the Lord is wisdom,/and to turn from evil is understanding.
Job 28.28

10 Teach us to order our days rightly,/that we may enter the gate of wisdom.
Ps. 90.12

11 Wisdom is more profitable than silver,/and the gain she brings is better than gold.
Prov. 3.14

12 The first thing is to acquire wisdom;/gain understanding though it cost you all you have.
Prov. 4.7

13 A fool thinks that he is always right;/wise is the man who listens to advice.
Prov. 12.15

14 Walk with the wise and be wise;/mix with the stupid and be misled.
Prov. 13.20

15 Wisdom prevails over strength,/knowledge over brute force.
Prov. 24.5

16 Do you see that man who thinks himself so wise?/There is more hope for a fool than for him.
Prov. 26.12

17 For in much wisdom is much vexation, and the more a man knows, the more he has to suffer.
Eccl. 1.18

18 Wisdom shines bright and never fades; she is easily discerned by those who love her, and by those who seek her she is found.
Wisd. 6.12

19 The true beginning of wisdom is the desire to learn.
Wisd. 6.17

20 She is the brightness that streams from everlasting light, the flawless mirror of the active power of God and the image of his goodness.
Wisd. 7.26

21 Age after age she enters into holy souls, and makes them God's friends and prophets, for nothing is acceptable to God but the man who makes his home with wisdom.
Wisd. 7.27–28

22 If virtue is the object of a man's affections, the fruits of wisdom's labours are the virtues; temperance and prudence, jus-

tice and fortitude, these are her teaching, and in the life of men there is nothing of more value than these.
Wisd. 8.7

1 Wisdom was first of all created things;/ intelligent purpose has been there from the beginning.
Ecclus 1.4

2 To all mankind he has given her in some measure,/but in plenty to those who love him.
Ecclus 1.10

3 If you long for wisdom, keep the commandments,/and the Lord will give it you in plenty.
Ecclus 1.26

4 If you discover a wise man, rise early to visit him;/let your feet wear out his doorstep.
Ecclus 6.36

5 Wisdom appeared on earth and lived among men. She is the book of the commandments of God, the law that stands for ever.
Baruch 3.37; 4.1

6 Divine folly is wiser than the wisdom of man, and divine weakness stronger than man's strength.
1 Cor. 1.25

7 The wisdom of this world is folly in God's sight.
1 Cor. 3.19

8 The first step of wisdom is to know what is false.
Latin Proverb

9 God grant me the serenity to accept things I cannot change, courage to change things I can, and wisdom to know the difference.
REINHOLD NIEBUHR

WORK

10 You shall gain your bread by the sweat of your brow/until you return to the ground;/for from it you were taken.
Gen. 3.19

11 Man comes out to his work/and to his labours until evening.
Ps. 104.23

12 Unless the Lord builds the house,/its builders will have toiled in vain.
Ps. 127.1

13 Go to the ant, you sluggard.
Prov. 6.6

14 One man wins success by his words; another gets his due reward by the work of his hands.
Prov. 12.14

15 Honest work bears glorious fruit, and wisdom grows from roots that are imperishable.
Wisd. 3.15

16 Do not resent manual labour or farmwork,/for it was ordained by the Most High.
Ecclus 7.15

17 They maintain the fabric of this world./ and their daily work is their prayer.
Ecclus 38.34

18 Hard work is the lot of every man.
Ecclus 40.1

19 The man who will not work shall not eat.
2 Thess 3.10

20 Grant that this day we fall into no sin, neither run into any kind of danger; but that all our doings may be ordered by thy governance, to do always that is righteous in thy sight.
BOOK OF COMMON PRAYER From the *Collect for Grace*

21 To work is to pray.
Benedictine motto

22 There is a kind of Church worker for whom our age even more urgently calls, and on whom the life and example of Christ set more immediately the seal of

discipleship—the man who, to the glory of God and for the good of his fellows, does honest work of the everyday sort.
A. C. CRAIG *University Sermons*

1 O Lord God, when Thou givest to Thy servants to endeavour any great matter, grant us to know that it is not the beginning but the continuing of the same, until it be thoroughly finished, which yieldeth the true glory.
SIR FRANCIS DRAKE

2 Knowledge we ask not—knowledge Thou hast lent,/But, Lord, the will—there lies our bitter need,/Give us to build above the deep intent/The deed, the deed.
JOHN DRINKWATER *Collected Poems*

3 He who sees how action may be rest and rest action; he is wisest among his kind; he has the truth. He does well—acting or resting.
Hindu saying

4 God give me work/Till my life shall end/And life/Till my work is done.
WINIFRED HOLTBY

5 Not alone in the darkness of grief do we need Thee,/Not alone in the splendour of joy,/Not alone in the wild open-air would we thrill to thy presence,/Not there alone would we know ourselves Thine;
But here in the dull monotonous round,/Here in the steady rhythm of everyday work,/Here where so little uplifts and so much degrades and oppresses,/Here above all do we need Thee, our God.
JOHN S. HOYLAND

6 O God, who hast ordained that whatever is to be desired, should be sought by labour, and who, by thy blessing, bringest honest labour to good effect; look with mercy upon my studies and endeavours.
SAMUEL JOHNSON

7 God does not measure men's lives only by the amount of work which is accomplished in them. He who gave the power to work may also withhold the power.
BENJAMIN JOWETT *Select Passages from the Theological Writings*

8 We need not bid, for cloistered cell,/Our neighbour and our work farewell,/Nor strive to wind ourselves too high/For sinful man beneath the sky;
The trivial round, the common task,/Would furnish all we ought to ask,—/Room to deny ourselves, a road/To bring us daily nearer God.
JOHN KEBLE *Hymn*

9 Thou, O God, dost sell us all good things at the price of labour.
LEONARDO DA VINCI

10 These things, good Lord, that we pray for, give us Thy grace to labour for.
SIR THOMAS MORE

11 When Christ to manhood came/A craftsman was he made/And served his glad apprentice time/Bound to the joiner's trade.
So God, our labour take,/From spite and greed set free;/May nothing that we do or make/Bring ill to man or thee.
NORMAN NICHOLSON *100 Hymns for Today*

12 Lord of all eagerness, Lord of all faith,/whose strong hands were skilled at the plane and the lathe,/Be there at our labours, and give us, we pray,/your strength in our hearts, Lord, at the noon of the day.
JAN STRUTHER *100 Hymns for Today*

13 Every citizen should have a voice in the conduct of the business or industry which is carried on by means of his labour, and the satisfaction of knowing that his labour is directed to the well-being of the community.
WILLIAM TEMPLE *Christianity and the Social Order*

14 O Lord, let us not live to be useless, for Christ's sake.
JOHN WESLEY

WORLDLINESS

1 The worldly are more astute than the other-worldly in dealing with their own kind.
Luke 16.8

2 Whoever chooses to be the world's friend makes himself God's enemy.
Jas. 4.4

3 Everything the world affords, all that panders to the appetites or entices the eyes, all the glamour of its life, springs not from the Father but from the godless world. And that world is passing away with all its allurements, but he who does God's will stands for evermore.
1 John 2.16–17

4 Whoever marries the spirit of this age will find himself a widower in the next.
W. R. INGE

5 Secularism has this age by the throat.
WALTER LOWRIE

6 The world is too much with us: late and soon,/Getting and spending, we lay waste our powers,/Little we see in Nature that is ours;/We have given our hearts away, a sordid boon!
WILLIAM WORDSWORTH *Sonnets*

WORLD, UNSEEN

7 Meanwhile our eyes are fixed, not on the things that are seen, but on the things that are unseen: for what is seen passes away; what is unseen is eternal.
2 Cor. 4.18

8 We know that so long as we are at home in the body we are exiles from the Lord; faith is our guide, we do not see him.
2 Cor. 5.6–7

9 Some in one way, and some in others, we seem to touch and have communion with what is beyond the visible world.
F. H. BRADLEY

10 Let us urge forward our spirits, and make them approach the invisible world, and fix our mind upon immaterial things, till we clearly perceive that these are no dreams, nay, that all things are dreams and shadows besides them.
HENRY SCOUGAL *The Life of God in the Soul of Man*

11 O world invisible, we view thee,/O world intangible, we touch thee,/O world unknowable, we know thee,/Inapprehensible, we clutch thee!
FRANCIS THOMPSON *In No Strange Land*

WORSHIP

12 Hold the Lord in awe then, and worship him in loyalty and truth.
Josh. 24.14

13 Choose here and now whom you will worship: . . . But I and my family, we will worship the Lord.
Josh. 24.15

14 Worship the Lord with reverence.
Ps. 2.11

15 Come! Let us throw ourselves at his feet in homage,/let us kneel before the Lord who made us;/for he is our God,/we are his people, we the flock he shepherds.
Ps. 95.6–7

16 Let all be done decently and in order.
1 Cor. 14.40

17 God said: In whichever form any worshipper wishes to worship with faith, in that form I strengthen his faith.
The Bhagavad Gita (Hindu)

18 Jesus, where'er Thy people meet,/There they behold Thy mercy-seat;/Where'er they seek Thee Thou art found,/And every place is hallowed ground.
WILLIAM COWPER *Hymn*

19 The glory of God is a living man; and the life of man consists in beholding God.
ST IRENAEUS *Against Heresies*

1 It cannot be that the instinct which has led to the erection of cathedrals, and of churches in every village, is wholly mistaken and misleading. There must be some great truth underlying the instinct for worship.
SIR OLIVER LODGE

2 In our worship, Lord most holy,/hallowed be thy name;/In our work, however lowly,/hallowed be thy name,/In each heart's imagination,/In the Church's adoration,/In the conscience of the nation,/hallowed be thy name.
TIMOTHY REES *100 Hymns for today*

3 We worship and adore the framer and former of the universe; governor, disposer, keeper; Him on whom all things depend, mind and spirit of the world; from whom all things spring; by whose spirit we live; the divine spirit diffused through all; God all-powerful; God always present; God above all other gods; Thee we worship and adore!
SENECA

4 God reveals His presence:/Let us now adore Him,/And with awe appear before Him./God is in His temple:/All within keep silence,/Prostrate lie with deepest reverence./Him alone/God we own,/Him our God and Saviour:/Praise His name for ever.
GERHARD TERSTEEGEN *Hymn*

5 Dear Lord and Father of mankind,/Forgive our foolish ways;/Reclothe us in our rightful mind;/In purer lives Thy service find,/In deeper reverence, praise.
JOHN GREENLEAF WHITTIER *Hymn*

YEARNING

1 If I could only go back to the old days,/ to the time when God was watching over me.
Job 29.2

2 O Lord, to find Thee is my desire/But to comprehend Thee/Is beyond my strength. . . . I call upon Thee night and day.
ABDALLAH ANSARI (Sufi)

3 Reveal Thyself to me, reveal Thyself to me./I seek not wealth nor power, I yearn to see Thee alone./O God, I care not for renunciation or enjoyment; I yearn to see Thee alone./O God, I am neither anxious for home, nor for the forest life;/ I only yearn to see Thee./Yea I seek for naught save Thee, O God, I yearn for Thy vision alone; grant my prayer.
DADU (Hindu)

4 I thirst for Thee, O God; when shall I meet with Thee?/Is there a Friend, a Saint, a God's-Own who'll take me to the Lord?/Without Him I'm comforted not.
The Granth (Sikh)

5 The heavens are still; no sound;/Where then shall God be found?
SHAO YUNG (Shinto)

YOUTH

6 Do not remember the sins and offences of my youth,/but remember me in thy unfailing love.
Ps. 25.7

7 The glory of young men is their strength,/ the dignity of old men their grey hairs.
Prov. 20.29

8 Start a boy on the right road,/and even in old age he will not leave it.
Prov. 22.6

9 Rod and reprimand impart wisdom,/ but a boy who runs wild brings shame on his mother.
Prov. 29.15

10 Delight in your boyhood, young man, make the most of the days of your youth.
Eccl. 11.9

11 Remember your Creator in the days of your youth, before the time of trouble comes and the years draw near when you will say, 'I see no purpose in them.'
Eccl. 12.1

12 If you have not gathered wisdom in your youth,/how will you find it when you are old?
Ecclus. 25.3

13 The new generation is morally braver, more truthful, more serious, intelligent, candid and frank.
ANTHONY CHEVENIX-TRENCH

14 One other thing stirs me when I look back at my youthful days, the fact that so many people gave me something or were something to me without knowing it.
ALBERT SCHWEITZER *Memories of Childhood and Youth*

15 Heaven lies about us in our infancy!/ Shades of the prison-house begin to close/Upon the growing boy.
WILLIAM WORDSWORTH *Intimations of Immortality*

Source Index

Entries taken from the Bible and the Book of Common Prayer appear separately at the beginning and they follow the order in which they fall within these books; other entries are listed alphabetically by author or (if the author is not known) by source. In each case the subject heading and the page number on which each entry will be found is given.

Subject Index

This index lists the main subject headings in small capital letters thus: COMMITMENT. Entries to be found under these headings are not listed again in the index except by way of cross-reference to another subject. Thus, 'No morality can be founded on authority, even if the authority were divine' (A. J. Ayer *Essay on Humanism* 7: 5) will be found in the index under 'morality' and 'divine' but not under 'authority' since that is the heading under which it appears.

(References are given thus: 63:11, indicating, page 63 entry 11.)

Abandon: a. hope . . . enter here 98:18
Abased: we must know how to be a. 100:3
Abba: to cry 'A.! Father!' 96:7
Abide: changest not, a. with me 14:5
Abiding: the holy Lord, a. within himself 87:16
Abraham: before A. was born, I am 17:17
   by faith A. obeyed the call 52:10
Abroad: a saint a. . . . devil at home 144:6
   thou wert within, and I a. 87:11
Absalom: A. my son, my son 91:14
Accept: a. one another 12:3
Acceptable: say and think . . . a. to thee 157:6
Accomplished: 'It is a.!' 43:19
Account: if thou, Lord, . . . keep a. of sins 150:1
Acknowledge: we a. and bewail 37:6
Acquainted: vital . . . become a. with God 72:3
Action: a. may be rest and rest a.166:3
   faith; if it does not lead to a. 52:11
   life is an a., not a thought 159:14
ADAM: SECOND ADAM 1
Addressed: God . . . only be a., not expressed 75:15
Adore: a. God as if you could see Him 80:1
   learn to a. the Divine Spirit 109:14
   O come let us a. Him 32:1
   thee we a., O hidden Saviour 94:18
ADULTERY 1
ADVERSITY 1–2
ADVICE 2
Advocate: friend . . . act the part of an a. 57:18
Affection: full of brotherly a. 30:9
Afflicted: those, who are in any way a. 154:8
Affliction: bread of a. 11:14
   the furnace of a. 65:14
   love . . . a.s for the love of God 154:11
Afraid: always a. of Christ 21:14
   I am a. of saying 'yes', Lord 36:3
   in God I trust . . . not be a. 85:13
   it is I; do not be a. 22:4
Against: he who is not a. us 30:6
Agony: is there any a. like mine? 3:4
Agrippa: A. said to Paul, '. . . it will not take much to win me over' 133:1
Alarms: I sink in life's a. 29:6
All: a. this, and Heaven too! 94:10
   Christ is a., and is in a. 18:7
Alleviate: a. a father's or a mother's grief 123:8
Alms: a. are . . . vehicles of prayer 59:21
Almsgiving: a. atones for sin 59:10
   Let your a. match your means 59:9
Alone: never forget that you are not a. 79:14
Alpha: the A. and the Omega 18:10
Altar: bringing your gift to the a. 59:12
   mean a. of my heart 17:14
Always: I am with you a. 17:15
Amazing: behold the a. gift of love 77:3
Ambassadors: as Christ's a. 25:3
Amends: a fool is too arrogant to make a. 136:1
Anchor: hope set before us . . . like an a. 98:15
Angel: entertained a.s without knowing 107:2

holy A.s guard thy bed 15:8
   in action how like an a.! 115:9
   lower than the a.s 6:17
   strange . . . a.s . . . announced Peace 124:14
ANGELS 2
ANGER 2–3
Anger: better be slow to a. than a fighter 162:2
   who nurses a. . . . judgement 120:9
ANGUISH 3
Anguish: how long must I suffer a. 91:15
Animal: meditation frees man from the a. nature 117:10
ANIMALS 3–4
Anointing: Thou the a. Spirit art 97:5
Answer: before they call to me, I will a. 118:10
   soft a. turns away anger 2:17
Antioch: in A . . . name of Christians 30:7
Antique: constant service of the a. world 148:8
ANXIETY 4
Anything: I have strength for a. 153:17
Apollos: I planted . . . and A. watered 77:6
Apology: a. for the Bible 10:1
Apple: like the a. of thine eye 80:12
Apprehension: immediate a. . . . of God as King 71:2
   in a. how like a god! 115:9
Argue: I should still a. my cause 84:4
ARGUMENT 4
Arguments: these are not a. . . . sacraments 144:1
ARIDITY 4–5
Arise: a. and come to our help 65:5
ARMOUR OF GOD 62
Arrogance: a. before a fall 133:16
   a. is hateful to God and man 133:20
Arrows: the a. of the Almighty . . . in me 154:3
Art: a. . . . expression of the profoundest thoughts 157:11
Artist: not an a. . . . not a Christian 30:10
ASCENSION, THE 5
Asceticism: Christianity is A. without Rigorism 29:14
Ascribe: a. glory to the Lord 68:6
Ashamed: I am not a. of the Gospel 90:8
   I'm not a. to own my Lord 25:16
   never be a. to admit your mistakes 98:4
Ask: a., and you will receive 128:13
   what we ought to a. of Thee 129:4
   Whatever you a. for in prayer 128:14
ASPIRATION 5–6
Ass: humble and mounted on an a. 123:1
Assent: we a., but we do not believe 8:11
Astronomy: turn topsy-turvy the whole Art of A. 145:10
ATHEISM 6
Athlete: every a. goes into . . . training 112:6
ATONEMENT, THE 6–7
Auschwitz: so far as A. is concerned 115:3
Author: a. of life divine 96:1
Authorities: supreme a. 7:4

Fear: any man who f.s the Lord 67:16
  f. nothing, for I am with you 79:10
  I have a sinne of f. 56:6
  man who f.s the Lord keeps his friendships in
    repair 57:13
  man who f.s the Lord . . . nothing else to f. 67:21
  the f. of the Lord is wisdom 164:9
  we all have secret f.s to face 91:9
FEAR OF GOD 67
Fearful: free ourselves from f. doubt 50:6
Feet: those f. in ancient time 21:3
Fell: if we never f., we should not know how feeble
  . . . we are 151:9
Fellow-Christians: never cease to love your f.-C.
  112:22
Fellowship: f. your homes may bind 53:7
Fence: 'How long will you sit on the f.?' 62:13
Festival: Ascension is a f. of the future 5:6
Fêtes: no f., no bazaars . . . *for Justice* 105:19
Fetters: loose . . . f. of injustice 105:14
Fictitious: Christianity . . . discovered to be f. 29:11
Fidelity: f. in little things 53:15
  love and f. have come together 112:10
Fight: f. gallantly, armed with faith 62:10
  f. to the death for truth 159:1
  our f. is not against human foes 51:3
  to f. and not to heed the wounds 132:8
  your little f. against your avarice 89:1
Fighteth: none other that f. for us 124:5
Find: f. a wife . . . f. a good thing 163:14
  I said: 'I will f. God' 82:4
  your sin will f. you out 149:13
Finger: my little f. is thicker 11:4
  the Moving F. writes 126:9
Finished: it is not f., Lord 125:5
FIRE 54
Fire: for lack of fuel a f. dies down 49:21
  kindle f. in his bosom 1:11
  my inner f. is quenched 72:16
  pure celestial f. 17:14
  round disk of f. 2:13
  the Lord was not in the f. 84:3
Firm: if you feel sure . . . standing f., beware 99:9
  truth . . . stands f. for ever 158:14
First: I am the f. and . . . the last 66:9
  I, the Lord, I am the f. 66:8
Fishers: f. of men 16:12
Fitness: science . . . innate sense of the f. of things
  145:6
Flame: f. of sacred love 17:14
  the f. of Thy love glows 73:15
Fled: I f. Him, down the nights 74:10
Fleeting: is not my life short and f.? 110–111:19
Flesh: f. is weak 26:13
  the two shall become one f. 115:18
  whoever eats my f. 94:15
Fleshpots: sat round the f. 11:9
Flights: no supersonic f. to the Celestial City 127:9
Flock: there will then be one f. 32:13
Flower: cut down, like a f. 45:19
  man . . . blossoms like a f. . . .withers 111:1
  St Francis . . . cultivation of f.s 42:5
FOLLY 54–55
Folly: doctrine of the cross is sheer f. 42:11
  f. of the Gospel 90:9
  f. to Greeks 42:12
  God calleth preaching f. 133:7
  wisdom of this world is f. 165:7
Food: proper f. of all inward religion 136:12
FOOL 54–55
Fool: a f. thinks that he is always right 164:13
  f. says in his heart 6:4
  f.s rush in 2:15
  f.s . . . came to scoff, remain'd to pray 129:7
  we are f.s for Christ's sake 30:8
  'You f., this very night . . . surrender your life'
  119:8
Foolish: the f. man is full of selfishness 146:13
Footfall: He can hear even the f. of an ant 132:2

Footprints: f. in the sands of time 158:2
  f. of thy well-beloved Son 17:11
Forefathers: stood by his oath to your f. 76:12
Forget: He f.s our sins when we repent 138:6
  I never f. thy law 72:9
  if I f. Thee, do not f. me 132:6
  if I f. you, O Jerusalem 103:2
  lest we f.—lest we f.! 137:17
Forgive: Father, f. them 43:14
  f. our foolish ways 168:5
  wilt thou f. that sinne 56:6
Forgiving: the Lord . . . f. iniquity . . . and sin 63:6
FORGIVENESS 55–57
Forgiveness: sin . . . Man's f. give—and take!
  151:14
Form: f. of the earthly . . . Christ 20:4
Forsake: Lord, do not thou f. me 79:8
  pride is to f. the Lord 133:21
  thou, Lord, dost not f. those who seek thee 81:12
  though my father and my mother f. me 63:1
Forsaken: my God, why hast thou f. me? 43:13
  never have I seen a righteous man f. 142:4
Fortitude: what credit . . . in f. when you have done
  wrong 154:6
  with what . . . f. . . . bear the sufferings of other
  folks 155:1
Fortunes: my f. are in thy hand 85:12
Forward: if I go f., he is not there 48:4
Foundation: built upon the f. 33:8
  Christ is made the sure f. 34:2
  the Church's one f. 34:10
  there can be no other f. 33:3
  thou didst lay the f.s of the earth 66:7
  so is repose the f. of action 143:8
  where were you when I laid the earth's f.s?
  63:17
Foundation-stone: Christ Jesus himself is the f.-s.
  33:8
Foxes: F. have their holes 152:11
Fragrance: as f. dwells in a flower 87:17
Framer: we worship . . . the f. . . . of the universe
  168:3
Francis: F. . . . began saying funny things 144:11
  (F.) . . . sing . . . praises of the Lord 144:12
  St F. ordered a plot . . . for the cultivation of
  flowers 42:5
Free: Christ set us f., to be f. men 57:2
  the truth will set you f. 159:3
FREE WILL 57
Free-will: sin is evil . . . springing from f.-w. 151:4
FREEDOM 57
Freedom: all theory is against f. of the will 57:6
  I walk in your f. 83:16
  whose service is perfect f. 83:7
FRIEND 57
Friend: God. He is your f. 79:15
  he wants not f.s that hath Thy love 35:4
  O that as f.s we might agree 48:9
  'Teresa, that is how I treat my f.s' 158:12
  the rich have f.s in plenty 141:9
FRIENDSHIP 57
Friendship: greatest f. . . . that between man and
  wife 116:9
Frightening: money is f. It can serve or destroy man
  119:12
Frontiers: a God without f. 85:1
Fruit: f. from the tree 1:1
  kindly f.s of the earth 40:7
Fulfils: God f. himself in many ways 62:2
Fulness: in thy presence is the f. of joy 79:6
  Lord, in the f. of my might 25:7
  men may have life . . . in all its f. 108:18
Furnace: save us from the blazing f. 74–75:16
FUTURE, THE 58

Gaiety: wine brings g. 164:5
Gain: what will a man g.? 145:13
Gaining: by g. his life a man will lose it 108:17
  not with the hope of g. aught 148:5

Galilean:
Thou hast conquered, O pale G. 16:9
Gambler: He was a g. too, my Christ 7:2
Garden: God . . . first planted a g. 40:12
 nearer God's heart in a g. 41:8
Gate: enter the g. of wisdom 164:10
 g. that leads to life is small 108:16
 lift up your heads, you g.s 75:5
 swinging between Hell G. and Heaven G. 33:15
Gaze: fix your g. upon what lies ahead 58:1
Generation: the new g. is morally braver . . . 169:13
GENEROSITY 59
Genial: bestow. . . . a g. spirit 14:12
Gennesareth: not of G., but Thames 65:11
Gentle: Oh sleep! it is a g. thing 152:8
Gentleman: only the Almighty can make a g. 115:4
Gentler: find some means of making men g. 93:12
Getting: g. and spending, we lay waste our powers 167:6
Gift: all good g.s around us 40–41:18
 excellent g. of charity 14:9
 offered him g.s 31:8
 only of thy g.s . . . we give to thee 68:11
 thy great g. . . . g. of silence 149:8
GIFTS 59–60
Give: give all you can 119:13
 g. me the strength . . . bear my joys 85:6
 g. when you are asked to g. 59:13
 to g. and not to count the cost 132:8
 we g. Thee but Thine own 83:12
 what can I g. Him? 25:11
 what God g.s, and what we take 131:9
Given: man who has will . . . be g. more 90:11
 where a man has been g. much 59:6
Giver: lavish g. has the world for his friend 59:8
GIVING 59–60
Giving: happiness lies more in g. 93:1
 it is in g. that we receive 148:3
Gladdens: fear of the Lord g. the heart 67:20
Gladness: as with g. men of old 31:13
Gladsome: let us with a g. mind 79:4
Glass: my g. is half unspent 119:1
Glorious: g. company of the Apostles 78:4
 g. things of thee are spoken 34:7
 how bright these g. spirits 35:8
 O Lord . . . how g. is thy name 75:4
Glory: afterwards wilt receive me with g. 111:10
 earth . . . filled with the g. of God 81:4
 g. fills the skies 23:1
 g. is perfected grace 91:8
 G. to Man in the highest! 115:12
 hope of a g. to come 29:2
 in the Cross of Christ I g. 43:2
 king of g. may come in 75:5
 Lord, let Thy g. be my end 87:8
 Moses prayed, 'Show me thy g.' 76:4
 my gown of g., hope's true gage 127:7
 paths of g. lead but to the grave 46:9
 the g. of the spring how sweet 41:7
 the hope of g. 156:14
 we saw his g. 26:3
GLORY OF GOD 68
GLORY TO GOD 68
Glutton: 'Look at him! a g. and a drinker' 19:9
Go: where you g., I will g. 53:9
GOD 60–62
God: apart from Christ . . . we do not know what G. is 16:4
 by G.'s grace I am what I am 90:16
 complete being of G. 18:6
 even if G. is not 'there' 66:11
 for right is right, since G. is G. 142:7
 G. is the way to man 114:13
 G.'s in His heaven 40:16
 G., whose centre is everywhere 41:11
 G. would not be G. if he could be fully known 72:4
 in one G. I believe 8:6
 like g.s knowing . . . good and evil 88:8

made him little less than a g. 114:5
man without G. is no longer man 114:14
no one has ever seen G. 26:4
no room for G. in him who is full of himself 146:16
O G., if there be a G. 50:9
O G., if you are there 50:8
one G., one law, one element 161:1
Son of Man standing at G.'s right hand 152:13
the G. who rules this earth 12:19
to thee, O G., we turn for peace 124:16
what will G. say to us, if some . . . go to him without the others? 160:10
where then shall G. be found? 169:5
you cannot serve G. and Money 119:7
GOD, ARMOUR OF 62
GOD, BELIEF IN 62
GOD, CARE OF 63
GOD, COMPASSION OF 63
GOD, CREATOR 63–64
GOD, DELIVERER 65
GOD, DISCIPLINE OF 65–66
GOD, ETERNAL 66
GOD, EXISTENCE OF 66
GOD, FAITHFULNESS OF 67
GOD, FATHERHOOD OF 67
GOD, FEAR OF 67
GOD, GLORY OF 68
GOD, GLORY TO 68
GOD, GOODNESS OF 68–69
GOD, GUIDANCE OF 69
GOD, HEALER 69
GOD, HOUSE OF 69–70
GOD, JUSTICE OF 70
GOD, KINGDOM OF 70–71
GOD, KNOWLEDGE OF 71–72
GOD, HIS KNOWLEDGE OF US 72
GOD, LAW OF 72
GOD, LIFE IN 72
GOD, LIGHT 73
GOD, LOVE OF 73–74
GOD, LOVE TOWARDS 74
GOD, LOYALTY TO 74–75
GOD, MAJESTY OF 75
GOD, MYSTERY OF 75–76
GOD, NAME OF 76
GOD, OBEDIENCE TO 76
GOD, PEOPLE OF 76–77
GOD, PRAISE OF 77–79
GOD, PRESENCE OF 79–80
GOD, PROTECTOR 80–81
GOD, PURPOSE OF 81
GOD, REFUGE 81
GOD, SEEKING AND FINDING 81–82
GOD, SERVANT OF 82–83
GOD, SERVICE OF 83
GOD, SPEAKING WITH 83–85
GOD, STRENGTH FROM 85
GOD, SUPREMACY OF 85
GOD, TRUST IN 85–86
GOD, UNIVERSAL 86
GOD, WAITING FOR 86
GOD, WILL OF 87
GOD, WITHIN 87–88
GOD, WORD OF 88
Godfearing: man who is g. . . . is acceptable to him 76:17
Godhead: prayer . . . essence of the G. 130:9
Godless: hope of a g. man 6:5
Godly: g., righteous and sober life 109:1
Gold: g., frankincense, and myrrh 31:8
Golden: g. lads and girls 47:1
Gong: without love . . . sounding g. 112:17
Good: a g. man's prayer is powerful 128:19
 a g. wife means a g. life 164:2
 contemplation of the G. 37:14
 do all the g. you can 90:7
 everything . . . God created is g. 64:10
 God has told you what is g. 89:8

Man (*cont.*)
  what is m. and what use is he? 111:6
  what sort of m. is this? 19:8
  what was in a m. 19:14
Manhood: m . . . better thing than boyhood 119:2
Mankind: all m. is grass 88:4
  dear Lord and Father of m. 168:5
  I have never been able to conceive m. without
  Him 60:19
  the proper study of m. is man 147:4
  to all m. he has given her (wisdom) 165:2
Manna: Israel called the food m. 11:11
  nothing . . . except this m. 11:12
Mark: Lord put a m. on Cain 80:5
MARRIAGE 115–116
Marries: whoever m. the spirit of this age 167:4
Marry: when they rise from the dead, men and
  women do not m. 138:11
Martyr: noble army of M.s 78:4
  true m. . . . instrument of God 117:1
MARTYRDOM 116–117
Marvellous: tell the story of thy m. acts 77:11
  the Lord has shown me his m. love 73:7
Mary: 'Here am I,' said M. 101:13
Master: dear M. in whose life I see 22:10
  depths of our M.'s character 27:1
  I am the m. of my fate 133:22
  men at some time are m.s. of their fates 153:11
  m. over all thy creatures 114:5
Material: attainment of m. riches . . . the supreme
  object 141:17
Materialist: Christianity is the most . . . m. of all
  the great religions 30:2
  Christians . . . most sublime of m.s 5:6
Maze: here in the maddening m. of things 74:11
Me: Adam is m. 1:7
  Christ be with m. 16:7
Meal: no ordinary m.—a sacrament awaits us
  143:14
Meaning: as far as m. is from speech 41:15
  love was His m. 113:10
Measure: good m., pressed down 59:16
Meat: will no one give us m.? 11:12
  some ha'e m., and canna eat 131:7
Medes: law of the M.s and Persians 108:2
Mediator: the living M. 139:3
Mediocrity: sign of m. to be niggardly with praise
  128:5
Meditate: m. in the field 117:4
  O my soul, m. on God 8:7
MEDITATION 117
Meditation: drynesses . . . in . . . m. 4:13
Meek: Christ offends us by calling on us to be m.
  100:1
  exalted the humble and m. 99:10
  God . . . bestows his favour on the m. 99:2
  make me m., Lord: Thou wert lowly 100:6
Meeting: real life is m. 109:15
Melody: sweetness of m. . . . make some entrance
  for good things 84:12
Mercies: for his m. aye endure 79:4
  when all Thy m., O my God 78:7
Merciful: the Lord your God is a m. God 137–
  138:18
Mercy: Lord, in M. grant my soul to live 68:17
  M. has a human heart 114:16
  that m. which . . . your Master . . . bestows on
  you 107:6
  the abundance of thy m. 68:16
  the quality of m. 36:16
  to M., Pity, Peace and Love 114:16
Mercy-seat: approach, my soul, the m.-s. 130:8
Merry: a m. heart makes a cheerful face 93:17
Message: the m. of reconciliation 136:3
MESSIAH 118
MESSIANIC AGE 118
METHODS OF PRAYER 131–132
MIDDLE AGE 118–119
Midge: you strain off a m. 126:2

Might: faith that right makes m. 142:8
  for the m. of Thine arm 33:18
Mills: dark satanic m. 21:3
  m. of God grind slowly 61:6
Mind: keep in peace men of constant m. 123:17
  let the m. run on 117:9
  money never made any man rich, but his m.
  119:11
  my m. reels . . . in the darkness 49:6
  my m. to me a kingdom is 104:1
  possess the m. of Christ 28:14
  quiet m. is worse than poverty 38:9
  serve thee with a quiet m. 55:14
  stuff not the ear of your m. 87:13
  this m. of mine went . . . wandering 157:10
  with m. one-pointed 117:6
Minister: truly and indifferently m. justice 105:18
Minstrels: m. and maids, stand forth 32:8
Miracle: Incarnation would be . . . a m. however
  Jesus entered the world 102:1
Mirror: puzzling reflections in a m. 110:5
Mirth: m. that has no bitter springs 13:2
Misdeeds: blot out my m. 55:4
Miserable: m. creature that I am 150:18
Misery: how deep I am sunk in m. 65:4
Misfortunes: I never knew any man . . . could not
  bear another's m. 158:13
  the good man's m.s may be many 158:9
Mist: your life . . . no more than a m. 111:7
Mock: m. on, m. on, Voltaire, Rousseau 160:1
MONEY 119
Money: getting m. is not all a man's business
  107:8
Month: this is the m., . . . happy morn 32:6
Moon: God made the m. as well as the sun 127:8
Moral: belief is a m. act 8:8
  middle age . . . m. stagnation 119:3
  m. advance moves in a spiral 119:15
  m. law within me 153:10
MORALITY 119–120
Morality: no m. can be founded on authority 7:5
Morning: blest m., whose first dawning rays 139:16
  course of the righteous . . . like m. light 142:5
  every Christian . . . up early in the m. 31:1
  in the m., when I say my prayers 132:4
  joy comes in the m. 103:17
  whose justice dawns like m. light 70:10
  wish us good m. when we wake 132:7
MORNING PRAYER 132
Mortal: m. must be clothed with immortality 101:9
MOTHER 120
Mother: as a m. comforts her son 63:12
  be thou then, O thou dear/M. 162:7
  M. of the Fair Delight 162:8
  my m. and my brothers 17:2
  our m. the earth 41:5
  stood the mournful M. weeping 162:9
  the Church for his m. 33:12
Mountain: dwell on thy holy m. 142:3
  England's m.s green 21:3
  faith strong enough to move m.s 112:18
  how lovely on the m.s 47:14
  the 'Delectable M.s' 126:15
  they shall not hurt or destroy in all my holy m.
  118:8
Mountain-top: if Christ . . . retire . . . to the m.-t.
  132:3
Mourners: m. go about the streets 45:9
Mouth: Christ in m. of friend 16:7
  God be in my m. 6:1
  keep your m. shut and show your good sense
  149:2
  out of the same m. come praises and curses
  128:4
MURDER 120
Music: Lord, who hast revealed thyself in m.
  140:11
Mustard-seed: faith no bigger . . . than a m.-s.
  52:3

Tempted: one thing to be t., another . . . to fall
156:9
we must not be surprised that we are t. 156:10
Tender-hearted: be generous to one another, t.-h.
59:7
Terrestrial: dark t. ball 40:8
Terror: from all that t. teaches 48:2
Tested: t. above your powers 156:5
Thames: not of Gennesareth, but T. 65:11
Thank: now t. we all our God 157:1
Thankful: let us . . . be t. for health 157:5
Thanking: sigh in t. God 156:15
Thanks: give t. whatever happens 156:13
  Lord . . good to give thee t. 77:15
  t. be to God for his gift 90:18
THANKSGIVING 156–157
Thanksgiving: enter his gates with t. 77:18
Theology: social gospel needs a t. 25:9
  starting point for natural t. 4:10
Think: t. oftener of God than you breathe 84:8
  we may t. those things . . . good 89:12
  whoso t.s thoughts of ill 157:9
Thinking: humility . . . freedom from t. about your-
  self 100:11
  nothing . . . good or bad, but t. makes it so 89:6
  prayer is a fundamental style of it. 130:5
  thoughts of God's t. . . . we need 157:12
Thirst: I t. for Thee, O God 169:4
Thirsty: if anyone is t. 26:7
Thorns: God placed t.s among roses 157:4
Thou: God is the T. 60:17
  in each T. we address the eternal T. 66:10
  there is only Thou . . . O God 86:16
  T. in me and I in thee 46:18
  T., my God, who art Love 74:6
  T. wast with me 79:13
Thought: act on our first t.s 157:2
  be one in t. and feeling 30:9
  offer . . . service of my t.s. 83:8
  universe . . . like a great t. 41:12
THOUGHTS 157
Throne: Heaven is my t. 94:5
  him who sits on the t. 21:1
  Thy t. shall never . . . pass away 71:1
  to Him who sits upon the t. 21:5
Through: Thou knowest me t. and t. 72:6
Throw: t. away Thy rod 66:2
Thyself: give me T. 5:9
  Thou hast made us for T. 60:12
TIME 157–158
Time: darkest t. in the year 102:3
  fill, fill deserted t. 118:14
  fixed t.s for all things 79:18
  from out our bourne of T. 47:7
  last syllable of recorded t. 47:3
  the t. has come 27:15
  t. and chance govern all 14:1
Toad: t. ugly and venemous 2:7
Toil: to t. and not to seek for rest 132:8
Tomorrow: things he intended/to do—T. 58:5
  t., and t., and t. 47:3
  t. will look after itself 4:4
Tongue: keep my t. from evil-speaking 152:1
  O for a thousand t.s 24:9
  the slanderous t. kills three 152:5
  t.s like flames of fire 96:4
  t.s of men or of angels 112:17
Torment: t. shall not touch them 110:3
Touch: if I can only t. his cloak 18:16
  Thy t. has . . . ancient power 19:6
Towering: t. o'er the wrecks of Time 43:2
Traditional: forget everything t. . . . about God
  62:5
Train: t. your children 14:16
Tranquillity: dispose our soul for t. 37:13
Transcendence: the language of 't.' 61:2
  the old doctrine of t. 61:16
Transgressions: He was pierced for our t. 83:3
  He . . . wipes out your t. 63:11

Treasure: do not store up . . . t. on earth 141:7
  guard your heart more than any t. 93:16
  pots of earthenware to contain this t. 140:8
  where your t. is 141:8
  within the cave of the mind is an inexhaustible T.
  71:11
Treat: t. others . . . like them to t. you 121:4
Treaty: we have made a t. with Death 45:12
Tree: eat from the t. of life 110:8
  every t. speaks through thee 40:13
  finds tongues in t.s 90:3
  Saviour, as thou hang'st upon the t. 43:4
  t. . . . moves some to tears 40:14
  t. of the knowledge of good and evil 88:7
Trials: t. or corrections of heaven 66:4
Tribulation: in all time of our t. 48:1
Tribunal: all stand before God's t. 105:5
TRINITY, HOLY 97–98
Triton: old T. blow his wreathed horn 42:10
Triumph: he has risen up in t. 65:2
Triumphing: t. over death, and chance 110:15
Trivial: the t. round, the common task 166:8
Troth: thereto I plight thee my t. 116:6
TROUBLE 158
Troubler: Ahab . . . 'Is it you, you t. of Israel?'
  134:3
True: all that is t. . . . whatever is excellent 157:8
  God must be t. 159:5
  to thine own self be t. 159:15
  t. to Thee in my distress 48:8
  what is t. in the lamplight 159:12
Trumpet: the t. shall sound 101:8
  t.s sounded for him on the other side 46:3
Trumpet-call: if the t.-c. is not clear 163:4
Trust: curse on the man who t.s in man 114:10
  t. in him and he will act 35:10
Trusted: who it is in whom I have t. 77:7
TRUST IN GOD 85–86
Trustworthy: 't. in a small way' 53:13
TRUTH 158–159
Truth: his t. is marching on 105:7
  Holy Spirit, T. divine 97:4
  I am the t. 18:1
  I asked for T. 5:12
  no one has from himself the t. 68:18
  now stands no more between the T. and me 61:1
  of the one light of T. . . . in every religion a several
  ray 137:13
  simple t. his utmost skill 93:6
  some great t. underlying the instinct of worship
  168:1
  speak the t. and shame the Devil 49:16
  the belt of t. 62:7
  t. himself speaks truly 28:3
  when he comes who is the Spirit of t. 96:3
Truthfulness: the commandment of absolute t.
  159:9
Trying: what made these Sundays . . . t. 143:4
Tumult: the t. and the shouting dies 137:17
Tunes: why should the Devil have all the good t.?
  49:14
Turn: t. back all of you by God's help 138:2
  when a man t.s to God 148:2
Turned: once I t. from thee and hid 125:4
Tutor: the law was a kind of t. 108:6

UNBELIEF 160
Understand: help us not to despise . . . what we do
  not u. 98:8
  I believe . . . that I may u. 8:5
  seek not to u. that thou mayest believe 160:8
UNDERSTANDING 160
Understanding: bestow . . . u. to know Thee 71:8
  do not rely on your own u. 85:15
  gain u. though it cost you all . . . 164:12
  peace of God . . . beyond our . . . u. 124:4
  religion . . . small enough for our u. 136:9
  to be patient shows great u. 123:10